THE
BEST
OF
PAPE'S
NOTES

ALSO BY GORDON PAPE

Investment Advice

Building Wealth in the '90s
Low-Risk Investing in the '90s
Retiring Wealthy
Making Money in Mutual Funds
Gordon Pape's 1998 Buyer's Guide to RRSPs
Gordon Pape's 1998 Buyer's Guide to Mutual Funds
The Canadian Mortgage Book (with Bruce MacDougall)

Consumer Advice (with Deborah Pape)

Gordon Pape's International Shopping Guide

Humour

The $50,000 Stove Handle

Fiction (with Tony Aspler)

Chain Reaction
The Scorpion Sanction
The Music Wars

Nonfiction (with Donna Gabeline and Dane Lanken)

Montreal at the Crossroads

THE BEST OF PAPE'S NOTES

15 Years of Sound Financial Advice

GORDON PAPE

I(T)P® Nelson

an International Thomson Publishing company

Toronto • Albany • Bonn • Boston • Cincinnati • Detroit • London • Madrid • Melbourne
Mexico City • New York • Pacific Grove • Paris • San Francisco • Singapore • Tokyo • Washington

I(T)P° **International Thomson Publishing**

The ITP logo is a trademark under licence
http://www.thomson.com

Published in 1998 by
I(T)P° Nelson
A division of Thomson Canada Limited
1120 Birchmount Road
Scarborough, Ontario M1K 5G4

Visit the ITP Nelson Web site at http://www.nelson.com/nelson.html

Canadian Cataloguing in Publication Data

Pape, Gordon, 1936–
    The best of Pape's notes : fifteen years of sound advice

ISBN 0-17-606822-8

1. Finance, Personal.   2. Investments.   I. Title

HG179.P37 1997   332.024   C97-931134-9

Cover photo by Dave Starrett and Craig Copeland

Printed and bound in Canada
1 2 3 4 (WC) 00 99 98 97

*To all the talented people
I've worked with
at CBC over the years,
and to all my dedicated listeners.
Thank you all.*

CONTENTS

PREFACE

None of this was my idea. I never planned to become a financial commentator on CBC Radio. I was pushed into it.

It happened back in the autumn of 1984. After many years of political and general-interest writing, I started to develop an interest in specializing in personal finance. My long-time friend Tony Aspler, with whom I had collaborated on three novels, suggested I approach CBC about doing a regular feature on the subject.

I demurred. Although I had done a great deal of radio work in the past, I felt I wasn't ready at that point to undertake the responsibility of advising Canadians on how to manage their money and invest for success. Give it a couple more years, I said.

Tony, who was well connected in the Corporation from his days as a producer, disagreed. He made a couple of phone calls, and suddenly I was invited to appear on Toronto's *Metro Morning* with Joe Coté to discuss the pros and cons of the new issue of Canada Savings Bonds.

Metro Morning's producers must have liked what they heard, because they started inviting me back on a regular basis. A few months later I got a call from Infotape, CBC Radio's in-house syndication unit. Would I be interested in doing a national weekly commentary, along the lines of what I doing on *Metro Morning*?

Why not? At this point I was becoming increasingly confident about my knowledge of personal financial matters, and was enjoying some success with my personal investments. I felt I had something useful to say, and that my thoughts might help people who were struggling to cope with the financial complexities of the 1980s.

So it began—and it's been going ever since, 52 weeks a year, no repeats. Almost 15 years of watching our country's financial and economic fortunes unfold, and offering suggestions to Canadians on how to prosper in ever-changing circumstances.

Over that time, I've seen a lot. A spiralling tax burden that has resulted in greatly diminished personal incomes. Broken promises by one government after another. Scams and rip-offs of all types. Stock market booms and stock market crashes. Plunging interest rates.

Mutual funds mania. Tax shelters that cost investors thousands. The collapse of great financial empires.

You'll find that fascinating cavalcade of events reflected in these pages, plus a lot more.

Doing these weekly broadcasts hasn't always been easy. I've worked with some excellent CBC Radio producers, and with a few know-it-alls who figured they understood personal finance better than I did and had to rip every script apart. I've had run-ins with CBC management, especially over comments I wanted to make on the economic implications of Quebec separation. Too sensitive, I was told. Mustn't roil the waters too much. Preserve national unity and all that. I'm all for national unity. But I felt I had a responsibility to warn Canadians about what they might be in for from a personal finance point of view if things went wrong. In the end I was allowed to say most of what I wanted to, but some of my comments were censored before they went on air. I contemplated quitting the show but decided I could do more good for my listeners by staying on.

But these squabbles are just sideshows. What's important is that over the years I've developed a rapport with tens of thousands of Canadians who listen faithfully to my commentaries. As one lady gushed to me at a reception: "Oh, Mr. Pape, I wake up with you every Monday morning!" My wife wasn't amused.

So popular have the commentaries become that CBC stations across the country maintain a stock of transcripts for listeners who want the text of a broadcast. Someone years ago labelled these "Pape's Notes"—hence the title of this book. More recently, the transcripts have been posted at my Internet Web site, where hundreds of surfers download them daily.

The idea to go the next step and compile the best broadcasts into a book came from Tim Sellers of ITP Nelson. It probably never would have occurred to me, but as I began to read through some of the old commentaries, I realized that much of the advice I gave a decade ago is still valid today. Only the numbers have changed. I also became aware of just how badly Canadians have been treated by their governments over the years—as you'll discover in the pages that follow.

Special thanks for the preparation of this book goes to my two researchers, Wanda Ottewell and Deborah Pape. Together they read through every commentary I have given over the years (which I calculate to be somewhere around 750), selecting the ones they found most interesting and appropriate.

I hope you enjoy the fruits of these labours, and that the advice in these pages helps you to achieve a better financial life.

GORDON PAPE
North York, Ontario

Gordon Pape's CBC Radio transcripts are available every week at his Web site. The address is www.gordonpape.com

CHAPTER
1

Growing Up with the Pape Family

Over the years, many of the inspirations for my broadcasts came from the everyday experiences of my own family. Like most Canadian householders, my wife, Shirley, and I had to deal with mortgages, budgets, the costs of raising children, and all the other financial concerns that arise from day-to-day living. As a result, CBC listeners across the country became familiar with our personal financial problems and experiences, as well as what our kids were getting up to. One cousin in Vancouver, whom we were able to see only infrequently, remarked that she could always keep in touch with what we were doing just by turning on the radio.

This chapter offers a selection of some of those family items. I'll start with a trip we took to the States with the kids back in 1984, when they were all in their teens. (How long ago that seems!) The newspapers at that time were full of articles bemoaning the weak Canadian dollar and the high cost of vacationing abroad. It turned out not to be so bad after all. And most of what we experienced then still holds true today.

TRAVELLING IN THE U.S.
JULY 1984

Earlier this month we packed up the family and went for a week-long holiday in the States. With what's been happening to the dollar, I wasn't thrilled with the idea. But we'd been planning it for some time and I didn't want to disappoint the kids, so off we went.

Well, we're back and I have to report I'm not about to declare bankruptcy. It's true, our dollar bought less than it did a year ago. But none of the prices really shocked me, and in fact some things were a lot cheaper, even with the big exchange differential.

Let me give you a few examples. We travelled by car, so obviously we were interested in the price of gas. Well, it's cheaper in the States, no question about it. We paid an average of $1.21 U.S. for regular unleaded gas at self-serve stations. With the exchange rate and the conversion to metric, that works out to about 42.5 Canadian cents a litre. That's a substantial saving—about 17 percent—over what I'm paying at home right now.

Another example. We enjoy the occasional drink and glass of wine with our dinner. Liquor is much cheaper south of the border, whether you buy it in a bar or restaurant or at a store. One of the highlights of our trip was enjoying a bottle of Pouilly-Fuissé, a fine white Burgundy I haven't been able to afford for years. I picked up a bottle in a grocery store in Maine for under $12 Canadian. That may sound expensive, but the same bottle in Ontario costs almost $18.

We hit some rainy weather, so the kids went shopping for clothes. I don't pretend to be an expert on the price of children's clothing, and obviously prices will vary depending on where you buy. But my wife found prices were generally cheaper for comparable brand names in the stores we visited.

Not everything costs less, of course. We found food prices more or less comparable to those in Canada, whether we were buying in a grocery store or eating out.

Accommodation tended to be more expensive, although not a lot. We paid $35 to $40 U.S. for rooms in good-quality motels in New England, which works out to between $46 and $54 Canadian. You can sleep much cheaper than that, of course, if you stay at one of the budget chains like Days Inns. We just didn't happen to hit any of them.

Now, obviously, one family's experience isn't the final word. But what we found tended to confirm some price comparisons I'd obtained for a magazine article on tourism I had written just before we left. With the help of a number of organizations, including Travel USA, the Ontario Motor League, and the State of New York, we estimated the cost of a one-week holiday for a family of four in the U.S. and Canada. We used New York and Ontario, because of the physical proximity and more or less comparable attractions. We factored in all the various costs that would be involved—accommodation, meals, sports, an amusement park, evenings out, gas, alcohol—and used average prices supplied by the various organizations. You know what the result was? The cost worked out to be almost exactly the same when the exchange rate was taken into account, with a very slight advantage going to New York.

So let's keep things in proportion. Sure, it would be nice if the dollar were higher and our vacations cost a little less. But things aren't as bad as the headlines might lead you to believe. If you've got holiday plans in the States this summer, don't let the ups and downs of the dollar scare you off. There are many good reasons for choosing to visit Canada instead, but exchange-rate panic isn't one of them.

UPDATE

It's surprising how little has changed more than a decade later. The price of gas in the States is slightly higher, but not a lot. You can still find decent motel rooms for the equivalent of $50 Canadian. Children's clothes are still cheaper in the U.S. (now it's our grand-children who are the beneficiaries of this). When we did a survey for my *International Shopping Guide* last year, we found food prices to be comparable, with a slight edge to Canada. About the only thing that's changed dramatically are the wine prices. A bottle of Pouilly-Fuissé for $12 Canadian! I weep.

INTRODUCTION

One of the bittersweet experiences of family life is watching the children grow older. Experiencing them as young adults is fascinating. But it lacks the magic of childhood. They get too practical!

CHRISTMAS GIFTS
NOVEMBER 1989

I'm feeling just a bit sad about Christmas this year. Our youngest daughter turned 18 last month and for the first time in years we don't have any children in the house. Just three young adults who haven't married yet—so no grandchildren either.

Now, I have to confess: I'm really a kid at heart. One of the things I always enjoyed was wandering through the toy departments at Christmastime, picking out gifts for the children. I had more fun watching them open a new game on Christmas morning than from any of the gifts I received, nice as they were.

But now they're too old. They're not interested in that sort of thing any more. They want gloves and scarves and sweaters and all that stuff they used to think was boring—and I still do.

I guess my only consolation is the fact they're now much more appreciative of my financial gifts than they ever were when they were young. In fact, they're now asking for them on their Christmas lists, with some clever embellishments of their own.

My 19-year-old son, who started university this year, is perhaps the most imaginative. He went out of town and he's discovering just how expensive living on his own can be. So his Christmas list has all kinds of suggestions that really come down to money—but money in a more acceptable form than plain cash, although he wouldn't mind that either.

If you're thinking about giving your children or grandchildren some financial gifts this year, let me share some of his requests with you. They might give you some ideas.

First on his list are long-distance gift certificates. Since he's out of town, he finds he's running up some pretty hefty phone bills between calling us, his girlfriend, and heaven knows who else. Any gift that reduces those costs will be gratefully accepted.

Then there's the high cost of dating. When I was his age, a movie, popcorn, and a snack afterward cost maybe $5. Today, it's more like $30. So he's got cinema passes and McDonald's gift certificates way up on his list. Not money, but just as good.

His new appreciation of the high cost of living has also made him more conscious of the need to save. After all, he's got at least two more years of school after this, maybe more.

So he's put mutual funds, guaranteed investment certificates, and bonds on his list. Any of these would make him happy. He's even gone so far as to ask for property—but I think he's just kidding. At least I hope so.

Anyway, there are some ideas for older kids. If your children or grandchildren are younger, here are a couple of other things to consider.

One is to set up a Registered Education Savings Plan. Many people want to help their children save for college or university. The problem is that if you give them a gift of cash for that purpose, even at Christmas, you're exposing yourself to a tax risk. If Revenue Canada finds out about it, they'll attribute any interest earned on that money back to you for tax purposes.

An RESP is a way to get around that. So there's one idea.

If the children are still very young and you want to give them a gift that's more fun, look at something like those gumball machines that double as banks. They'll enjoy playing with them. And every so often you can empty the money with them, count it together, and then deposit it in a special bank account for them. Even if you buy some of the gumballs yourself, I doubt Revenue Canada is going to get too upset.

Happy shopping.

UPDATE

It turned out that Kendrew *wasn't* kidding about property. We ended up buying a house in London, Ont., which he occupied during his university years (along with boarders to pay the cost). In retrospect, I would no longer recommend RESPs. There are better ways to save for a child's education. But a gumball machine still sounds like fun. Fortunately, we now have grandchildren around, so we can get back to buying some *real* Christmas gifts again.

INTRODUCTION

The cost of postsecondary education is soaring as governments cut back their support to colleges and universities. But all this has done is to magnify a problem that has been around for a long time, as the following item shows.

THE HIGH COST OF LEARNING
SEPTEMBER 1990

Boy, am I beat! I spent most of the first week of September schlepping my two youngest children off to university, and I still haven't recovered. It seems like I've done nothing but load the family wagon, drive for hours, unload at the other end, carry heavy boxes, and help assemble build-it-yourself furniture.

Anyway, we finally got our son established in the house we bought and our daughter safely settled into residence. Now all I have to do is write cheques—for tuition fees, books, residence costs, meal plans, you name it.

Postsecondary education may be relatively cheap in Canada compared to the States, but it still costs a heck of a lot of money. I estimate it will take about $8,000 to see *each* of our kids through the year—and that's with no frills.

They're paying some of that themselves, of course, out of their summer wages. But not many college students can earn *that* much over four months. Someone has to help out, and it's usually mom and dad. That's why it's important to take advantage of every education tax break you can get. Unfortunately, our tax system doesn't bend over backward to help students. You're not allowed to deduct the cost of residence, for example. Nor can you claim a credit for books or necessary school supplies. The only direct college expense you can claim is the tuition fee. That's it—nothing more.

The federal government *does* allow postsecondary students an education credit, but it's pitifully small. For someone who's at school for an eight-month term, it ends up being worth about $80 off your federal tax payable. You're not going to buy very much with that.

There are a few indirect ways you can save some money, though. Moving costs are one. If a student attends a college or university that's more than 40 kilometres away, he or she can claim moving expenses. Those include the cost of transporting and storing personal effects, travelling costs, temporary lodging, and similar expenses.

There's just one small catch—only the student can claim this deduction. It can't be transferred to anyone else. So unless a student makes enough money to pay taxes in the first place, the moving deduction won't be much help.

Just about every student should be able to benefit from the new Goods and Services Tax credit that starts next year, however. It will be worth up to $290, payable in quarterly installments. But you have to claim it—the cheques won't arrive automatically.

One other place students can look for money is your provincial tax-credit system. Some provinces have refundable credits that students can take advantage of. For example, Ontario offers a small credit for residence fees as part of the property tax credit.

See if there's anything that applies in your province. Every dollar helps.

UPDATE

The Liberals took steps in 1996 and 1997 to provide more tax relief to students and their parents. The value of the education credit has been significantly increased and the tuition fee credit has been extended to cover other mandatory costs as well. But you still can't claim a credit for residence costs or, surprisingly, textbooks. Those are areas that need to be revisited.

Parents should also be sure their college-age children file a tax return to claim the GST credit. Many still don't.

INTRODUCTION

Our family has always included a dog as well as, on various occasions, assorted fish, turtles, birds, and even a ferret. So we know only too well the high cost of keeping a pet.

PET INSURANCE
FEBRUARY 1991

We got a new puppy last summer—a little Shetland sheepdog whose legs were still so short he bounced instead of walked. It had been years since we'd had a puppy in the house, and naturally we all immediately fell in love with him. It's hard not to react when a tiny ball of fluff settles down comfortably in your lap for a snooze.

And then our new puppy got sick. We never knew how, but something he ingested poisoned him. Naturally, we rushed him to the vet. He didn't know what was wrong, but he did all the things good vets do to pull our puppy through. It was touch and go for about 48 hours, but the good news is, he made it. He's been fine ever since, and is growing into a typical playful, friendly Sheltie, with legs long enough that he can now run.

The bad news was the bill.

It cost us over $500 to get the treatment the pup needed. That's a lot of money. For some pet owners, it might have been simply out of reach.

That's one reason why veterinarian associations across the country are welcoming the introduction of a new type of insurance— peticare, you might call it. These are plans that cover you for exactly the kind of emergency we had with our puppy. They'll pick up the tab for vet fees, X-rays, surgery, prescriptions, emergency boarding—just about any contingency you can imagine.

The veterinarians like the idea, because, as their costs increase, they're aware that it's becoming more difficult for people to provide the kind of care and treatment their pets require. That's why you'll find applications for this insurance in many veterinarian waiting rooms.

There are three programs currently being offered in Canada: Pet Plan, Pet Sure, and Medipet. All provide basic health- and accident-insurance coverage. But some go even further, offering pet life insurance—which isn't as silly as it might at first sound if you think about the cost involved in replacing a pedigreed dog or cat. You can also get coverage for any advertising costs or rewards if your pet strays.

Obviously, the more frills you choose, the higher your premium. So if you *are* interested in one of these plans, give some careful thought to exactly what you need. Also, take a close look at the terms of these programs before you sign up. Generally, they won't cover your pet for any preexisting condition, including hereditary problems, which can be quite common in highbred animals. They also won't pay for things like neutering, routine checkups, vaccinations, and the like. Those are still your responsibility.

Essentially, you should look on these plans as disaster coverage. If something really bad happens—say, your dog gets hit by a car and is hurt but not killed—you'll know the money is there to provide the care required.

I wish we'd had it when our pup took sick.

UPDATE

Surprisingly, pet insurance hasn't turned out to be very popular. There are still some plans around, but they come and go. Check with your vet to see what's available now. By the way, the Sheltie (his name is Misha) is still around. He's now middle-aged but still acts like a pup—he cries like a baby when we go out for the evening.

INTRODUCTION

The marriage of the first-born child is always a joyous event. But in our family the practical implications had to be considered too.

KIM'S WEDDING
DECEMBER 1991

My oldest daughter is getting married in January. Naturally, we're all excited about it—she's the first of our children to walk down the aisle.

My wife has been busy looking over catering menus, visiting the dressmaker, arranging for a minister, planning a wedding cake, sending out invitations, and all the rest. Somehow, Christmas seems to have been lost in the shuffle, although I'm sure we'll find it before the 25th.

Now, originally, the kids wanted to have a holiday-season wedding. Fortunately, we managed to talk them out of that idea. Not only would the logistics have been overwhelming, it would have cost them a small fortune in tax dollars as well.

There was a time when it was good financial planning to get married just before New Year's. In the days of single-income families, the husband could claim a tax deduction for his new wife for the full year—even though they'd been married only a couple of days.

But that's ancient history. Now the rules say that if you wed at any time during the year, you have to reduce your claim by your spouse's net income for the whole year—not just the time you were married.

So, if your spouse earned more than about $5,700 before you got married, forget it—you won't get any tax credit. In fact, you may end up with a tax penalty. The Goods and Services Tax credit is one example. Two single people can each apply for the GST credit. The amount they receive is based on their individual incomes. For example, two single people, each earning $24,000 a year, would each qualify for the maximum credit of $290.

When they marry, however, their combined income gets taken into account. If they keep working, earning a total of $48,000 between them, they'll both lose their GST credits. That's a loss of $580 a year, in after-tax dollars.

Your eligibility for the GST credit is based on your marital status on December 31, so getting married before year-end could mean you're both ineligible for payments in the next year. By waiting just a couple of days, you'll ensure that doesn't happen.

Let's take another example. Suppose you're a single parent. You're eligible for the equivalent-to-married credit, which is worth a tax reduction of about $1,300 this year. The rule is that as long as you were single at any time during the year and supported a child, you can claim this credit. So if you got married before year-end, you could still make a claim for that year.

But suppose you waited until the New Year. The tax guide says you can make the claim if you were eligible *at any time in the year*—even for only a couple of days. So by waiting, you can claim the equivalent-to-married exemption in both this year and the next. You end up with an extra $1,300 in your pocket for being patient—almost enough to pay for the honeymoon.

That particular credit doesn't apply to my daughter, but the GST rule does. So by waiting until January, they've gained several hundred dollars in income—and preserved their mother's sanity.

Thanks, kids.

UPDATE

The actual dollars have changed slightly, but the tax rules are much the same as when this commentary was delivered. Avoid December weddings!

INTRODUCTION

After the wedding came the first house. It had been a long time since Shirley and I purchased a home, so we rediscovered what was happening in the marketplace when Tim and Kim went shopping in the midst of the recession of the early nineties.

FIRST HOUSE
MAY 1992

My daughter and her husband are homeowners. I never thought it would happen—but two weeks ago they closed the deal on a pleasant little townhouse just a couple of kilometres or so from where we live. It's actually something of a miracle. Under normal circumstances, they never could have done it. They've been out of college only a couple of years and haven't had time to save a lot of money. But three factors combined to make it all possible.

First, prices. We all know they're low in many areas. But you may not realize that, with some hard bargaining, you can drive them down even more. There are a lot of would-be sellers whose homes have been on the market a long time. In some cases, they've already bought another place and are desperate to get out from under.

That was the situation with the house my daughter bought. It was sitting vacant, costing the owners a lot of money to carry. It had already been reduced a couple of times, but even so her agent recommended going in with an offer well below the asking price.

She got it—and I think in a couple of years it's going to turn out to have been a great investment.

So the message here is, be tough. Asking prices are only that, nothing more. You can often get the house for several thousand dollars less, especially if it's been on the market for some time—and, most especially, if it's unoccupied.

Remember also that it's in your agent's interest to have you pay the highest possible price—it means more commission for him or her. So listen to the agent but use your own common sense when drawing up an offer. Don't be pressured into putting in too high a bid. If there ever was a time to drive a hard bargain, this is it.

The second reason my daughter bought is low mortgage rates. It's less expensive to carry a property today than it has been for many years. The key is whether to stay short or lock in for the long term.

I would normally advise people to go with a six-month or one-year term right now. With the economy still a disaster zone in many parts of the country, interest rates should fall still more in the coming months.

But the constitutional mess suggests caution. If a sudden increase in interest rates would put your home at risk, locking in a five-year rate at around 10 percent is the safest course at present.

But here's a way to hedge your bets. Find out what your monthly payment would be if the interest rate were, say, 11 percent. See if you could afford it. If so, take a six-month term at a lower interest rate, but make your payments as if it were at the higher rate. The difference goes toward reducing your principal. If rates drop over the next six months, you can lock in then. If they go up, your budget covers the increased cost.

The clincher in my daughter's decision to buy was the RRSP withdrawal plan announced in the February [1991] budget. Since I'm a firm believer in the value of RRSPs, I've urged my children to invest in them from the time they started to earn income. They've listened.

Of course, none of us expected such a fast payoff. But the money my daughter and son-in-law had accumulated in their plans gave them that little extra they needed to meet the down payment. It wasn't a lot—just a few thousand dollars. But it made the deal possible. So just in case you're listening, Mr. Mazankowski [Don Mazankowski was the finance minister at that time], your plan has helped at least one young couple become homeowners.

What really impressed me was the ease with which my daughter was able to make the arrangements. This is a program with a minimum of red tape, and the repayment terms are quite reasonable. Normally, I don't advocate dipping into RRSP money. But there are times when I'll make an exception. This is one of them.

Happy house-hunting.

UPDATE

Housing prices have firmed somewhat since this was written, but interest rates are much lower than they were at the time. My advice on mortgage management still stands: Pay the lowest amount of interest possible and use the difference to reduce your principal. As for the Home Buyers' Plan, it's become a permanent part of the landscape and is immensely popular. But unless you manage the repayments properly, it will end up taking a big bite out of your retirement income.

CHAPTER

2

The Tax Man
Cometh . . .

Taxes are an inevitable consequence of government. Politicians and
bureaucrats, by their very nature, always want to introduce new programs or expand existing ones. Such initiatives bring power, status,
publicity, and, if popular, can be useful in obtaining reelection—the
ultimate goal of every government. But new or expanded programs
must be funded, and the only source for the money is the Canadian
taxpayer, whether as a corporation or an individual.

Because we allowed our governments to play this game for so
long, we have reached the point where we are among the most
heavily taxed people in the world. When the United States, which
many Americans feel is guilty of overtaxation, looks like a tax haven
to Canadians, you know something is seriously amiss.

Newly elected governments are especially guilty of piling on
taxes. They've just received a mandate from the electorate, usually as
a result of lots of promises. Contrary to popular belief, politicians
usually do take such promises seriously and strive to implement as
many as possible. Since the new government won't have to face the
voters again for another four years, the time to gather the money to
achieve those objectives is in the early stages of the mandate.

The commentary that follows was delivered shortly after the
first Progressive Conservative government led by Brian Mulroney
took office in 1984 and the finance minister of the day, Michael
Wilson, was pondering his options and deciding what steps to take
to try to get the deficit under control—one of the Tories' campaign
promises. As you read this, remember that it was written a decade
before we actually got a budget that seriously addressed the deficit
problem.

TAX REFORM
AUGUST 1984

Taxes. It's a subject nobody likes, but one you're going to be hearing a lot about as our new government tries to come to grips with our financial mess. One of the first items on the agenda has to be a program to get our runaway deficit under control. Part of that must be a plan to increase revenues. That's why there's going to be a lot of talk about the tax system in the months ahead.

The government is really in a bind here. Canadians are already among the most heavily taxed people in the western world. Piling on more is not going to sit well. So what I suspect is coming is a lot of talk about tax reform. I suggest you be very suspicious: Often what that really means is a rearrangement of the tax system so governments can take more of your money without your being aware of it. A political flimflam, if you like. Let's look at some of the things that might happen.

First, I'll be very surprised if the government doesn't quickly introduce some variation of Ed Broadbent's minimum tax [Broadbent was NDP leader at the time]. That's the concept whereby anyone earning over a certain amount—Broadbent set the figure at $50,000—would have to pay a minimum income tax each year; the NDP leader suggested 20 percent. [Liberal leader] John Turner has also picked up the idea, and although his numbers are different, the concept is the same. The idea is to prevent high-income earners from using a variety of deductions to reduce their income tax to zero. That sounds laudable on the surface. The problem is that when you start to analyze why those people aren't paying taxes, you often find it's because they've invested in some area of the economy that Parliament felt was in need of a financial shot in the arm. Tax concessions are a way of achieving that. Remove them, and you cut back the flow of money, leaving yourself with the original problem.

Nonetheless, I think a minimum tax is inevitable. For one thing, it would raise a substantial amount of cash—$150 million to $200 million, according to estimates I've seen. For another, it would be politically popular—a soak-the-rich device that might deflect attention from other steps that soak everyone else. And, finally, there's a precedent—the United States already has such a tax in place.

One other consideration that I think will make a minimum tax irresistible: It would create a precedent that could then be applied to corporations. And that's where the real money is.

Another thing you'll hear a lot about is a flat-rate tax. That's a system in which most deductions are eliminated and everyone pays a single rate—say, 25 percent of their earnings. You may remember that Peter Pocklington raised the idea during the Tory leadership race [he was a leadership candidate]. Some critics accused him of being financially naive. But support for the idea has been quietly building. It's getting a lot of attention in the States—there are several bills in Congress supporting it and President Reagan seems to favour the idea.

Many tax lawyers and accountants in this country think it could work. It's a political minefield—remember what happened to Allan MacEachen when he tried to cut out some deductions in 1981. But if the idea catches on in the U.S., don't be surprised to see it move up the political agenda here.

The problem with a flat-rate tax is that the people it will hit hardest are the lower- and middle-income groups—the ones that make up the majority of voters in this country. Once people start to recognize this, the idea may not be quite so appealing. Furthermore, with the government needing to increase revenues, any flat-rate tax would probably be set at a level that would ensure that the total take is higher than it is now. That's what I mean by using tax reform to disguise real increases.

UPDATE

We did indeed get a minimum tax from Mr. Wilson, albeit in a watered-down form. The flat-tax debate rages on, but no government, either here or in the U.S., appears to be anywhere close to implementing the idea. One other point to remember: During their eight years in office, the Progressive Conservatives, who were theoretically opposed to high taxes, increased the tax burden on Canadians more than any previous post-war government had done, culminating with the introduction of the GST. And while they were doing that, the deficit climbed and climbed and climbed. History will brand that government and its members as one of the most profligate we've ever experienced.

INTRODUCTION

The effort to escape heavy taxes led Canadians to take evasive actions, some of which technically turned us into criminals. Here's an illustration.

UNDERGROUND ECONOMY
AUGUST 1985

I have a couple of questions for you. Now be honest when you answer.

First question: Have you ever done any work for which you were paid in cash and which you didn't declare on your income tax? Think about it—it could be anything from a baby-sitting job to an article you wrote in your spare time.

Second question: Have you ever done any work on a barter basis that you didn't declare for income-tax purposes? Maybe you're a dentist who fixed an auto mechanic's teeth in exchange for work on your car, or a lawyer who swapped services with a plumber.

Final question—and if you answered no to the first two, this one may catch you: Have you ever accepted an offer to have work done at a discount if you paid in cash? Maybe it was a carpenter who did work at your home, or a hairdresser who gave you a perm after-hours in his or her apartment, or a cleaning person—anything of that nature.

If you answered yes to either of the first two questions, you're a member of Canada's mysterious but growing underground economy. If you answered yes only to the third one, you're an accomplice in it. In either case, Revenue Canada is becoming more interested in you, so watch out.

The underground economy is simply tax evasion on a grand scale. It's a twilight zone of cash deals, moonlighting, and barter transactions that are never reported for tax purposes. Revenue Canada has known about it for some time. They haven't been talking a lot about it, though—perhaps because they've been afraid that by calling attention to it, they'd just encourage more people to participate.

That's changing, though—maybe because the underground economy has gotten so big the government can no longer afford to pretend it doesn't exist. No one knows exactly how large it is. How can you measure the unmeasurable? But some estimates suggest Ottawa may be losing $10 billion a year in tax revenue because of it. That's almost a third of our swollen deficit.

So now Revenue Canada is beginning to make noises about a crackdown. Revenue Minister Perrin Beatty has a personal interest in the subject and his department is responding accordingly. Beatty would like to deal with the problem by restoring confidence and a sense of fairness in the tax system. He recognizes, quite rightly, that you can't put a taxman in everyone's home. We operate on an honour system in this country, and if that breaks down—as it may be doing—we're in trouble.

I'd be delighted to see some basic tax reform that took us in the direction of restored confidence and fairness. That's one reason I hope that Ronald Reagan gets his tax proposals through in the U.S.— they will force us, finally, to rethink our chaotic system. In the meantime, though, my guess is that if Revenue Canada is going to make any inroads into the underground economy, it will be by getting tough. One thing they may do is to take an especially close look at some areas in which tax evasion has become quite systematized and launch some test cases.

Those won't be hard to find. Last year, for instance, a prominent Quebec contractor stated publicly that as much as 25 percent of the construction work in the province is done by workers who get paid reduced rates in cash, under the table. He estimated the total wages at between $500 million and $600 million per year, most of which is not declared.

So if you answered yes to any of those questions I asked at the beginning, be warned. I don't know where Revenue Canada will swoop, or how they'll do it—but it's coming. A word to the wise.

UPDATE

Ottawa has still not figured out how to deal effectively with the underground economy. In fact, the problem has become much worse since the introduction of the GST, which was only a glint in Michael Wilson's eye at the time this commentary was delivered. Canada's auditor general has complained about the revenue drain on several occasions, and the tax department has zeroed in on specific sectors of the economy to try to catch evaders. But the practice continues on a broad scale.

INTRODUCTION

With a little distance between us and the Mulroney years, it's sometimes easy to forget just how effective that government was at reducing our take-home pay. The following two items, prepared after Michael Wilson's first budget, serve as a reminder.

MORE TAXES

DECEMBER 1985

I don't really want to play the Grinch who stole Christmas. After all, this is supposed to be a happy time of year. But I have to tell you this:

After all the presents are opened and all the turkey eaten, there are some unpleasant surprises coming. When you wake up New Year's morning, it won't just be a hangover you'll have to contend with. There will also be a whole new batch of tax increases to add to your discomfort. Some may be courtesy of your provincial or territorial government. But most will be the doing of Brian Mulroney's Tories—their holiday gift to the Canadian people.

Remember last May? The grass was turning green, the tulips were in bloom—and Michael Wilson was presenting his first budget. It was a very clever budget. There was a lot of talk about fairness and toughness, and a headline-grabbing proposal on capital gains. There were also a lot of tax increases. But most of them were hidden. When you got up the morning after, nothing very much seemed to have changed.

Well, I'll let you in on a secret. Our politicians have gotten smart. They've figured out that most Canadians are fed up with paying higher and higher taxes. So what are they doing? They're burying those taxes. They're hiding them away, hoping you won't notice that they're sticking their hand even deeper into your pocket. The worst thing is, they seem to be getting away with it. It's all happening so subtly that we're only dimly aware of what's taking place.

It used to be that the impact of tax increases was painfully obvious. A finance minister read his budget speech and announced higher rates of personal income tax. A few weeks later your paycheque was less because more tax had been taken off. You knew how hard you'd been hit, and you knew who to blame. That's no longer true. And this last Conservative budget has taken the art of hiding taxes to a new high.

Let me give you an example. On January 1, a whole range of federal sales taxes will go up by a percentage point. The general tax will rise to 11 percent. The tax on construction materials will increase to 7 percent. The tax on cable- and pay-TV services will also go to 7 percent. And the tax on alcohol and tobacco will go to 14 percent.

Now, your first reaction may be, So what, what's 1 percent? Well, it's not 1 percent. The tax on your cable-TV services will actually go up 17 percent. The general sales tax is levied at the manufacturer's level. Let's take an appliance company. It produces a quality refrigerator that it sells for $500. At a 10 percent rate, it would be assessed $50 in tax. But when the rate increases to 11 percent on January 1, that assessment goes to $55—a 10 percent increase.

You may never notice that increase. It will be passed along to the wholesaler and then to the retailer, and finally to you. But you *will* end up paying—not knowing why, perhaps grumbling about the return of inflation, never realizing that the blame should be placed squarely on Mr. Wilson.

There's a bit more to this particular story. The former Liberal government raised the federal sales tax from 9 percent to 10 percent as a "temporary" measure shortly before it was voted out. That temporary tax was to have expired at the end of 1988. Mr. Wilson made that increase permanent in his budget—and then added a new one on top of it.

So if you notice prices are starting to creep up during 1986, don't be too quick to blame the retailer or the manufacturer. It may just be Mr. Wilson's budget starting to work its magic.

UPDATE

The taxes referred to here relate to the old manufacturers' sales tax, which was buried in the sale price of the goods and services you bought. When the GST replaced this tax, it was hailed as a great improvement because the new sales tax was transparent—you could see how much you paid the government. When people saw how much they were being hit for, they didn't like it. So the Liberals have gone back to the idea of trying to bury the tax again, which was a key part of the GST harmonization with the Maritime provinces in early 1997. Then they'll be able to slip through unseen increases again, in the same way Michael Wilson did a decade ago. Things never change.

STILL MORE TAXES
DECEMBER 1985

For the past couple of weeks I've been talking about some of the tax changes that become effective in 1986. Let me wrap up this unpleasant subject with a quick look at a few more of the measures from last May's federal budget that are about to take hold.

First the surtax. It's been in place since last July, but for 1986 the rate doubles. Perhaps more to the point, it's now going to be taken into account in your tax deductions at source, which it hasn't been until now. That means that if your income is high enough, you're about to start feeling the bite.

The surtax will amount to an additional 5 percent on your basic federal tax between $6,000 and $15,000. If you pay more than $15,000 in federal tax, you'll pay an additional 10 percent on the balance.

Now, this is supposed to be a temporary tax. When Finance Minister Wilson announced it, he promised it would die at the end of 1986. If that's true, and you're going to be hit by it, you should try to delay some income until 1987 if you can. But temporary taxes have an odd way of becoming permanent, so I wouldn't try anything too complicated to avoid it.

The surtax will affect only those people making pretty good incomes, probably over $60,000. But another change will hit us all. The old federal tax deduction that used to save us a few dollars a year has finally bitten the dust. It was worth $100 in 1985, but now it's gone. Rest in peace.

If you're eligible for the child tax credit, there are some changes here as well. Starting in 1986, the maximum income your family can earn and still receive the full credit drops from $26,330 to $23,500.

The good news is that the credit itself goes up by $70, to $454 per child. But for every $100 in family income over the $23,500 level, the value of the credit drops by $5. That means if your family earns over $32,500, the credit has no value.

What else? Well, things aren't all bleak; there are a couple of goodies if you have some money. The first is that the maximum RRSP contribution goes up to $7,500 or 20 percent of earned income in 1986, if you're not a member of a company pension plan. It's the first stage in the government's plan to eventually increase the contribution levels to $15,500 a year by 1990.

If you are a member of a company plan, the RRSP rules are the same as they were last year. There were some changes proposed, but they've been delayed until Ottawa deals with the protests they generated. That means you can still contribute a combined maximum of $3,500 to your pension plan and your RRSP in 1986.

The allowable capital gains exemption also jumps in 1986, to $50,000. This is stage two in Mr. Wilson's plan to eventually allow each of us lifetime tax-free capital gains of half a million dollars. If you're one of the fortunate ones who can benefit, this can go a long way toward offsetting all those nasty budget tax increases that are now starting to bite.

On that optimistic note, Happy New Year.

UPDATE

The "temporary" surtax is still around, and figures to be for a long time. Income tax was supposed to be a temporary measure too, when it was introduced to help pay for the First World War. The bit about RRSPs is interesting—we were supposed to move to a $15,500 maximum contribution by 1990. The current timetable will have us there around 2005. Don't you believe it! As for the $500,000 lifetime capital gains exemption, Michael Wilson backtracked on that within a year, reducing it to $100,000 and hedging it with all kinds of conditions. Paul Martin completed the demolition job in his first budget after the Liberals came to power. So what are we left with in the late nineties? The tax breaks are all gone, but the tax increases are still in place. O Canada!

INTRODUCTION

The next item conveys a sense of the frustration that I, and many other Canadians, was feeling about the ever-mounting tax burden more than a decade ago—a frustration we still feel today.

ENOUGH TAXES
JUNE 1986

Let me ask you a question. How much do you think you're paying in taxes out of every dollar you earn? I'm not just talking about income tax here. Add in sales taxes, property taxes, gasoline taxes, liquor taxes, corporation taxes—the whole bit.

According to a calculation done recently by the Bank of Montreal, the average Canadian this year will give our various levels of government 41 cents out of every dollar earned.

Think about that. Forty-one cents of every dollar. And then think about this. The average American will pay governments about 25 cents of every dollar earned. That's a heck of a gap. If you look at it in percentage terms, it means we're paying out about 64 percent more in taxes than the average American is.

The other day at lunch, a friend asked me when Canadians were going to stop passively accepting this incredible tax burden and start protesting. I find myself wondering the same thing. The tax burden in this country is becoming stifling. And it just gets worse, not better. Last year we were paying about 39.3 cents of every dollar earned to governments. We desperately need a major tax reform in this country, similar to what's happening in the U.S.

But we need more. We need major cuts to government spending if we are ever going to start getting taxes down to reasonable levels. I don't mean by that the kind of cosmetic cuts the Conservatives have been content with to date. I mean some *real* cuts—starting with the universality of our social welfare system, which is a luxury we can no longer afford. Until we do that, we haven't a hope of being able to enjoy more of our earnings. Let me tell you why.

In 1970—just 16 years ago—the total cost to the federal government for interest payments to service the national debt amounted to just 6 percent of revenues. Now that amount is up to 36 percent. With an annual deficit of close to $30 billion, another $3 billion or so is added to those interest costs each year.

So far, the Conservatives have tried to reduce that deficit mainly by raising taxes. If they keep on that way, we're all going to be handing over an even larger chunk of our pay in the years ahead. That's why, as far as I'm concerned, it has got to stop. Remember the movie *Network*? People throwing open their windows and yelling: "I'm fed up and I'm not going to take it anymore!"?

Well, the friend I had lunch with was feeling that way. I'm feeling that way. I suspect a lot of Canadians are feeling that way. If you're one of them, drop a note to your MP. Maybe if there are enough of us, someone will listen.

UPDATE

Taxes have moved higher still since that broadcast, but at least our political leaders finally came to the realization that spending cuts were needed. Maybe the long-awaited process of tax reduction is next on the agenda.

INTRODUCTION

One of the most unpopular acts of the Mulroney government, and the one that perhaps contributed most to the annihilation the Conservatives suffered in the 1993 election, was the introduction of the Goods and Services Tax. I never liked the GST for a number of reasons, as I explained to CBC Radio listeners in the following commentary.

BEWARE THE GST
MAY 1990

Whether we like it or not, the GST is coming.

Let me start by saying yet again that I am adamantly opposed to this tax. I began speaking out against it several years ago, when Michael Wilson first hinted he wanted to go this route, and my mind has not changed since. It's not that I'm a fan of the existing manufacturers' sales tax. It's a mess, no question about it. But there are several problems with the GST.

One is its complexity. It's going to take years before we understand exactly how this tax applies in every situation. And the paperwork involved for small businesses is going to be brutal.

Second, it's an easy way for governments to squeeze more tax money out of us. There's speculation that several provinces will jump on board pretty quickly, now that the federal Tories have taken all the political heat. And why not? It's easy money for provincial treasurers. They can extend their sales tax base while lowering the rate of provincial sales tax at the same time. It's a politician's dream—they can take credit for a lower tax rate while putting their hands still deeper into our pockets.

My third concern is that the GST is going to have a much greater impact on inflation than Ottawa is suggesting. I don't believe the estimate of a modest 1.25 percent impact on the CPI. I lived through the imposition of the Value Added Tax in Britain, and if the U.K. experience is any indication, the effect of the GST on prices here is going to be much worse than anyone expects.

I think those are all very good reasons to scrap the GST. Unfortunately, Mr. Wilson isn't listening to me—or to the millions of other Canadians who share my view. Like it or not, we're going to have this tax. So I think the time has come to stop trying to hold back the tide and to start figuring out how best to live with this new beast that's about to become part of all our lives.

For starters, we're all thinking in terms of the GST taking effect next January 1. In fact, you're going to have to make decisions on some items before September 1 if you want to avoid paying GST on them.

These are things you pay for this year but benefit from, either in whole or in part, in 1991.

One example is magazine subscriptions. If you renew before September 1, you'll escape the tax. If you wait until after that date, you'll pay GST on that portion of your subscription that covers the period after January 1, 1991. That tax won't be collected from you right away—under the legislation, Ottawa can't start raking in money until the New Year. So the magazine publisher will send you a special invoice in 1991, covering the GST due on that part of your subscription. You can avoid that hassle, and save a little money, by acting now.

Club memberships are another item affected by the September 1 cutoff.

The GST will apply to all club expenses: initiation fees, activity fees, a club share—the works. So if you're thinking of joining a club, do it before September 1—you'll save yourself a lot of money, especially if it's an expensive membership. If you're already a club member, consider pre-paying your 1991 dues before September 1 to save on tax.

There's one catch here, though. This pre-September tax saving applies only to individuals. If your company pays your fees, there's no way out. The GST will have to be paid.

UPDATE

The GST turned out to be every bit as complex and unpopular as I predicted. Fortunately, the impact on the CPI was not as severe as I had forecast, but that was mainly due to the fact the tax was launched in the midst of a deep recession. Sellers simply couldn't pass on the costs to customers, because of heightened price sensitivity. I continue to believe the tax should be scrapped, not just because of the huge number of dollars it sucks out of our pockets but also because of the immense amount of bookkeeping and paperwork it imposes on self-employed people and small businesses that don't have the resources to keep up with the government's reporting requirements.

INTRODUCTION

If you voted for the Liberals in 1993 because of their promise to scrap the GST and were disappointed when they didn't, you probably didn't hear the following broadcast made two years earlier.

GST ISN'T GOING
JANUARY 1991

As those of you who listen regularly know, I've never been a fan of the GST. But now that it's here, it's here forever.

Let's not kid ourselves about that. It doesn't matter what party is in power in Ottawa—the Liberals, the Reform, the NDP, the Tories, the Bloc Québécois. None of them will abolish the GST. I don't care what they say during an election campaign. It's never happened anywhere else in the world. So why should it happen here?

The reason is simple. The GST is a wonderful money machine for cash-strapped governments. No one is going to give that up. So if you've been deluding yourself into thinking this nightmare will go away after the next election, forget it. Like income tax, it's here to stay.

The challenge now is to make it more tolerable, because, as things stand, this tax is a mess. It needs a drastic overhaul, and quickly. The biggest favour our politicians could do for us is to get started *now*.

Here's my wish list of what I'd like to see done. First, the responsible governments should bring in regulations to standardize the way the tax is applied at the retail level right across the country. Top priority should be given to the way in which GST is applied to consumer prices. Let's have all retailers either include it in the sticker price or—and this is my preference—add it on at the register. The chaos we're now seeing—where some stores do one thing and some do another—simply can't be allowed to go on. Action on this has to be a priority. Manitoba has already introduced some rules. The other provinces should do so as well.

By extension, the same policy should apply also to advertising. Right now, trying to compare advertised prices from one store with those from another is pure guesswork. Do both include GST? Neither one? The ad may tell you—or it may not. In most provinces, there are no laws requiring retailers to state whether the prices in their ads are GST inclusive. There should be. Let's get with it.

After we get these immediate problems dealt with, we need to come to grips with the way GST is applied to food. As things stand now, what we're experiencing is the stuff of high farce. My wife was at the supermarket meat counter the other day when an elderly stranger came up to her holding two seemingly identical jars of peanuts. He couldn't get over the fact that one was subject to GST because the nuts were salted, while the unsalted variety escaped.

This nonsense can't go on. It's no use saying we'll get used to it—we won't. We'll just be constantly reminded how silly the bureaucrats in Ottawa really are. Either tax all food at the same rate—at a rate lower than 7 percent, as some other countries do it. Or don't tax food at all—any food, anywhere.

Last on my GST wish list is an appeal to the provincial governments to act responsibly and integrate their sales taxes with the GST sooner rather than later. Every province now has a two-tax system except Alberta, which has no provincial sales tax, and Quebec, which is already integrating its sales tax with the GST.

Do our lives really have to be this complicated? Isn't paying the damn tax bad enough? Can't we at least have our pockets picked without having to reach for our calculators every time?

As I said at the outset, the GST is here to stay. So let's stop the political posturing and get down to making the situation a little more tolerable.

UPDATE

As predicted, the Liberals didn't abolish the GST, despite their campaign promises. The tax continues to create absurdities. The battle over whether to include it in the sticker price just had a rerun in the

Maritimes. And provincial harmonization in the rest of the country still seems a long way off.

INTRODUCTION

The government is always tinkering with tax rules in an effort to keep them abreast of social changes. Here's an example that affected 1.5 million Canadian families.

WHAT'S A SPOUSE?
MARCH 1994

It all goes back to the 1992 budget. That's when the finance minister of the day, Don Mazankowski, told the House of Commons that couples living together in a common-law relationship would be considered as "spouses" for tax purposes.

The change was made necessary by a high-profile court case in which a Hamilton, Ont., couple showed that they were paying thousands of dollars a year more in taxes because they were legally married. The case brought home to all Canadians something a few people had quietly known for years—that "living in sin," as it used to be called, had some definite economic advantages.

Once the cat was out of the bag, Ottawa decided something had better be done about it before the tax revolt expanded into a marriage revolt as well. So Mr. Mazankowski decreed that, starting with the 1993 tax year, unmarried couples living together would be treated exactly as if they were duly married.

It's too soon to know how this is going to work out, because 1993 tax returns are only now being filed. But it wouldn't surprise me to see a lot of common-law couples come out of the closet—at least in terms of what they say to Revenue Canada—while others stay discreetly hidden. That's because declaring common-law status will mean lower taxes for some people, but higher taxes for others.

The winners will be traditional single-income households, where one spouse works and the other stays home with the kids. For the first time the working spouse—let's say it's the man, in this case—will be able to claim a married tax credit for his common-law wife. If the wife's net income was less than $538 last year, that produces a reduction in the husband's federal tax of $915. With provincial taxes added in, the total savings will be in the $1,400 range. Not bad. Couples in this situation should love the new rule.

You'll also come out ahead if one partner has tax credits he or she can't use—these include the age, pension, disability, education, and tuition credits. Any of them can now be transferred to a common-law spouse.

Who loses under the new rules? Generally, two-income couples. They'll have to combine their incomes to determine eligibility for the GST rebate or the Child Benefit. Many people who qualified for either or both in the past, when each income was looked at separately, will see their payments reduced or even eliminated. The new rules also end income splitting between common-law couples—a technique designed to get more income into the hands of the partner with the lower tax rate.

So what's the definition of a common-law spouse? The tax guide says it's the parent of your child, if that person is living with you. Or it can be someone of the opposite sex who has lived with you continuously for 12 months. What the guide doesn't say—maybe Revenue Canada was too embarrassed to add this—is that you have to be together in a conjugal relationship. Two people of the opposite sex who are simply sharing an apartment as roommates—which happens more frequently these days—aren't common-law spouses, even though the tax guide makes them appear to be.

The obvious question is how Revenue Canada decides you're in a conjugal relationship if you have no children. I thought the state had withdrawn from the bedrooms of the nation. Maybe I was wrong.

UPDATE

These rules are still essentially the same. The next problem the tax people will have to face is same-sex couples.

CHAPTER
3

... And the Government Taketh Away

Over the years, successive governments have pulled off a deft sleight of hand on the unsuspecting Canadian public. They have successfully picked our pockets for billions of dollars in additional revenue by stripping away many of the benefits that in happier times had offered a spoonful of sugar to help make the tax medicine go down. In doing this, they have been able to create the illusion that they weren't really raising taxes at all—which of course was the furthest thing from the truth. This chapter documents some of the ways in which various finance ministers managed this trick, starting with the move to do away with the deduction on interest income.

SUPPORT CANADA AND PAY MORE TAX
NOVEMBER 1987

If you bought Canada Savings Bonds this year, I have good news and bad news for you.

The good news is you made a tremendous investment. In fact, you won't find anything else that pays as good a return while offering both safety and immediate cash if you need it. The bad news is you're probably going to pay more tax on those bonds. That's because tax reform has really dealt a blow to small investors.

The problem is the plan to do away with the $1,000 investment income deduction, beginning in 1988. That deduction meant that most of us didn't have to pay tax on the interest we earn on our savings accounts or CSBs. Starting next year, we will.

All the interest you earn on your bonds is going to get caught in Revenue Canada's net. That means that for every $100 bond you bought, you have to pay $2.30 in tax next year, assuming you are in the lowest bracket. If you are in the highest bracket, you'll pay about $4. It doesn't make those bonds look quite as attractive, does it?

This change will force you to think carefully about how you want to declare the income on your compound interest CSBs. You have a choice. You can declare the interest every year and pay tax accordingly. Or you can save it up and declare the interest every third year. Under the old rules, most people were better off declaring the interest yearly. This was because the investment income deduction could be used to shelter it.

The new rules may change your thinking, though. Since you're going to have to pay the tax anyway, you might as well postpone it for as long as you can. That means you might want to take advantage of the three-year rule. The only thing to watch out for is that the accumulated interest doesn't push you into a higher tax bracket. You'll have to make that calculation yourself. Remember, this applies to compound-interest bonds only. If you have regular bonds, you have to declare the interest every year.

Now this change doesn't come in until 1988, but it may affect your thinking about how you prepare your 1987 tax return. Obviously, you want to take full advantage of the investment income deduction while it's still around. After all, this is your last kick at the can.

So if you have any older Canada Savings Bonds that are earning interest this year, and you haven't made full use of the investment income deduction, be sure to include your CSB interest on your 1987 tax return.

These days you need every edge you can get.

UPDATE

It's interesting to note that tax reform always seems to consist of making people pay more tax. Governments claim that they are targetting only the wealthier segments of society, but this is a classic example of a "reform" that hit small investors hardest of all. The government wasn't fooling around, either. Having made this decision, they were determined to go after every cent they could get, as the next commentary explains.

It's a SIN
December 1988

It's another fall-out from tax reform.

As of January 1, you have to give your social insurance number whenever you open a new bank account. You'll also have to give your SIN if you purchase a guaranteed investment certificate, invest in mutual funds, buy stocks, or, in fact, make any kind of investment. If you don't, you're liable to be hit with a $100 fine. Obviously, the government means business here.

What's all this got to do with tax reform? Well, you may remember that one of the casualties of tax reform was the old $1,000 investment income deduction. That deduction was enough to shelter all the interest and dividends most people earned. But it was wiped out effective with the 1988 tax year. That meant that every penny of interest earned in your savings account suddenly became taxable.

That's a lot of potential new tax revenue for Ottawa. The trick is to collect it. Many people never bothered declaring small amounts of interest on their tax return—either because there were only a few dollars involved or because they knew the investment income deduction would cover them. And the government didn't worry, also because of that $1,000 deduction. So no serious effort was made to ensure the income was reported.

Now everything's changed. The government wants to hear about every cent your deposits and investments earn. They expect financial institutions to issue T-5 slips for all such income—and they want your social insurance number on those slips so they can trace the money back to you. That's the reason for these tough new rules.

You know, I was a political journalist when the social insurance number concept was first introduced in the 1960s. I remember the debate at that time. The government of the day—it was Lester Pearson's Liberals, as I recall—kept insisting social insurance numbers would never be used for anything other than keeping track of pension and welfare payments. They were indignant when the opposition parties said it was just the thin edge of the wedge—that eventually SIN would be used in virtually every aspect of government, including tax collection.

Well, the critics were right, of course. In fact, Ottawa started asking for social insurance numbers on tax returns in 1967. They've been gradually extending the use of them ever since—to the point where now you can't even open a bank account without giving one, unless you're prepared to run the risk of being hauled into court and fined.

Of course, it all makes bureaucracy function that much more efficiently. But when I look back on the original purpose of these numbers and the promises that were made, I can't help but feel a little betrayed.

UPDATE

Matters have progressively become even worse. These days you need to give your SIN for just about every financial transaction you make. It's not yet required for a trip to the bathroom, but wait a bit. The government is everywhere.

INTRODUCTION

Many of the benefits and tax advantages Ottawa has taken away over the past decade relate directly to the growing number of seniors in the Canadian population. Successive governments realized that our once-prized principle of universality in social problems was inevitably going to result in a cash drain on the federal treasury that could be met only by imposing huge tax increases on a population that was already convinced it was paying too much. The only alternative was to abandon universality in favour of selectivity. But it had to be done oh so carefully to avoid inflaming public opinion. The challenge the Finance department faced was to find some way of maintaining the fiction of universality while actually dumping the whole concept. After much soul-searching, the clawback was chosen as the solution.

THE END OF UNIVERSALITY
APRIL 1990

Something new has been added to your tax return this year, and you're not going to like it very much. It's a section titled "social benefits repayment"—a rather innocuous term for the notorious clawback provisions relating to family allowances, unemployment insurance benefits, and Old Age Security payments.

You may remember that Michael Wilson announced in his 1989 budget that the government was going to start taxing back various benefit payments from people with higher incomes. Well, now you're seeing it in action. The program is being phased in over a three-year period; by the 1992 tax year it will be fully operational.

What we've got now is bad enough, though. While I've long been in favour of the principle of reducing social benefits to higher-income people, I have very serious reservations about the way it's being done. On top of that, Ottawa has added yet another level of difficulty to what is already an unnecessarily complex tax system. If you look at line 235 in the tax guide, you'll find three charts with over 20 lines of calculations that you may have to complete if you received any of these payments during the year.

I can just hear the bureaucrats who devised this idea muttering, "What's he going on about? It's not all that complicated." Well, when you pile this on top of tax credits, capital gains forms, CNIL, minimum tax, and all the other new items this government has added to our overburdened system, it's too much. It's about time someone gave a little thought to the poor taxpayer who actually has to fill out all these forms every year.

But until that happens, we're stuck with this. So let's see if I can help lead you through the clawback. For starters, the key number that determines whether you'll be hit by this measure is not your total income. There's been some confusion about that. What counts is your net income before adjustments. That's the figure that appears at line 234 of your return.

That's important, because it allows you to make a number of deductions from your income before your obligation to repay your social benefits is determined. Some of these deductions are potentially quite large—pension and RRSP contributions, child-care expenses, alimony and separation payments, union dues, and so on. If you're on the borderline, this may save you from the clawback. And if you're hit this year, take some time to study the list of deductions carefully to see if you can increase them—perhaps by adding to your RRSP contribution.

Once you arrive at a figure for line 234, see if it's over $47,190. If it's not, you're off the hook entirely—the clawback won't apply in your case. If it's over that amount but less than $50,000, only unemployment insurance benefits will be affected. Beyond $50,000, payments from all of the programs will be hit. In that case, the only good news I can give you is that, for 1989, you can lose only up to one-third of your benefits.

Next year, it'll be worse—unless you can find some additional deductions to bring your income under the magic number.

UPDATE

The clawback has now become a fixture in our tax system, with variations of it used to reduce other benefits and credits, such as the age tax credit. So far, it has not been applied to such sacred cows as the Canada Pension Plan. But don't expect that to last forever. As the bill mounts for CPP premiums every year, Canadians are going to become increasingly restless about the program.

INTRODUCTION

The idea was immensely appealing: a big lifetime capital gains exemption that would allow even small investors to potentially get rich without Revenue Canada thrusting its hand deep into their pockets. In his first budget after the Progressive Conservatives came to power in the early eighties, the finance minister of the day, Michael Wilson, unveiled plans for a half-million-dollar capital gains tax exemption for everyone. For tax-weary Canadians, it was a huge psychological boost, and the government obviously figured it would pay off by funnelling more money away from nonproductive GICs and into the lagging equity markets.

Then someone in the Finance department sat down and looked at the costs. The retreat was on. The $500,000 exemption suddenly became $100,000. Then the Tories started to hedge even that by bringing in tortuous concepts like the Cumulative Net Investment Loss (CNIL), which had the effect of reducing or eliminating the exemption under certain circumstances.

It became apparent over time that the cash-strapped Mulroney government wished it had never heard of the capital gains exemption. But it was their baby, so they were stuck with it.

But the Liberals weren't. So when they turfed out the Tories in the fall of 1993, it was clearly only a matter of time before the new government took away yet another goodie from the taxpayers.

GOODBYE TO THE
CAPITAL GAINS EXEMPTION
DECEMBER 1993

Every time the Conservatives brought in a budget, people would ask me the same question: Are they going to abolish the capital gains exemption this year? And every year I'd give the same answer: No, I don't think so.

My reasoning was simple. It was the Conservatives who originally brought in the exemption, in the first budget speech Michael Wilson ever delivered. They'd have looked pretty stupid if they'd announced at the end of their mandate that it wasn't such a good idea after all, and they were killing it. So they did what politicians usually do in these situations. They fiddled around with it. They reduced the amount you could claim, they declared that real estate was no longer eligible, they introduced silly concepts like the Cumulative Net Investment Loss—but they kept it.

Now they're gone and someone else is running the show. The Liberals have no political baggage here. This wasn't their baby, it's complicated to administer, and it's draining away badly needed tax dollars. Furthermore, they can at least make an argument that it hasn't been doing the job it was designed for. Low interest rates have been a far greater incentive for people to invest in the stock market than the capital gains exemption ever was.

So it wouldn't surprise me to see it disappear in the first Liberal budget. In fact, the prudent investor should consider that a strong possibility and take appropriate precautions.

This doesn't mean you have to rush out tomorrow and sell everything that's made a profit for you. For one thing, a budget is some time away. Parliament won't even meet until mid-January, so I wouldn't expect a federal budget until March or April. More important, I doubt that the finance minister would just slam the window shut if he abolishes the exemption. He's more likely to invoke the Mazankowski formula.

That's the plan former Finance Minister Don Mazankowski used in 1992 when he announced real estate would no longer be eligible for the exemption. What he did was to start a tax clock ticking on March 1 of that year. The effect is that the longer you hold real estate after that date, the greater your potential exposure to tax on your capital gain when you sell. The same formula could be extended to all other types of investments. So the exemption would be wound down over time, with everyone given fair warning.

That would be the best way to do it. But if you're worried the Liberals might not be so generous toward investors, then you should take steps to crystallize any capital gains before the next budget.

There are several ways to do that. You could simply sell the security and then, if you wish, buy it back. There's no mandatory waiting period involved; that applies only if you're claiming a capital loss.

Another possibility is to contribute the securities to a self-directed RRSP. That immediately triggers a capital gain for tax purposes. Or you could give the securities to a family member—your spouse or a child. That's also considered a deemed disposition for tax purposes. One other way to trigger a capital gain is to die—but that seems a little extreme under the circumstances.

The point is, you should start to give some thought to what you want to do. Your solution shouldn't be a drastic one—after all, Mr. Martin could surprise us and leave the exemption alone.

But frankly, I wouldn't want to take bets on that. Forewarned is forearmed.

UPDATE

Mr. Martin did indeed abolish the exemption in his first budget, but he gave Canadians who had gains they hadn't yet crystalled one last chance to use it. The end result of the whole fiasco is that we now pay more tax on a capital gain than we did before Mr. Wilson made his original announcement. At that time, only 50 percent of gains were taxable—the rest were ours to keep. As a price for the exemption, Mr. Wilson raised the "inclusion rate" to 75 percent in two stages. That's where it stands today. So people who didn't make extensive use of the exemption when it was available now must pay a higher tax cost for their profits—subsidizing, in effect, those who were able to benefit while it was around.

INTRODUCTION

The effective elimination of universality from Old Age Security, family allowances, and unemployment insurance was an initiative of the Progressive Conservative government led by Brian Mulroney. But

Jean Chrétien's Liberals obviously thought the idea was a good one, and Finance Minister Paul Martin picked up on the theme in his first budget, in 1994. This commentary was delivered a few weeks later.

TAXING TIMES FOR SENIORS
APRIL 1994

On April 27, 1989, the finance minister of the day, Michael Wilson, rose in the House of Commons to deliver his annual budget speech. It's a date that every Canadian over 65 should circle in black. We didn't realize it at the time, but in that speech Mr. Wilson set in motion a chain of events that would cost older Canadians millions of dollars and create what I believe is the potential for major social problems in the years ahead.

In that speech, Mr. Wilson announced a new tax that would hit seniors hard. It was called the social benefits repayment—better known today as the clawback. The idea was to tax back government payments to people Mr. Wilson described as "high-income tax-payers." Among the programs hit was Old Age Security—a universal plan that provides monthly support to people 65 and up.

When he introduced the tax, Mr. Wilson soothingly told the House of Commons: "It will affect about 4 percent of the 3 million seniors who receive Old Age Security pensions; less than 2 percent will have the full amount recovered." The implication was obvious. Only a few wealthy seniors would be affected. It's nothing to get excited about. The universality of Old Age Security would be pre-served.

There was some grumbling about the tax, but nothing compared to the angry response of a few years before, when Mr. Wilson tried to de-index OAS payments. The new measure went through and is now being fully applied. That might have been dismissed as a one-shot effort. But a new finance minister, representing a different party, has shown us it wasn't.

In his February budget, Paul Martin introduced stage two of the tax attack on seniors. He announced that the age credit would be reduced for people whose net income exceeds $25,921. The age credit provides additional tax relief to people over 65. It's a recogni-tion of the fact that many Canadians at this point in their lives have to live on a fixed income that may be substantially lower than incomes they enjoyed in their working years. In hitting the age credit, the finance minister effectively raised taxes on the older segment of the population. Like his predecessor, he claimed only higher-income people would be affected.

But the reality is somewhat different. Next year, in 1995, an older Canadian with an income of just $30,000 a year will have to pay about $150 more in taxes because of this change. At $35,000 a year, the increase will be in the $350 range. That's a lot of money for someone living on a fixed income.

And it's not the end of the story. Provincial governments, picking up on Mr. Wilson's precedent, have been targeting seniors for spending cutbacks. The reduction in medicare payments for services outside Canada was directed mainly at seniors who spend part of the winter in warmer climates. Some provinces have cut back on drug benefits for seniors.

In its February budget, the Alberta government proposed what is perhaps the most drastic step of all—to eliminate provincial government benefits to single seniors whose net income is higher than $18,200. The cutoff level for couples is $27,600.

The average annual family income in Canada is about $43,000 right now. So clearly, it's not just wealthy seniors who are being targeted. It's anyone who has managed to save enough money to live above the poverty line.

The pattern is now well established, and it's going to get worse.

UPDATE

It has gotten worse. If the proposed Seniors Benefit comes into effect as planned, in 2001, millions of middle-income Canadians will not only lose some or all of their government support but will face effective tax rates of up to 70 percent in some cases as their payments are clawed back.

INTRODUCTION

Eliminating tax breaks isn't always a bad thing. In some cases, government action helps to save people from themselves. Here's an example.

SOFTWARE LIMITED PARTNERSHIPS
DECEMBER 1994

The federal government has announced it's closing down one of the most popular tax shelters of 1994—the software limited partnerships.

Frankly, I'm not surprised. Many of these tax shelters were questionable at best. When someone tells you that you can deduct three dollars for every one you invest, it should make you at least a *little* suspicious. Revenue Canada isn't in the giveaway business.

The idea behind these tax shelters was to raise money to promote and market software programs that were supposedly sure-fire hits. Sounds OK—except that some of the deals were based on software packages that were acquired by the promoter at a bargain-basement price and had very little chance of success. In other words, the deals were created strictly for the write-offs involved. Not all of them were like this—but there were enough marginal offers to cause some prominent tax advisors to start raising warning flags. The concern was that Revenue Canada could come back and reassess your deductions on the grounds there was never any "reasonable expectation of profit." That's a catchall term the government uses to disallow investment tax claims it thinks are unreasonable.

I know people who have been caught on this hook in the past. A few years ago, a number of investors found themselves facing huge tax bills after Revenue Canada rejected their deductions for a yacht deal in the Caribbean. Some of them received reassessments totalling tens of thousands of dollars. Believe me, that's not the kind of notice you want to get in the mail.

So if you're thinking of buying a last-minute tax shelter to reduce your 1994 taxes, be very careful. Choose the type of shelter that's well established and has a track record with Revenue Canada. You may find some film deals or some oil-and-gas shelters still available. Some of these are OK, but others are highly speculative. Before you invest any money, take a close look at the investment projections, ask questions about the promoter's track record, and see how much money is being taken off the top to pay for initial expenses.

Also, make sure you won't be on the hook for more money if the deal runs into financial problems. Sometimes there's a clause in the contract that allows the promoter to come back to the unit holders for additional cash—and there may be no limit on the amount you'll be asked to put up.

The best advice I can give you, if you're considering a tax shelter, is to get an independent opinion from a financial professional you

trust before going in. These deals are usually extremely complex—
and often fraught with danger, both from an investment and a tax
point of view.

If in doubt, stay out. Better to pay 50 cents in taxes than lose a
dollar in capital.

UPDATE

Many people who bought into some of the more aggressive software
deals did in fact end up being audited by Revenue Canada. Meantime,
the Liberal government continued to close down more types of tax
shelters, including the extremely popular mutual fund limited partnerships, which had their last gasp in the early months of 1997.
There are still some tax shelters on offer in this country—but the
quality is often highly questionable. Be wary.

CHAPTER
4

RESP Risks

Saving for a child's future education is one of the most common financial concerns of young parents. They know the cost of attending university is rising at a rate that greatly exceeds inflation, and they know they should be putting money aside to ensure that their youngsters are able to go on to a postsecondary institution. But finding the right way to achieve that goal is difficult. Many parents (and grandparents) have opened Registered Education Savings Plans (RESPs) for their children. But these highly promoted plans have some serious flaws. When I pointed them out in the following commentaries, I unexpectedly unleashed a wave of criticism, both from some RESP sponsors and some investors who are in the plans. See what *you* think.

RESP DANGERS
APRIL 1996

It's hardly news that a college education is becoming more expensive every year. One of the prices we're having to pay for deficit reduction is a cutback in the funding of postsecondary schooling. As a result, university tuition fees are rising at an almost breathtaking rate. That has prompted angry student protests in many parts of the country, but don't expect them to have any impact. The reality is that there just aren't enough tax dollars to spread around. So the price of a college degree is going to keep going up.

By the time today's grade-school students are ready for college, only four groups of people are likely to go on to higher learning:

- Group one will be the very rich, whose parents can afford to send them anywhere.
- Group two will be the very smart, who will be able to win scholarships to pay for their education.

- Group three will be the very industrious, who are prepared to work long hours to earn the money needed to supplement their student loans.

- And group four? They'll be the ones whose parents started saving for their education early and regularly, and who invested the money wisely along the way.

It was this last group that Finance Minister Paul Martin was playing to when he brought down his budget in March. One of the measures he announced was an increase in the contribution limits to Registered Education Savings Plans—RESPs, as they're known. You're now allowed to contribute a maximum of $2,000 a year to one of these plans, up from $1,500 before. The lifetime contribution limit has been pushed up to $42,000.

What the finance minister was effectively saying is that since the government can no longer afford the same degree of educational support, they'll make it easier for individual families to do so. All well and good, as far as it goes. But if you have young children and are concerned about their future education, I suggest you think long and hard before opening one of these plans. Mr. Martin's increased contribution limits could actually end up costing you more money.

There's one fundamental problem with RESPs. They're a gamble. Literally. I call them education roulette. Why? Because if the plan's beneficiary doesn't go on to college, you lose *all* the income that the plan has earned over the years. That's right. All of it—perhaps tens of thousands of dollars.

The reason is that the Income Tax Act states that money earned in an RESP can be used only for purposes of furthering education. If the child doesn't make use of it, you have an expensive problem. Some plans allow you to change the beneficiary, so that the money can be directed to a sibling or another family member who wants to continue studies. But suppose no one in the family fits the bill? You're out of luck. In some programs, your money goes into a pool to be used to pay for the education of other participants—worthy students, perhaps, but no one you know.

Other plans require that you designate an educational institution to receive the income your child can't use. You'll get your contributions back, but that's all.

We're talking about a lot of money here. If you set up a plan when a child is born and contribute annually until you reach the maximum, the RESP will be worth just under $90,000 when the child is 21, assuming a 7 percent average annual return. That means if the child does not go on to college, you lose almost $48,000! That's 21 years of investment income down the drain because you guessed wrong.

And you wonder why I call it education roulette?

RESP Solutions
April 1996

RESPs can be great ways to save for a child's education—*if* the youngster goes on to college. If he or she doesn't, these plans could cost you tens of thousands of dollars in lost investment income.

There's no need for this. All it takes is for someone in the Finance department to wake up to the reality of the situation and ask the minister to introduce a small amendment to the Income Tax Act. That amendment would simply strike out the requirement that all income earned in an RESP must be used for purposes of education. It's *that* provision that turns these plans into such a gamble. If no one in your family can use the money for that purpose, then some one else's child is going to be the beneficiary of all your years of saving and personal sacrifice. That is simply not fair, and it's time the government acknowledged the fact—that is, if they really want to encourage Canadians to save for an education in this way.

The solution is very simple. If the accumulated investment earnings cannot be used for an educational purpose, introduce a requirement that the plan be collapsed when the beneficiary reaches a certain age—say, 24. Return the capital to the parents, tax-free, which is what happens right now. Then tax the balance in the plan at the beneficiary's marginal rate.

In all probability, the government will recover between 40 and 50 percent of the plan's earnings over the years in taxes by using this system. That's fair enough—after all, that money was earned on a tax-sheltered basis. But the balance of the money would be available to help the young person get a start in life, perhaps by putting it toward the down payment on a home. And the family won't have been deprived of perhaps two decades of investment income.

I think this approach is fair from everyone's point of view—the government gets back a big chunk of that tax-deferred income, and the lottery aspect is removed from what should be a popular, widely used savings plan.

But unless and until the government gets around to doing this, what should you do? Let me make some suggestions. For starters, don't open an education savings plan for an only child. The odds are stacked against you; the great majority of students do not go on to university.

If you have two children, you might consider setting up a plan for one of them. Just make sure you can change the beneficiary at any time, if need be. Of course, the problem with this approach is that if both kids go on to college, you won't have saved enough. Unfortunately, that's the kind of risk the government is forcing us to take.

Alternatively, save for your children's education in some other way. Our tax rules make this difficult, because without the sheltering of an RESP, any investment income you earn is going to be taxed. That means the savings will grow more slowly.

But there is a way around this problem. Invest the money in your child's name, in trust, and put it into securities that generate mainly capital gains. Any interest or dividend income earned from this type of investment is attributed back to the parents. But capital gains are not. They stay with the child. That means that there should be little or no tax payable on these earnings, because the children won't have much other income.

You'll have to manage the money carefully, realizing and declaring some of the gains along the way. That's because if you wait until the child is ready to go to college to take profits, the amount could be so great that it would push your youngster into a high tax bracket. So be careful how you handle the money, or get some professional advice.

All this shouldn't really be necessary, though. RESPs are a fundamentally sound concept. The government simply has to recognize their fatal flaw and remove the provision that confiscates years of investment income, all because a parent guessed wrong.

UPDATE

Whether prompted by these broadcasts or some other consideration, the federal government did in fact decide that RESPs were flawed. In his budget of February 1997, Finance Minister Martin attempted to remedy the problem. Unfortunately, his solution fell short of the mark, as the following commentary points out.

UNSATISFACTORY COMPROMISE
FEBRUARY 1997

It's costing a lot more money each year to send a student to college or university, and that's not likely to change anytime soon.

The reason is simple—government cutbacks, both federal and provincial, have left postsecondary institutions scrambling to find other sources of revenue. One of the ways they've been doing this is to raise tuition fees at a rate that's far in excess of inflation.

This threatens to create a situation in which the advantages of a college education are restricted to students from wealthy families. That's clearly not acceptable in a country that seeks to provide equal opportunity for all. So that's why Finance Minister Martin moved so aggressively in his budget to provide more tax relief for students and their parents.

The improvements he announced to the education and tuition tax credits will certainly be welcome. But the most important change is the overhaul of the Registered Education Savings Plan system. The federal government is doubling the allowable annual contribution to an RESP, to $4,000.

But to my mind, the most significant rule change is the one dealing with what happens to education plan earnings if the child does not go on to college. Last year, I said on this program that I wasn't a big fan of RESPs because I felt they represented a Las Vegas-style roulette game. If the beneficiary of the plan chooses not to go to college, all the money that has been earned in the program over the years is effectively lost. I suggested at the time that if the federal government really wanted to make education plans popular, they should dump that restriction. Well, now Mr. Martin has done that—sort of. Under the proposed new rules, if the money can't be used for education purposes, the plan's contributor can transfer the assets into an RRSP.

Unfortunately, the finance minister has hedged his bets here. You can make such a transfer only if you have enough RRSP room available—and then the limit is set at $40,000.

This is completely unrealistic. If you invest $4,000 a year on a child's behalf until you reach the lifetime maximum of $42,000, and it earns 10 percent annually, the plan will earn about $145,000 in income over 21 years. That's a lot more than you're allowed to transfer to an RRSP if the student decides not to go on and there's no alternative beneficiary available.

The government has proposed a change that will allow you to withdraw the unused income from an RESP directly. But you'll pay tax on the withdrawal at your marginal rate plus a 20 percent excess tax penalty. That means that in some provinces you could end up paying more than 70 percent tax on a withdrawal of this type, based on current rates. Generous of them to let you keep the rest, isn't it?

So while the finance minister has come around to the view that losing the income from years of saving in an RESP is too onerous a penalty for a family to face, he hasn't gone far enough toward solving the problem.

The answer is really quite simple. Allow an unlimited transfer of unused education plan funds into an RRSP, or allow the money to be withdrawn and taxed at the contributor's normal marginal rate without any penalty.

The budget proposal is an unsatisfactory halfway house that does not solve the basic problem.

UPDATE

The problem remains unsolved to this day. So be very careful if you're considering an RESP to help save for a child's college costs. They're still a gamble.

CHAPTER
5

Going Down
in Flames

The eighties and nineties saw more failures among major financial institutions than in any previous 20-year period in our history. Time and again, the Canada Deposit Insurance Corporation (CDIC) or some counterpart had to come to the rescue, at a cost of hundreds of millions of dollars. On other occasions, only a last-minute takeover prevented a financial calamity, such as the Royal Bank buyout of a once blue-ribbon company, Royal Trust. Here are just a few of the commentaries I've made on this topic over the years, beginning with the demise of the Canadian Commercial Bank in the mid-eighties.

CCB COLLAPSES
SEPTEMBER 1985

I hope you weren't one of the many thousands of people who were involved with the Canadian Commercial Bank. If you were, then I hope you were a depositor and not a shareholder. At least that way you'll get your money back.

This whole bank collapse is a sorry mess, and it really does shake my faith in the integrity of our banking system. We may never know who the real villains were in this affair. But it's pretty clear who the victims were—a lot of innocent people who had a right to expect something better.

I'm not going to attempt to analyze what went wrong here—that's for people who are far more knowledgeable than I am about the intricacies of the banking system. What I want to talk about today are the lessons to be learned from this fiasco—and there are plenty of them.

First, if you're a depositor, the CCB collapse drives home yet again the importance of deposit insurance. Wherever your money is, make certain that it's protected. Make it a point to learn the rules covering deposit insurance, and use them.

In this particular case, the federal government is bailing out all CCB depositors, regardless of how much money they had in the bank. But don't bet on that happening again. For one thing, we can't afford it—this particular bailout will end up costing hundreds of millions of dollars. Ottawa isn't going to undertake many more of those.

So it's up to you to protect yourself. And that means being alert to changes in the deposit insurance program, changes that I think will come pretty soon. I'll talk about them in more detail when that happens, but be alert to the possibility.

For investors, the CCB failure just reinforces all those rules you've heard before. This is as good a time as any to go through them again. For starters, never take anything for granted. There is no such thing as a riskless stock. In this situation, both common and preferred shareholders of one of the top ten chartered banks in Canada have seen their entire investment wiped out. The fact that such a thing hadn't happened in over 60 years didn't help.

Second, pay close attention to your investments. Be alert to signs of trouble. If you own shares that begin to fall in price, make the effort to find out why. It may be just a general market correction. Or it may be that something is seriously wrong with the company. If that's the case, cut your losses and run. When CCB preferred shares began to fall from last year's $25 level, a lot of people held on in the hope that things would improve. They ended up with nothing. I've made the same mistake in the past so I know from bitter experience that it can happen. Don't get caught.

Third classic rule: Diversify. Don't put all your investment eggs in one basket, no matter how attractive that basket may look. Spread your risk around. That way, if the worst happens—as it did in the CCB case—you won't end up being wiped out.

All of this may sound like pretty basic investment advice. The problem is, people are constantly ignoring it—and paying a heavy price for doing so.

UPDATE

There have been many more failures since. The precautions I suggested more than a decade ago are still valid today.

INTRODUCTION

Although deposit insurance offers a measure of protection in situations where a financial institution goes under, many people don't understand how it works and what its limits are. That was the case when the Alberta-based Principal Group went down in 1987. Many people who thought they owned GICs that were covered by the CDIC found to their dismay that wasn't the case.

UNDERSTANDING DEPOSIT INSURANCE
JULY 1987

This is happening too often—small financial institutions or investment firms going belly-up and leaving thousands of unsuspecting people holding the bag. I don't know the reason—although it may be that the laws and regulations governing these firms should be much tougher. I do know that it's more important than ever to protect yourself against becoming one of the victims of these bankruptcies. Let me tell you how.

First, and most essential, you must be absolutely certain that your money is protected by the Canada Deposit Insurance Corporation—the CDIC. Now, that's not as easy as it sounds, as this debacle in Edmonton is showing. Many of the people who stand to lose their life savings thought their money had been placed with Principal Savings and Trust—a company that is protected by deposit insurance. In fact, they were holding investment certificates issued by related companies not covered by insurance. In other words, every cent was at risk.

If you're putting money into any type of deposit account, guaranteed investment certificate, term deposit, or anything similar, the onus is on you to be certain that your money is protected by deposit insurance. If there's any doubt in your mind, don't sign anything.

Typically, what happens in these situations is that uninsured companies offer higher rates of interest to get your money. When you hear of a deal like that, be very suspicious. An additional point or two on your interest rate won't be much consolation if the firm goes under.

Now, please understand me. I'm not suggesting the offer of a higher interest rate is an automatic signal of trouble. Many smaller trust companies routinely offer premium rates to get business, and they're fully covered by deposit insurance. Just be sure.

The second point is to be very clear on what's covered by deposit insurance—and, even more important, what's *not* covered. Your bank or trust company may be a member of the CDIC—but a lot of the financial products it sells aren't covered by deposit insurance.

For example, U.S.-dollar accounts and term deposits have become quite popular in the last few years. But a lot of people don't realize that those deposits—and any others held in a foreign currency—are not protected.

If you have an RRSP with your local bank, the funds you have in it may not be fully covered. If the money is all in savings accounts or guaranteed investment certificates, you're OK. But if any of your RRSP holdings are in things like bonds, stocks, mortgages, or mutual funds, you have no coverage.

And, of course, if you have more than $60,000 on deposit in any one financial institution, the balance over that amount isn't protected. That may seem like a lot of money, but many people who are approaching retirement age may be surprised to find their RRSPs have reached that level and beyond. If you're in that situation, you should switch some of your funds to another bank or trust company. That $60,000 limit is per financial institution. You could have five accounts of that size scattered around and all $300,000 would be covered.

Let me finish by cautioning you once again to take nothing for granted. There's too much turmoil in the financial world right now to take any chances. Even our major chartered banks aren't immune—they're in the process of putting more money aside to cover themselves against unexpected debt losses in Third World countries.

In times like this, you can't be too careful. Don't you end up like those unfortunate people in Alberta the next time a financial company goes down.

UPDATE

The deposit insurance rules described here are still in place. The good news for Principal Group depositors was that in the end they recovered most of their invested money—but it took time and a lot of frustration before that happened.

INTRODUCTION

The need for people to protect themselves in the face of the various crises in the financial world was a theme I returned to again and again over the years. Let's fast-forward to the early nineties.

BANKING TURMOIL SPREADS
JANUARY 1991

I saw some numbers the other day that shocked me. Of the ten biggest bank failures in the history of the United States, half took place within the past year.

That's frightening. We've been hearing horror stories about the savings-and-loan debacle across the border, but these failures show it's not just the little guys who are at risk. Some very big financial institutions are going belly-up. The Bank of New England is the latest casualty—it had over $23 billion in assets. People were lining up around the block trying to get their money out before the doors closed.

In Rhode Island, the new governor closed down half the financial institutions in the state on New Year's Day after the company that insured their deposits declared insolvency. Depositors wanting to withdraw their money found state troopers guarding the doors.

Sounds like the Great Depression revisited, doesn't it? It was the collapse of a large segment of the U.S. banking system in the 1930s that wiped out many people's life savings and helped transform a downturn in the economic cycle into a financial calamity.

The reasons behind today's problems in the U.S. banking system are much the same as those in the thirties—overly aggressive loan policies during the previous decade, which came home to roost when real estate markets collapsed and overextended businesses went under.

So is history repeating itself? It is indeed—but with one major difference. The difference is deposit insurance. In the Depression, people were wiped out. Today, they're protected—at least in theory. That's the only reason we haven't seen mass panic and a run on the banks in the U.S.

But the deposit insurance system itself is now under pressure. For starters, not all states require their banks to be covered by the federal deposit insurance program. Some—Rhode Island is one—allow private insurers to do the job. We've just seen what can happen in that situation.

And even the U.S. Federal Deposit Insurance Corporation is under pressure. The rising number of bank failures across the U.S. has pushed its resources to the brink. There's now talk in Washington that the administration may impose new limits on the protection available to depositors in the event of a bank failure.

What does all this mean to us? Fortunately, not a lot—so far. Our banking system is more concentrated and our regulations are tighter than in the U.S. But we're starting to see some of our institutions come under pressure. Standard Trust has had serious problems and there are rumours on Bay Street of a possible major bank merger. The message is that while we're better protected against bank failures than the U.S., we're by no means immune. And we are in a period of escalating risk.

What should you do? For starters, make sure your assets are covered by deposit insurance—don't take anything for granted. Now, most people won't have $60,000 in a savings account—that's the deposit insurance limit. But what about your RRSP? If you've been putting money aside for several years, it's quite possible your retirement plan is approaching that amount. If your money is in a savings RRSP or guaranteed investment certificates, it's covered by deposit insurance—but only to $60,000. If you have more in any single financial institution—especially if it's a small one—you might want to consider opening another plan somewhere else and shifting some of the assets to it.

This is a time to be ultra-cautious. We won't experience the problems here that they have in the States. But one or two financial institutions may not survive this difficult year. Don't put yourself in a position where you'll get hurt if one of them is yours.

UPDATE

Fortunately, the banking system survived in both the U.S. and Canada. But there are plenty of scars that attest to the traumas it experienced. And it wasn't long after this commentary was delivered that another financial institution with operations in Canada went down in flames and scandal.

THE BCCI SCANDAL
JULY 1991

The scandal surrounding the Bank of Credit and Commerce International keeps growing. On Monday, a New York district attorney described it as "the largest bank fraud in world financial history" as he announced criminal charges against the bank's U.S. operations.

It's really hard to believe this mess was allowed to fester for so long. If only a fraction of what we're now hearing is true, the operations of BCCI have amounted to a scam of incredible proportions. Stop and think about what's happened here.

The Bank of Credit and Commerce International was a major financial institution. It operated in 69 countries around the world, including Canada. Its assets were purported to be in the neighbourhood of $20 billion. Its shareholders and officers included many wealthy and powerful men. In fact, the principal owner at the time of the bank's collapse was the Sultan of Abu Dhabi, one of our allies in the Gulf War. Former U.S. Defence Secretary Clark Clifford was also involved with the bank. So were many prominent Middle Eastern businessmen.

You have to wonder why all these people agreed to be part of an organization that was privately referred to in financial circles as the Bank of Crooks and Criminals. Based on the information that's been revealed to date, there was certainly plenty of warning that some strange things were going on.

For instance, at the Florida trial of former Panamanian dictator Manuel Noriega, it was established that he had moved millions of dollars through BCCI. As a result, several bank officials were convicted of laundering over $14 million in drug money. And that's only the beginning:

- The bank has been accused of paying $3 million in bribes to officials in Peru to encourage them to deposit government money with it.

- The U.S. indictment charges it with illegally acquiring blocks of shares in prominent American financial institutions.

- A former executive of the bank's British operations has claimed BCCI systematically helped clients evade that country's Value Added Tax.

- There have been strong suggestions that BCCI had links to international terrorism and that one of its clients was the notorious Abu Nidal.

- Other good customers are said to have included Ferdinand Marcos, various Colombian drug lords, and even Saddam Hussein.

How much of all this is true we'll know only after the dust settles. What is clear is that a lot of people stand to lose a lot of money as a result of all that's happened.

Which leaves us with the question: How could this have been allowed to go on for so long? The answer seems to be a lack of tough international financial regulation.

It had apparently been known for some time that BCCI's auditing practices left much to be desired. The bank is reported to have insisted that different accounting firms conduct audits at the head office in Luxembourg and a major branch in the Cayman Islands, and that neither auditor talks to the other. It's also reported the auditors were not allowed to use anyone who spoke Urdu, even though many of the bank's key memos were written in that language.

The implication is that the bank was able to avoid major disclosures about its business practices in this way—and there was no regulatory agency to blow the whistle. Obviously, this is a problem that must be addressed by the international financial community. This sort of outlaw activity simply can't be allowed to go on.

In the meantime, Canadians who had deposits with branches in this country have problems of their own. I'll talk about those next.

HOW THE BCCI COLLAPSE HIT DEPOSITORS
JULY 1991

When the Bank of Credit and Commerce International went under in early July, it had four branches operating in Canada and a purported $200 million in assets. For the most part, its clients were institutional, including a number of foreign embassies—some of which, it's been reported, have had difficulty paying their bills since BCCI was closed down.

But there were also some ordinary customers involved, whose deposits totalled about $20 million. That's small potatoes by banking standards. But it's a lot if you happen to be one of those depositors and you arrive to find the bank's doors locked and your assets frozen. It's about then that panic starts to set in.

This is the second time this year we've seen a financial institution close down in Canada. The first was the demise of Standard Trust a few months ago. The circumstances surrounding that collapse were much different from those of the BCCI affair, but the consequences for small depositors were the same—locked doors and frozen funds. In the Standard Trust case, many more people were affected. The company had over 100,000 depositors, with more than $1 billion in assets.

In both situations, small depositors are being bailed out by the Canada Deposit Insurance Corporation, which was set up to deal with financial crises such as these. So on the surface it appears that anyone who had less than $60,000 on deposit with either financial institution comes out all right.

Unfortunately, that's not quite true. Deposit insurance is a wonderful safety net, and we're fortunate to have it. But it won't solve all your problems if you get trapped in a bank or trust company failure like this.

To begin with, you can't walk in and collect your money the next morning. Your accounts are frozen until all the necessary legal and financial procedures are completed—and that can take several weeks. In the Standard Trust case, provision was made for people in hardship situations. But it involved making a special application for a cash advance, a process that inevitably takes time. The only way to protect yourself against this is to have money on deposit in more than one financial institution. That way, you'll always have cash available if something goes wrong.

Another problem faced by customers of failed banks and trust companies is early termination of guaranteed deposits. That happened to a number of people in the Standard Trust collapse. Here's how it works:

Suppose you invest in a five-year guaranteed investment certificate that pays 12 percent interest—as some clients of Standard Trust did last year when rates were higher. Then the bank or trust company folds and CDIC steps in. Your GIC is protected for principal and interest up to $60,000. But CDIC does not guarantee to continue paying interest for the remainder of the term. Instead, your GIC is cashed prematurely. You collect your interest to the date of termination, but that's it. If interest rates have fallen in the meantime, you stand to lose a lot of money.

For example, Standard Trust clients who had to reinvest GIC funds found that five-year rates had fallen to the 9- to 9.5-percent range. That's a big drop from what they had been expecting to receive for the next four years.

So while deposit insurance is valuable, it isn't a guarantee that you'll come out of a banking crisis unscathed. Keep that in mind when you're deciding where to put your money.

INTRODUCTION

The banking and trust company industries weren't the only ones experiencing upheavals during this period. The insurance industry, long an unshakable pillar of financial responsibility, also discovered that it too was vulnerable to earthquakes. The first company to go down was a big Quebec-based firm, Les Co-operants. Then came a small Calgary company, Sovereign Life.

CRISIS IN THE LIFE INSURANCE INDUSTRY
JANUARY 1993

We used to think of life insurance companies as the foundation of our financial community. Trust companies could fold, small banks might vanish, brokerage houses could disappear, but the insurance companies were always there, rock-solid. Well, not any more.

In the past couple of years, two insurance companies have run into serious problems. One, the Quebec-based Co-operants Mutual Life Insurance Society, which once had assets of $3 billion, collapsed in 1991 and has since been liquidated. Then, last month, came word that federal regulators had been ordered to take control of Calgary-based Sovereign Life Insurance and to wind up the company. That move is being contested in the courts. But regardless of the outcome, it's clear that all is not well in an industry that has always prided itself on its strength and stability.

This has important implications for you. Almost every adult Canadian has some dealings with a life insurance company, even if it's just a group policy at work. For some people, their financial survival depends on the ability of an insurance company to meet its obligations. They may have purchased a life annuity, or set up a Registered Retirement Income Fund, or be receiving a disability pension. If the company goes under, what happens?

The good news is that you do have some protection. A few years ago, the insurance industry set up a special fund to compensate policyholders if a company failed—a variation on deposit insurance, if you like.

The bad news is that, like deposit insurance, there are limits to the coverage. Here are a few examples:

- If you have a life insurance policy, you're protected for coverage up to $200,000 if the company goes under. That may sound like a lot, but it really isn't—not these days, when many people are carrying much more insurance than that.

- In the case of cash values built up in a life insurance policy, your protection is a maximum of $60,000.
- If you're using a life insurance company to accumulate a retirement savings plan, your coverage with any one organization is also up to $60,000.
- Perhaps the area of most concern, if an insurance company fails, are pension and annuity benefits. Many people rely heavily on these monthly cheques. If they're cut off, it can mean real hardship. The insurance fund protects this type of income to a maximum of $2,000 a month per company. That strikes me as low—and it's something to take into account if you're approaching retirement and are considering using your RRSP savings to purchase an annuity.

If your annuity income will be more than $2,000 a month, there are a couple of things you should do before making a commitment. First, make inquiries about the financial strength of the company. Standard and Poor's in the U.S. does ratings on insurance companies across North America. Another possible source of information is Dun and Bradstreet.

My other suggestion is to buy annuities from more than one company, staying under the $2,000-a-month limit for each. That would enable you to spread your annuity income among several insurance firms and be fully protected. I can't stress the importance of this enough. Sovereign Life has something like 60,000 annuity holders. It's a pretty good bet that some of them are going to be financially hurt by this debacle.

If you want to find out more about this fund and how it works, you can contact the Canadian Life and Health Insurance Association, known as CompCorp for short. Ask for a free copy of their consumer booklet. Their toll-free number is 1-800-268-8099. If you live in the Toronto area, call 777-2344.

It's worth the effort.

UPDATE

As it turned out, the Sovereign Life wind-up was just the preview to a much bigger insurance company collapse that was already starting to take shape. I alerted CBC listeners to the danger in a commentary that was broadcast the following year.

TROUBLE AHEAD
JUNE 1994

Twice this month, Canada's Superintendent of Financial Institutions, Michael Mackenzie, has set off alarm bells about the state of our life insurance industry.

The first time, he was right on the industry's home turf, as he spoke to reporters after delivering a speech to the annual meeting of the Canadian Life and Health Insurance Association. The second time he was appearing before the Senate banking committee in Ottawa. On both occasions, his message was the same.

He warned us that there are some insurance companies that are not as sound financially as he would like. And he wondered out loud about the ability of the industry's emergency fund to cope if a major firm went belly-up.

In a subsequent TV interview, Mr. Mackenzie stressed that he felt the insurance industry is in good financial shape and said he does not expect a big company to close its doors anytime soon. But he pointed out that, like other financial industries, insurance companies have had their share of problems from real estate investments recently. That has led to, in his words, "stresses and strains on the industry" that people should be aware of.

Obviously, the reports of his comments caused some concern. After all, we've seen two insurance failures in recent years, the Co-operants in Quebec and Calgary-based Sovereign Life. So the possibility of an insurance company going down is not just hypothetical speculation.

So what should you do if you're worried? Mr. Mackenzie advises checking the financial health of any company you deal with. One of the sources he suggests for that information are the annual reports issued by the companies. Unfortunately, that kind of information is meaningless to most people. You almost have to have a degree in accounting to make any sense of an insurance company balance sheet. Talking to your agent may not be much help either. An agent's job is to sell insurance, not to be an expert on the operations of billion-dollar financial empires.

But you're not helpless. There is information available, if you know where to go. The rating agencies are one source. They're the companies that keep watch on the financial solvency of governments and corporations—the ones that cause a flap when they downgrade the safety rating of government bonds. They also assess the claims-paying ability of insurance companies and, in many cases, provide that information without charge.

There are two Canadian-based firms—the Dominion Bond Rating Service in Toronto and the Canadian Bond Rating Service in Montreal. You might want to contact one of them if you'd like to know about the financial status of your particular insurance company.

For general information about how to evaluate a company, get a copy of a brochure titled "Financial Strength," which is produced by the Canadian Life and Health Insurance Association. While you're speaking to them, also ask them to send along a copy of their CompCorp brochure. CompCorp is the industry's emergency fund for compensating policyholders if a company goes bankrupt.

UPDATE

It didn't take long. Two months after that commentary went out, I delivered the next item. Hopefully, some listeners had used the intervening period to take evasive action.

THE CONFED COLLAPSE
AUGUST 1994

Ever since the news broke, we've been hearing soothing words from the insurance industry, assuring Confederation Life clients that they're protected. That's because the industry has its own insurance policy, in the form of CompCorp. This organization provides partial protection for investors if an insurance company goes under.

The problem is that CompCorp has never been put to this kind of test before. Long before Confederation went down, there were suggestions that CompCorp might not have the financial resources to handle a collapse of this magnitude. That's because it's funded entirely by other insurance companies—there's no government backing, unlike deposit insurance.

We're now assured CompCorp will pay off—but at what price? Confederation wasn't the only insurance company that's financially strapped. When the CompCorp assessments for this debacle come through, it may push some other firms to the brink.

So my first suggestion is to be very cautious if you're about to enter into any kind of an insurance contract. In this environment, it's essential to check out the financial strength of a company before proceeding. Look especially at the credit rating, as established by the bond-rating services. It should be A+ or better. If it doesn't measure up, consider alternatives.

Now, what do you do if you're a Confederation customer—either of the insurance company or Confederation Trust, which has also been affected? There are a number of possibilities, so let's look at them quickly.

If you have a life insurance policy, keep up the premiums. Confederation's active policies will almost certainly be bought up by another company, so you probably won't suffer any loss of coverage.

If you have money invested in one of Confederation Life's segregated funds, relax. Those funds do not form part of the company's assets—that means they can't be seized by creditors. The money belongs to the investors and you should get it all back.

If you have an RRSP, RRIF, or annuity with Confederation, contact CompCorp for details of your coverage. Unfortunately, some annuity holders may hard hit by this failure, because CompCorp protects your income up to only $2,000 a month.

Now what about your position as a customer of Confederation Trust?

In this case, you're covered by federal deposit insurance. Any accounts, term deposits, or GICs are protected up to $60,000. Don't call CompCorp in this case; they have nothing to do with it.

If you have investments in the trust company's mutual funds, you can breath easy. You should get back the full current market value of your mutual fund units. Most likely the funds will be sold to another financial institution—that's what happened in the case of other trust companies that went down, like Central Guaranty and Royal Trust. The funds will either be given a new name or merged with existing funds. Either way, you'll be all right.

So how you're affected by all this depends very much on what form your investments took. Let's just hope the financial damage to individuals is kept to a minimum.

UPDATE

Cleaning up the Confederation mess turned out to be a real nightmare, one that went on for a long time. Here's where things stood a year and a half later.

THE RIPPLE EFFECTS
DECEMBER 1995

It was just a small item on the business pages—most people probably didn't even notice it. But if you were one of those affected, it must have come like a punch in the stomach.

The story concerned an announcement from the big chartered accounting firm of Peat Marwick Thorne. They're the agent for the liquidator in the Confederation Life wind-up. That's a technical designation that simply means they've been given the responsibility for administering the cleanup of the mess.

Peat Marwick's announcement concerned those who had purchased annuities from the fallen insurance company. Until now, annuity holders have received full payment. Even though Confed went bankrupt over a year ago, the liquidator has kept the cheques coming on a regular basis. But that's about to change.

Peat Marwick says it will no longer be possible to continue to make full payment in certain cases. Sometime in the first six months of 1996—the company can't give an exact date—some annuitants will have their income cut back, on the basis of a rather complex formula. In some cases, the amount will be small. In other cases, it may amount to several hundred dollars a month.

Now, if you're a Confederation Life annuity holder, don't panic yet. Only a relatively small number of people will be affected by this. Out of over 28,000 Confederation annuitants, less than 700 will be hit. As long as your annuity payment is less than $2,000 a month, you probably won't get hurt. But if your annuity payment is higher, you're looking at a cut.

That's because $2,000 is the maximum monthly protection provided by the Canadian Life and Health Insurance Association, commonly known as CompCorp. This is the body that insures the insurers. If something goes wrong, as it did with Confed, CompCorp steps in to protect policyholders. That's why in most cases annuitants will continue to receive their regular payments up to $2,000 a month—and in some cases they may get more, depending on their policy.

But there are limits to the protection—as some Confed annuitants are about to find out. For example, CompCorp coverage doesn't extend to non-Canadians. As a result, about 100 people have no coverage at all.

Now, your first reaction may be—well, it's not me, and not too many people are involved. So, in the great scheme of things, this isn't all that serious. But stop and think about this a minute. When you purchase an annuity from a life insurance company, you are, in effect, buying your retirement income. You're handing over a lifetime of savings in exchange for the certainty of a cheque showing up in your mailbox every month for as long as you live. Those savings are gone. You have no more control over that money, or access to it. You've entrusted your financial security to the fiscal health of an insurance company.

There was a time in this country when that was even a better guarantee than depending on the government. But no more. Confederation was one of the oldest and biggest pillars of our insurance community. If it can go down, others can too.

Try to put yourself in the place of the people who are affected by this announcement. Their annuity is probably one of their main sources of retirement income—perhaps *the* single most important one. Now it's being cut back, through no fault of their own. They've been caught by the machinations of big business and now they have to pay the price.

What do you do in those circumstances? If you're retired, there's probably no way you can make up that income somewhere else. The only alternative is to cut your standard of living. No more presents for the grandchildren, no more roasts on Sunday. Maybe you'll even have to move, because you can't afford to stay in your present home.

These people have no effective lobby group, so you won't see them demonstrating in front of the legislature or read about their heart-rending stories in the newspapers. But they'll be happening. You can bet on it.

Unfortunately, it doesn't seem like much can be done for the Confederation annuity holders. But there are ways to prevent this from happening to anyone else in the future. Next, I'll tell you how.

INTRODUCTION

That next item was one of the most important I've done in recent years as far as retirees are concerned. If there's an annuity in your future, it's required reading.

PROTECTING YOUR ANNUITY
DECEMBER 1995

If you're considering a life annuity as your main source of retirement income, be very careful. Otherwise, you run the risk of finding yourself in serious financial trouble down the road.

That's what will be happening next year to some people who were unfortunate enough to buy large annuities from now-bankrupt Confederation Life. They handed over their savings in exchange for a lifetime guaranteed income. And now they're being told that there's not enough money to pay the full amount they expected. They have to take a cut.

The good news is that only a relatively few people will be affected—about 700. The bad news is that it could happen to many more people in the future—maybe even to you, if you're not careful.

For years, annuities have been one of the main sources of retirement income for Canadians. Their popularity has diminished somewhat over the past decade or so, with the emergence of Registered Retirement Income Funds—RIFFs—as a more flexible option. But this is still a big business—and one that's controlled exclusively by the insurance industry. Only an insurance company can issue a life annuity—no one else.

The industry has lobbied hard to retain this privileged position and to slow the growing popularity of RRIFs. For example, for years the only retirement income option available to holders of locked-in RRSPs was to buy an annuity. That meant that all pension credits transferred to RRSPs when a person changed jobs eventually ended up going to an insurance company.

Recently, as a result of pressure from a number of sources, another option has emerged—the Life Income Fund, or LIF. It's more flexible, but most Canadians still have to convert all their LIF assets to an annuity by no later than age 80. Alberta residents are the sole exception.

The collapse of Confed and, before that, the Co-operants in Quebec tells me that the life insurance industry no longer merits this kind of exclusivity. It's time our legislators took a long hard look at this situation and acted in the interest of retirees, not the well-being of insurance companies.

That would mean either ending all forced conversion of retirement savings to an annuity or opening up the life-annuity business to other financial institutions, such as the banks. The insurance industry has shown itself to be just as vulnerable to failure as any other segment of the financial community. So why should retirees be forced into such a high degree of dependence on these companies?

Another welcome step would be for the Canadian Life and Health Insurance Association—CompCorp, as it's called—to revisit the limits on its annuity coverage in cases of this kind. The current level of $2,000 a month is not a lot of money these days. If they can't provide any better protection than that, it's just one more reason for stripping the insurance industry of its monopoly position in this field.

But all of this will take time. What can you do to protect yourself in the interim? I'll go back to what I said at the beginning. If you're planning to buy an annuity, shop carefully. If there's a substantial amount of money involved, spread it around. Don't buy an annuity from any one company that exceeds the CompCorp coverage. If you need more annuity income than $24,000 annually, go to another insurance firm.

Be especially careful if you're about to retire and collect benefits from an employer pension plan. In some cases, pension plans arrange for the purchase of a life annuity to provide the payments to retirees. If that's the case, get involved in the process. Don't let the plan administrator use your credits to buy an annuity that will exceed the CompCorp coverage. Here again, spread the money around.

After all, it's *your* future. After the Confederation Life debacle, you have to do everything you can to protect it.

UPDATE

The life-annuity business remains the exclusive preserve of the insurance industry. No move has been made to extend CompCorp's coverage. Plan your retirement income accordingly.

INTRODUCTION

Without doubt, the greatest flameout of all during the years I've been talking about money on CBC was the incredible saga of Calgary-based Bre-X Minerals. No wonder movie producers were scrambling to option the story. It had everything. Rags-to-riches characters. An exotic setting deep in the jungles of Borneo. Political intrigue that reached into the office of the president of Indonesia. A mysterious fire that destroyed valuable records. An even more mysterious death when the number-two geologist plunged from a helicopter. The revelation that someone had pulled off the greatest scam in the history of mining. Billions of dollars in lawsuits. Wow!

But when all the smoke is cleared away, what it really comes down to is a basic tale of gold lust and greed. Here's what I had to say about the people who invested in the stock after the scope of the gigantic scandal was finally revealed.

THE BRE-X COLLAPSE
MAY 1997

The greatest scam in the history of mining! Billions of dollars worth of gold suddenly gone in a puff of smoke. That's not something we're going to easily live down. It will be a long time before reports of new finds by junior companies are taken seriously by anyone, unless those reports are independently confirmed.

Bre-X has given the Canadian mining industry a black eye, not just here but in the United States. The stock was listed on NASDAQ, and the unfolding saga has been closely watched by such influential media as *The Wall Street Journal* and *USA Today*. The impact on small Canadian exploration firms looking to raise capital will be severe, since a lot of that money traditionally flows from south of the border.

But what concerns me more than anything in this story is the impact this fiasco has had on many small investors. The media have been full of stories about people facing bankruptcy and even the loss of their homes. One man I saw interviewed on TV said he didn't know how he was going to explain to his family that their whole lifestyle would have to change.

It's a painful way to learn some of the basic rules of investing. Let's take a few minutes to look at some of the mistakes these people made, in the hope that you'll never repeat them.

Mistake number one. They bet the house—in some cases, literally. No matter how good an investment looks, never put too much of your wealth into it. The collapse of Bre-X was the most spectacular flameout we've seen in many years. But companies run into trouble all the time. That's why I've always recommended having a well-diversified portfolio of stocks, and never putting more than 10 percent of it into highly speculative ventures. That way, if you own a company that self-destructs, the damage to your financial well-being will be limited.

The second mistake made by many Bre-X investors was to leverage their holdings. They used borrowed money to buy shares, either on a margin account with their broker, or through a home equity line of credit, or even by the use of credit cards.

It's bad enough to take a beating on a stock that's fully paid for. But when you're up to your neck in debt, it's a disaster. There's no other word for it.

I've said many times that borrowing to invest can be very dangerous. It's a strategy that should be used only by experienced investors who understand the risks involved. But every time we get hot stock markets, I get questions from people who want to increase their profit potential by using other people's money. I can't think of a more graphic illustration of how it can all go wrong than the Bre-X crash.

The third mistake was to buy into Bre-X after the first negative report, in the hope that there was at least some gold out there in the jungle. One man who lost a bundle in this way compared it to buying a lottery ticket. That's a good analogy. But investing in the stock market isn't supposed to be just another version of Lotto 649. The wise investor buys shares for long-term growth and dividend income, not as some kind of get-rich-quick scheme.

The danger now is that many people will use the Bre-X story as an excuse not to invest in stocks or equity mutual funds. Too dangerous, they'll say. Let's stick with GICs. They don't pay much, but they're safe.

Well, Bre-X is *not* the stock market. If you get good advice and invest your money carefully, stocks still offer the best long-term growth potential. It's when people get too greedy and throw caution to the wind that they run into trouble.

UPDATE

Bre-X shares were delisted by the Toronto Stock Exchange shortly after this was written. Investors who still held them at that point (they last traded at around 9 cents) could burn their stock certificates or frame them, depending on their temperament.

CHAPTER

6

Let Me Look into My Crystal Ball

People are always looking to me to foretell the future—to predict stock market movements and interest rate increases before they happen. No one can know precisely what is going to happen. But we can see trends and patterns taking shape that give us some idea of what the future holds. "Coming events cast their shadows before," my father used to say. They do. Here are some of my crystal ball forecasts from years past.

THE YEAR AHEAD: 1985
DECEMBER 1984

This is the time of year for predictions, so let's spend a few minutes talking about what 1985 may do to your take-home pay and your bank account.

Prediction Number One. We'll be paying more tax, in one form or another, by year-end. The government has to take action to bring down the deficit, and it has very little room to manoeuvre. It's all very well to talk about achieving this goal through a combination of spending cuts and economic stimulation, but I just don't believe they can do it. At some point they'll have to increase revenues—and that means higher taxes.

Tax incentives for business will be a major target. The percentage of government revenues coming from corporation taxes has fallen significantly, and Finance Minister Michael Wilson has already said he's taking a close look at the situation.

But individuals are going to be hit too. The only real question is how. You may remember that last summer I said on this program that we could expect to hear a lot more about tax reform after the election. Well, that's beginning. Mr. Wilson has launched a new study into the feasibility of introducing a value-added tax in this country—a move that we can only hope will be rejected again, as it was after earlier studies under the Liberals.

Mr. Wilson is also looking closely at the U.S. tax-reform program recently proposed by Treasury Secretary Donald Regan. That plan would eliminate most tax shelters and deductions and create only three tax brackets with a top rate of 35 percent. It sounds good on the surface, but most tax-reform programs of this type end up generating more money for the government—which means that somebody ends up paying more than they are now.

However it works out, 1985 will be an interesting year on the tax front—and, unfortunately, a painful one.

Prediction Number Two. The federal government will either toss out or completely revamp its much-ballyhooed mortgage protection plan. This was the program that was introduced in Marc Lalonde's February budget to shield homeowners against big increases in mortgage interest rates. I criticized it at the time as being far too expensive for the protection it offered, and apparently a lot of people came to the same conclusion. As of the end of November only 83 homeowners in all of Canada had signed up for it. Can you imagine that? Only 83 people? Talk about massive rejection. But the basic concept is a good one. That means the Tories have a golden opportunity to score political points by overhauling the program and making it acceptable to homeowners.

Prediction Number Three. Competition for your mortgage money will continue to rage. 1984 saw a real breakthrough here. In an incredible scramble to expand business and increase market share, banks and trust companies came up with an amazing array of offers. It's become a real borrower's market, and I don't see that changing, at least for the early part of 1985. If you're looking for a mortgage right now, you're doing so at one of the best times in the past 20 years.

Prediction Number Four. Economic uncertainty will continue. That's cheating a bit, really, because economic uncertainty has become a fact of life. No one really knows where interest rates will be six months from now, or whether inflation is about to re-emerge, or if we're heading for another recession. So that means you must constantly be aware of what's going on, and you must be flexible. Be ready to change—your investments, the term of your mortgage, the type of bank account you have, your savings patterns, the works. It's the only way you're going to be able to protect yourself in the year ahead.

Happy 1985.

UPDATE

Under the Conservatives, Canadians experienced the greatest increase in their tax burden in history. The study of a value-added tax I referred to eventually led to the imposition of the GST—but only after the Tories had been safely returned in another election. The mortgage protection plan, which had been intended to shield home-owners against the scary rate increases of the early eighties, vanished as predicted. Few people remember it ever existed. And competition for mortgage dollars remains as fierce today as it was then.

INTRODUCTION

There have been a lot of changes in the way we spend our money in recent years—and even in the form the money itself takes. Here are some predictions in that area I made in mid-1985.

DOLLARS AND DEBITS
JULY 1985

I recently returned from a trip to France with the family. During the trip, I observed some uses of money that may well be harbingers of things to come here in Canada. One deals with the cash we carry around with us, the other with the credit cards most of us have in our wallet or purse. I'll talk about the cash first.

I'm sure most of you have heard by now about the plan to do away with our one-dollar bill and replace it with a coin. This idea is to phase out the bill over a three-year period, leaving only the new dollar coin. Well, all I can say is, you'd better get ready to lug a heck of a lot of metal around with you. You may end up listing to one side, it's going to weigh so much.

France has already done it—and believe me, it's annoying. Their lowest-denomination bill is a 20-franc note, which would be a little over $3 in our money. Below that, everything is coinage. The closest to our proposed one-dollar coin is a large silver five-franc coin, which is worth about 75 cents, and a copper-coloured ten-franc coin. Both of them weigh a ton. Even worse, the 20-franc notes seem to be in short supply, so when you get change for a 50- or 100-franc note, it's usually all in coins. I found it wasn't long before the accumulated weight in my pocket was literally pulling my trousers down on my hips.

As a result, I kept offloading the coins onto my wife to carry in her purse—and then wondered why she complained it was so heavy when we walked around castles and museums. When we finally unloaded all these coins on the dresser to count them, I couldn't believe how many we'd accumulated. I didn't have a scale to weigh them, but my guess is we were carrying about a kilogram of coins between us.

It might have been funny, except that's exactly the way we're heading here. Before you know it, the dollar bill will be gone. A lot of people don't like using the two-dollar bill—there's still a lingering feeling in some parts of the country, especially the West, that it's unlucky. So what may happen is that the five-dollar bill will become the basic unit of paper currency. If so, handling money is going to be a real pain. Maybe someone should start a POD campaign—Preserve Our Dollar—before it's too late.

The other thing I observed was more positive. I don't know about you, but I find most of our stores are incredibly slow and inefficient when it comes to handling credit card payments. I'm sure you've been through this scenario:

It's a busy Saturday at Canadian Tire and there's a big lineup of people waiting to pay. You arrive at the cashier and offer a Visa or MasterCard for your hose nozzle. Everyone behind you groans silently. The cashier takes your card and thumbs through the latest warning circular to see if it's been cancelled or stolen—as if you were going to stand there patiently waiting if it were.

When she's finally satisfied, she does up a slip, writing in most of the information manually. Finally, she gives you something to sign—and then insists you add your phone number, which takes still more time.

Sound familiar? Well, take heart. I've seen the future, and it works. In several places in France, we encountered machines that did all that in seconds. We just handed our Visa card to a cashier. She punched a couple of numbers, slid the card through so the machine could read the information that's magnetically encoded in that black strip on the back, and pressed a button. Out came an electronically printed slip, like a cash-register receipt, with all the necessary information. All I had to do was sign.

I hope we catch up with the French soon. I'm tired of being glared at.

UPDATE

Now we're just like the French—we have fast credit cards and heavy pockets. It's hard to believe credit card transactions were so primitive as recently as the mid-1980s.

INTRODUCTION

The mid-1980s were a time of general prosperity, falling interest rates, and a booming stock market. But as we approached the end of the decade, storm clouds began to gather on the horizon. The following warned listeners of trouble ahead.

TROUBLE AHEAD
DECEMBER 1988

When you reach a certain age, you develop a kind of sixth sense about things. It's a matter of having been there before, of having gone through similar experiences and remembering what it was like. My sixth sense is telling me there's financial trouble ahead in 1989.

I know, this isn't what you want to hear at the start of what we all hope will be a bright New Year. So let me hasten to add that my sixth sense isn't infallible. Maybe this is one of those times when it's wrong. But let me tell you why I'm concerned.

Over the holidays, I had a chance to talk with a number of friends in the newspaper and magazine business. They all said the same thing: Advertising is slowing down and they're worried about 1989.

Now, I know from my own experience in publishing that a weakness in advertising is one of the early warning signs of an economic slow-down. We knew we were headed for serious trouble in 1980, for example, long before that particular recession set in. A sharp drop in advertising commitments was the tip-off.

During the holidays, I also chatted with some people in the real estate industry. They told me that in November the market just seemed to die. If it doesn't start to pick up in January and February, they expect to see house prices soften in many parts of the country, especially where the markets have been overheated. Real estate is another leading indicator of where the economy is headed. If house prices start to drop, look out!

The conventional wisdom is that we aren't going to have any serious economic problems in 1989. The economy will slow down a bit, and we'll probably see a modest increase in the inflation rate. But nothing dramatic. Certainly none of the major economic forecasts I've seen are calling for a full-blown recession in 1989.

I hope they're right. But I'm getting twitchy. The current boom has been under way since mid-1982. That's a long time by historical standards. It may last a while longer, but sooner or later it's going to run out of steam. We're also seeing some of the classic signs of the late stages of an economic boom. Inflation is starting to take hold again. Wage demands are increasing. Interest rates are moving higher. Debt levels are rising. These are all traditional harbingers of trouble ahead.

So my advice for 1989 is to be cautious. This doesn't look like a good time for risk-taking in your financial affairs. Specifically, I suggest postponing any new borrowing if you can. Interest rates are high right now, and a large debt load is dangerous if the economy slows down. If you can, you should be paying off your debts rather than adding to them.

For those of you thinking of buying a house, I'd hold off for a while and keep a close eye on the market. If signs of price weakness start to appear, you may be able to get a bargain.

I think investors should avoid the stock market right now. You can earn over 10 percent on short-term investments, such as Treasury bills, without any risk. Bonds and bond funds may also be a good bet. If we do have an economic downturn, interest rates will drop and you'll realize a nice capital gain.

I hope 1989 turns out to be a lot brighter than my sixth sense is suggesting. But if it doesn't, these ideas may help you weather the storm.

UPDATE

It was a little late, but the recession I predicted hit like a hurricane in early 1990. Housing prices fell dramatically, and people who had taken my advice to wait were able to scoop up bargains. The stock market tumbled. Interest rates plummeted, creating terrific profits for bond investors in the early nineties. It took several years for the economic storm to abate, and many people still feel the effects of it.

INTRODUCTION

By the end of 1990 we were deep in the throes of the recession. When it came time to make my forecast for 1991, the situation was so uncertain that I almost passed, with the idea of using the excuse that the world was too confused to make any sense of it. But CBC wasn't paying me big bucks—all of $180 a commentary!—to cop out. So here's what I told listeners.

WAR, CHAOS, AND CRISIS
DECEMBER 1990

I've been making annual financial forecasts for several years, but this is the toughest one yet. There are so many wild cards in play that almost anything can happen in 1991. So the assumptions that are made going in are critical. If major events break differently, they will change all the patterns and set us off in another direction entirely.

Here's what I'm assuming will happen. If you don't agree, then ignore the financial advice that follows because it won't be relevant in your case.

First, I expect we *will* have a war in the Persian Gulf and that it will start around the third week of January. I think it will be relatively short—over by spring, I would guess. But I also expect it to be extremely violent and bloody.

Second, I believe our recession is going to drag on longer than many people expect. It could be autumn—or even later—before we finally start to pull out of it.

Finally, I think we'll find ourselves in a new constitutional crisis before the year is out, once the Belanger-Campeau Commission reports in Quebec. I expect a majority report that will strongly favour some form of independence. That will be followed quickly by a lurch toward sovereignty, or a variation of it, by the Quebec Liberal Party. That will be a purely political move, designed to avoid being left behind by the flow of events.

Those assumptions form the bases for how I see the year unfolding from a financial point of view. So let's see how they all come together.

I'll start with interest rates. They've been coming down in recent months, and I think we'll see more of the same, at least through the first half of 1991. Short-term rates will continue to lead the way. That means yields on Treasury bills, money market funds, term deposits of less than a year, and your bank accounts will decline during the winter, perhaps quite quickly. Longer-term rates, such as those on government bonds, will be slower to come down. But they'll also be less at mid-year than they are today.

Beyond that, it's difficult to see. However, given my assumptions, it would appear likely that rates will stay relatively low during the summer but start to move back up in the fall as the economy recovers and the constitutional crisis I'm expecting begins to put downward pressure on the dollar.

What does all this imply? For starters, if you are about to buy a house or have a mortgage coming up for renewal, I'd choose a six-month term. I expect rates will be cheaper by mid-year. If you're thinking about investing money—perhaps in an RRSP—I suggest including bond or mortgage mutual funds in your mix. They should do well in the type of climate I expect. When rates appear to have bottomed out, take your gains and move your money elsewhere.

If returns on short-term money keep dropping as I expect, you'll receive a lower return every time you roll over a Treasury bill or term deposit. Unless you have some reason for staying short, you'll do better switching some of your cash to longer-term GICs or into fixed-income funds.

UPDATE

We did have a short Gulf war, which started exactly when I predicted it would. The recession did indeed drag on longer than many people expected. The constitutional crisis came a year later then I expected, but it arrived in 1992 in the form of the ill-fated

Charlottetown Accord. Interest rates did in fact follow much the pattern I predicted.

INTRODUCTION

Many people in this business ignore their earlier predictions, especially if they're wrong. I think that's dishonest and unethical. So each year I report to CBC listeners on my report card for the previous 12 months, good or bad. Here's an example.

1993 LOOK-BACK
JANUARY 1994

The problem with making forecasts is that you're eventually called upon to account for them. Sometimes that can be embarrassing. Happily, this isn't one of those times.

1993 developed very much the way I thought it would when I made my investment recommendations last January. So if you followed them, you should have done pretty well.

At the time, I said I expected 1993 to be a better year than 1992 had been. I felt the economy would start to move, that interest rates would drift lower, and that the dollar would come under pressure.

My main concern was the federal election. I could see the rising strength of the Bloc Québécois and the Reform Party and I was worried that we'd come out of the campaign with a weak Parliament in which no one had a clear mandate to govern. I was so worried about this possibility that I strongly recommended that one of your key investment strategies in 1993 should be to move some of your money into foreign securities. The idea was to achieve two goals: to protect some of your assets against a further decline in the value of the Canadian dollar and to improve your profit potential.

Well, the dollar did indeed fall. It began 1993 at 78.68 U.S. cents. At current levels, it's down about 5 percent from that, which means the buying power of your Canadian dollar assets fell by that amount in U.S.-dollar terms.

As for increased profit, how well you did depended on what you invested in. But to give you an idea, the average international stock fund was up 27.5 percent in the 12 months to November 30. The average international bond fund gained about 13.5 percent in that time. Not bad returns, I'd say.

The other major strategy I recommended for 1993 was to invest some money in the Canadian stock market. I suggested this approach even for very conservative investors. My comment at the time was, "When the stock market turns, it can happen quickly. If you're not there, you'll miss out."

Well, the market did turn, and in a big way. The TSE 300 recorded its best one-year gain in a decade. You have to go all the way back to 1983 to find a better year. That's not a coincidence, by the way; 1983 was the year we emerged from the last great recession. Stock markets have a history of making their best gains in such conditions.

Not surprisingly, Canadian stock funds reflected that strength—and in many cases outperformed the TSE by a considerable margin. The average Canadian equity fund gained almost 34 percent in the 12 months to November 30.

Resource funds did even better. The average one-year gain there was—wait for it—more than 71 percent. The worst resource fund in the country—the worst—returned over 52 percent to its investors over that period.

So 1993 turned out to be a good year if you picked up on my recommendations.

UPDATE

This script speaks for itself. We didn't experience as good a year again until 1996.

CHAPTER
7

The Worst
of Times

When the recession of the early nineties finally hit, virtually no one escaped. It's doubtful that a single Canadian family was not hurt in some way or another, whether through layoffs or pay cuts or investment losses. It was a terrible time, and the impact wasn't confined to society's more marginal groups. This was a middle-class recession, one that hit white-collar workers every bit as hard as blue-collar ones. Here are some commentaries that were aired during that difficult period in our lives, starting with one I delivered shortly before the downturn began.

GET READY FOR TROUBLE
OCTOBER 1989

If you believe the doomsayers, next year is Armageddon. The Great Depression of 1990 and all that—and it's only months away. The recent plunge in the stock markets heightened those concerns and left many people thinking that maybe Black Monday two years ago wasn't just an aberration after all.

Well, I happen to think that next year *is* going to be a tough one. But I don't think it's going to signal the start of the 1930s revisited. In fact, I think the 1990s are going to be one of the most exciting decades of this century from a financial point of view. But we're going to have to get through some rough patches first.

The main problem we're facing right now is debt: We've all got too much of it and we're too dependent on it. It was debt that triggered the market slide of Friday the 13th, when it became apparent the U.S. junk-bond market was in real trouble. It's debt that's pushing our federal and provincial governments to keep raising our taxes. Third World debt is continuing to put pressure on the banking system, both here and abroad—the CIBC just announced it's writing off over $500 million in Third World loans.

There's no question all this debt is an economic time bomb. But there is some doubt as to whether it will actually explode. So far we've been able to manage it pretty well, and there's a great deal more consciousness of the problem now than there was five years ago. But it's going to cause difficulties and we'll see some of them if the North American economy moves into a recession next year as many people expect.

That's why I feel there's some rough sledding ahead and why I'd advise financial prudence for the next few months. Start by looking at your own debt situation. How would *you* be affected if the economy went into the dumps for six months or a year? Could you cope, or would you be in real trouble? If you're not sure, you'd better take some action right now.

Start with Christmas, which is just two months away. If you normally run up big credit card bills over the holidays, think about cutting back a bit this year. You can still have a great time without going into debt.

Once you've done your holiday planning, take a close look at other money you owe—credit card balances, your mortgage, car loans, and anything else. Interest rates are high right now and those loans are costing you a lot of money. If you can pay down some of them, do so. Start with those with the highest interest charges—usually that's the credit cards.

The point is to put yourself in as strong a financial position as possible so that if we do hit a recession, you'll be less vulnerable to its effects.

UPDATE

That advice turned out to be extremely timely. Six months later, the economy plunged into a prolonged recession. Families that carried heavy debt loads into those tough times struggled, and many of them lost their homes or had to declare personal bankruptcy.

INTRODUCTION

As the recession took hold, more and more Canadians began to understand that they were in for a long haul. Talk of a new Great Depression was everywhere. Here's what I had to say on that subject, as I returned again to the theme of financial prudence.

THE ECONOMIC NOOSE TIGHTENS
SEPTEMBER 1990

These are not happy times. Everywhere we look, it's bad news. The economy is slowing down. Oil prices are threatening to push up inflation. Unemployment figures are soaring. Consumer confidence is at its lowest point since the early eighties. Bankruptcies are way up. The stock market is way down.

Talk about doom and gloom. The last time we were this depressed was in 1981–82. Everyone's concerned, obviously. But younger people seem to be especially worried. They've never experienced this before. They came of age during the affluent eighties, when it seemed like the good times would roll forever and the bubble would never burst.

Well, all bubbles burst sooner or later. We can only hope they don't make too much of a mess in the process. It looks like the best we can hope for right now is that the recession will be soft and quick, and that we'll be back on track by mid-1991.

The worst-case scenario would be a repeat of 1981–82. Those were pretty rough times, as you may remember, but, mercifully, they didn't last too long.

I don't see us as being on the brink of a new depression. The potential is there, especially given the huge debt buildup that's taken place in recent years, not only in Canada but in many other countries as well. And the mess in the U.S. savings-and-loan industry doesn't fill me with confidence—the collapse of the American banking system contributed significantly to the Great Depression of the 1930s.

But I think there are enough pluses around to pull us through the coming crunch—more sophisticated financial management, freer international trade, less global dependence on the health of a single economy, the strengthening of Europe—all these will help.

Nonetheless, you might want to hunker down for the next few months until the picture becomes a bit clearer. For example, no more buying on credit. I know the holiday season is coming, but take it easy this year. You can have fun without being extravagant. Retailers will hate me for saying that, but this is a time for self-preservation. A lot of people could find themselves unemployed over the next few months as companies trim staff to cope with falling sales.

Others, especially the self-employed or commission sales people, may find their income drastically reduced. Just ask a real estate agent or a stockbroker about that.

The worst enemy when your income drops is debt. If you can't keep up the payments, there goes the sofa, the car, maybe even the house. We saw it happen in 1981–82, and we're seeing it again. Don't let it happen to you.

Once you stop buying on credit, your next priority should be to reduce any debt you already have. Begin with your credit card balances. You're paying over 20 percent interest on them in most cases. Go from there to paying down any demand loans. If everything else has been paid off, reduce your mortgage principal. The less you owe, the less vulnerable you are.

And start budgeting. I know, everyone hates budgets. But in hard times, it's an absolutely essential self-discipline. Know how much is coming in, what's going out, and how much is available each month for debt reduction.

And make sure you start putting something aside for an emergency fund—just in case. Ideally, you should have a cash reserve equivalent to six months' worth of after-tax income. Keep that money invested at the best rate you can get. Treasury bills or money market funds are good alternatives. Just make sure it's available if it's needed.

UPDATE

Although times were hard, the feared depression never came—thank heaven!

INTRODUCTION

The previous script deals mainly with defensive measures to take in tough times. But there are ways to actually profit from a recession. You just need to know how.

PROFITING FROM THE RECESSION
SEPTEMBER 1990

You've heard the old saying about how it's an ill wind that doesn't blow somebody some good. Well, this current economic slowdown may be just the latest example. A lot of people have already been hurt by it, what with job losses on the increase and personal bankruptcies soaring. And we may have seen only the beginning; I suspect there's worse to come this winter.

Your first priority in this kind of situation should be damage control. Pay off debts, budget your spending, build a cash reserve, and keep your head down. But those are all defensive tactics. There *are* things you can do to profit from a recessionary situation—if you're prepared to take some risks.

The fact is that many fortunes have been make in bad times by people who bought land or companies or stocks when they were cheap. If your financial house is in good order and you have little or no debt, you might consider making some financial moves over the next few months.

The stock market might be a good place to begin. I know, it's taken a terrible beating this year and there may be more bad news to come. And it's true that the worse things get, the more anxious people are to unload their holdings—and the lower prices fall. Last January, when I was giving my financial predictions for 1990, I said I expected the stock market to show weakness during the year. I also said that when that happened it would be a signal to go bargain-hunting.

Well, it has happened and I've started combing through some of the sale items on the Toronto and New York exchanges. You know, we have a rather perverse psychology when it comes to stocks. If K-Mart or Eaton's has a sale, we all flock to the store looking for deals. But let the TSE have a sale and we look the other way. We want to buy stocks only when they're expensive, because that's when everyone else wants them. So we end up paying too much. Then, when the market goes down, we sell, take a loss, and swear we'll never do it again. Crazy!

In fact, the time to buy stocks or equity mutual funds is when they're cheap. The people who had the faith and the nerve to buy quality stocks in 1982, or right after the 1987 crash, reaped huge rewards. I expect we'll see a similar opportunity in the next few months. If you have some money available and don't mind the risk, give it some thought. Don't invest everything immediately, though. Start small and watch how things develop.

Another depressed area that should rebound is real estate. Prices have taken a beating in many parts of the country. I don't expect them to turn around immediately, but a judicious investment in the next few months could pay off big down the road.

You might also still be able to make some capital gains by investing in bonds or bond funds as interest rates decline. However, the prospects aren't as good now as they were last winter and spring when I mentioned them on this program.

If you're wondering which part of Canada offers the best investment prospects, check out Alberta. It looks like oil prices may stay high for some time. That's bad news for most people but good news for petroleum companies. The Alberta economy was already showing signs of recovery before the Middle East crisis; we should now see that accelerate with greater exploration and development activity in the oil business.

Whatever you decide to invest in, stick with quality. I firmly believe that if you buy quality at a bargain price, you can't lose money. Sooner or later, you'll be able to sell at a profit.

UPDATE

The stock market began a comeback in 1991 and by 1993 it was surging. People who followed this advice and bought when prices were low made huge profits. The bond markets followed a similar pattern. The recovery in real estate took much longer to develop, and that sector started to produce good returns only after 1995.

INTRODUCTION

By mid-1992 it was apparent that the recession was starting to recede. But in the next commentary I suggested there were some important lessons to be learned from it. I restated some of the principles of good financial management I'd set out while the recession was on.

IGNORING HISTORY
JUNE 1992

We don't use the term austerity very much these days, but that's certainly what we've been going through for the past couple of years. These have not been fun times, by any stretch of the imagination. One result of these hard times is that many people have been rethinking how they handle their money. They're spending less, paying down debt, saving more—in short, practising good money management.

The question is, Will they keep it up when the good times return? If the last great recession is any indication, probably not.

Ten years ago, we were going through very much the same kind of situation we're facing now. The economy was in a mess, people were losing their jobs, companies were closing, and every dollar was precious. Then, in 1983, things turned around. Suddenly we were in the middle of what turned out to be a time of wild excess. People borrowed to the hilt, bought high-priced real estate, speculated in the stock market—in short, they did things with their money that they wouldn't have dreamed of a couple of years before.

I suspect things will be no different this time around. As the economy starts to pick up, we'll begin to get careless with our money, and a few years down the road we'll have to learn the same lessons all over again.

If you're determined that won't happen to you, here are some tips that may help. You're probably doing all this now. Just remember to keep doing it when conditions start to improve.

First, don't take on more debt than you can handle. In the eighties, individuals did it, companies did it, and, most especially, governments did it. It's one of the reasons why we're in so much trouble now. When times start getting better, don't take it as a signal to start piling up more debt on your credit card. Instead, use it as an opportunity to pay off existing loans. You'll be far less vulnerable when the next recession comes along.

Second, build an emergency fund. Many people were caught without any cash reserves when this slowdown hit. As a result, a layoff meant financial disaster. Put some money away for the proverbial rainy day. If possible, try to build a cash fund equivalent to six months' after-tax income. Invest the money in something safe and liquid—a premium savings account, a term deposit, or a money market fund, for example.

Third, have a contingency plan. When times are good, we tend to assume nothing will change. Our job will be there, the money will be there, and everything will be fine. Well, conditions do change—

sometimes amazingly quickly. Don't be caught off guard when they do. That means continually upgrading your skills, making yourself aware of other job opportunities, and having some idea of what you might do if your employer suddenly decides to downsize.

Finally, invest wisely. The investors who fared best during this recession are those who stuck with relatively low-risk, high-yielding securities, like bond and mortgage mutual funds. But when the economy heats up, I can guarantee that many of these same people will abandon their conservative approach and start speculating in overpriced investments. And they'll get hurt in the process.

The bottom line is that proper money management isn't something you practise only when times are tough. Too many people treat it like a diet: Once they've achieved some positive results, they think they can go on a binge. Don't you make that mistake when the good times return.

UPDATE

I don't need to add to this script. The principles laid out are fundamental to good financial management.

INTRODUCTION

Although the recession was winding down by the summer of 1992, the human casualties it left behind were many. Jobs were lost, careers destroyed, families disrupted. There was a great deal of despair in Canada during these days. I tried to offer some encouragement with the following item.

SILVER LININGS
JUNE 1992

It's not all good news, but the economy is showing some signs of recovery. Inflation is low, interest rates are down, exports are way up, productivity is improving, profits are edging higher, and the U.S. economy seems to be getting back on track.

These are all good signs—so why are we still so miserable? Basically because nothing much is happening to make us feel better.

The effects of a recession tend to linger long after the event itself has passed. Call it the hangover period, if you like. That's what we're in right now. It's a time when things aren't getting any worse—but they aren't getting much better, either.

Many companies that survived the recession are starting to turn around, but they aren't doing much hiring yet. That means unemployment stays high. In fact, we probably won't see any major improvement in the employment situation for a year or so.

Consumers, for their part, are still worried about the future, so they aren't spending any more than they have to. They're not buying cars, or furniture, or clothes they don't absolutely need. And they're certainly not spending money on luxuries.

That, in turn, means continued tough times for manufacturers, importers, retailers—anyone who relies on consumer spending for a living. So while we may finally be putting this long recession behind us, don't look for overnight miracles. The road back to prosperity still has a way to go.

In fact, this can be the hardest time of all for people who have been hit by the recession—those who have lost their job or even their business. If you're in that situation, the only advice I can give you is to hang in there. Don't become depressed, and above all don't give up. I know that's tough if you're out of work and can't find a job. But things *will* get better. They always do.

I've known a lot of people who have lost their jobs through no fault of their own. In many cases, they later claimed it was the best thing that ever happened to them. It got them out of a dead-end situation, opened new doors, forced them to acquire new skills, even turned them into entrepreneurs in some cases. I know. I've been through it.

Ten years ago this month, in the last great recession we suffered through, I was in exactly that situation, along with about a hundred other people. The magazine we were working for went belly-up and suddenly we were all without jobs. It was a traumatic experience, especially since some of us had been with the same organization more than 20 years. And it took a while to recover from the shock.

But, a decade later, I can tell you that many of those who lost their jobs that day have gone on to do very well for themselves. In some cases, it launched them onto an entirely new career path and they've ended up much better off as a result. So stick with it. There *are* better days ahead.

UPDATE

There were.

CHAPTER
8

The Trials of
the CPP

I was a parliamentary correspondent in Ottawa back in the 1960s when the Canada Pension Plan was introduced by the Liberal government of Lester Pearson. I recall the debate well. The left-of-centre wing of the Cabinet, led by such people as Judy LaMarsh and Paul Martin Sr., strongly supported the program, both as an important element of the social safety net and as a huge potential vote-getter. But others were more cautious, including clever business minds like Mitchell Sharp and Robert Winters. The fundamental concept of the CPP was flawed, the critics warned. A pay-as-you-go plan would eventually end up costing Canadians dearly as the years passed and the benefits started to flow out.

But the cautions went unheeded. If there were problems with the assumptions, a future generation could deal with them. The plan went ahead, and so did the Liberals in the polls.

Years passed, and not much debate was heard about the CPP. Then, in the latter part of the 1980s, the Conservative government of the day started to tinker with it. In retrospect, their moves accelerated the crisis we're now experiencing with the whole concept of public pensions. But at the time they were popular moves. Here are two commentaries from that period.

CHANGES TO THE CPP
APRIL 1987

Until this year, the Canada Pension Plan was pretty rigid. If you decided to retire early, you couldn't collect until you were 65. Working past the so-called "normal" retirement age was equally unheard-of—you became eligible to collect a pension at 65 whether you wanted it or not.

Well, all that's changed. As of January 1, there's a lot more flexibility built into the CPP. You can now retire early on a reduced pension, if you wish. Or you can keep on working up to age 70 and collect a fatter pension cheque.

The changes really bring the plan more into line with present-day reality. Here's how they work.

First of all, if you want to retire early and collect CPP benefits, you really have to retire. That means your income from employment or self-employment can't be more than about $6,200.

If you qualify, you can choose to start collecting early. But you'll pay a penalty in the form of a reduced pension. How much depends on your age. It amounts to about 6 percent a year for each year you're under 65 when you start collecting. So if you applied for benefits to start on your 60th birthday, your pension payment would be reduced by 30 percent. You won't ever get that back. That reduced pension is what you'll keep collecting for the rest of your life, with appropriate cost-of-living adjustments, of course.

OK, let's look at the other end of this sliding scale. Suppose you keep on working past 65 and thus delay collecting your Canada Pension Plan benefits. Now you've got some real flexibility. You can start your pension at any time and the rules about stopping work don't apply. In other words you could, if you wanted, keep on working and collect CPP benefits at the same time. For every year you wait past 65, your pension cheque goes up another 6 percent. So if you hold off until age 70, your monthly CPP cheque will be 30 percent higher than it would have been had you started collecting at 65. There are no further increments beyond age 70, so you might as well start collecting then. You don't have to stop work, though.

Another major change this year allows more flexibility in dividing pension payments between husband and wife. This can be a very useful way to split income for tax purposes, so if you're collecting CPP benefits you might want to check into it.

It works like this. First, both of you must be at least 60, and of course at least one of you must be collecting CPP benefits or have applied for them. Now, just to make this easy, let's say the wife has been contributing to the Canada Pension Plan for 20 years. The husband has never contributed. And let's say they've been married all that time and the wife has just starting collecting a pension of $500 a month. So she applies to the government to split her pension between them. They do two calculations:

- The first is how much the couple, combined, is collecting in pension plan benefits. In this case it's $500, since the husband isn't getting anything.
- The second calculation is the number of years they've been married as a percentage of the total number of years the wife was making contributions. In this case, they were married the whole time.

The husband would therefore be allowed to receive $250 a month—half the total. If they'd been married less than 20 years, he'd get something less than that. The result? The pension is split equally between them, and together they keep more because their tax bill is less.

It might seem a bit complicated, but if you're in that position, check into it. It could be worth your while.

UPDATE

Although the numbers have changed, the rules outlined in this commentary remain substantially in force. The real shock to government actuaries turned out to be the unexpectedly high number of Canadians who applied for reduced CPP benefits at an earlier age. The payments to that group greatly exceeded projections, contributing to the growing financial crunch the plan was facing. That crisis was already taking shape as these improvements were introduced, as the next item shows.

CPP BILL WILL RISE
APRIL 1987

I've been contributing to the Canada Pension Plan since it was first set up, back in 1966. The cost to me that year was $79.20. I remember at the time there were all kinds of dire warnings about how the CPP was underfunded. Future generations were going to have to pay through the nose as a result. We didn't think much about it then. And, in fact, during the first seven years of its existence, CPP contributions increased very little—an average of less than 2 percent a year. Hardly a big deal.

Well, all of a sudden those dire predictions are starting to come true. This year, my contribution is just under $445, which is the maximum level. Over the past five years—and this has been a period of low inflation, remember—it's been increasing at a rate of almost 11 percent a year. Four years from now, we'll be paying a maximum of $625 a year, assuming average wages continue to increase at around current levels. That translates into a yearly hike of about 9.5 percent. And if inflation drives average wages up, it will be a lot more than that.

Now, obviously, we're getting a lot of benefits for that money. And some of the programs, such as the disability pension, have been made much more generous. But it's important to look at the other side of the equation as well—what all this is costing us now and in the future.

Last year, our federal and provincial health ministers got together and decided that, yes indeed, the Canada Pension Plan was in fact underfunded. It needed a lot more money if it was going to maintain, much less improve, the benefits it offers. So the ministers quietly put together a long-term plan that, by the time it's finished, is going to mean a huge increase in the amount of your annual contribution. I say *your* contribution advisedly—*I* expect to be retired by then.

The reason these changes didn't generate a big debate at the time is that this is a really long-term plan—25 years. Since that's the time span usually considered to mark the passage of a generation, it really bears out the prophecies about high future costs that were made back in the 1960s. My kids may not be too happy when they find out what they've been saddled with.

Just to give you an idea, in 25 years the rate at which people contribute to the Canada Pension Plan is going to be double what it is today. This year, you'll contribute 3.8 percent of your earnings, up to the maximum level. You employer kicks in a similar amount. That's going to increase every year until 2011, when the contribution level will be 7.6 percent—twice what it is today and over four times what it was when the Canada Pension Plan started.

That's a very large increase over what we're paying now. Think of it in these terms: If those numbers were in force today, your maximum annual contribution would be almost $1,000. Of course, it will be many times that 25 years from now, because of the impact of inflation on wages subject to CPP. And your employer has to match your contributions, which means an ever-increasing burden on business.

That's why it pays to be familiar with all the benefits the Canada Pension Plan offers—and to apply for them if you're eligible. You and your children are going to pay a lot for them. You may as well use them.

UPDATE

That was a decade ago. Note the projection the finance ministers made at that time—that we'd be paying 7.6 percent of insurable earnings by 2011 if the CPP was to be kept solvent. Now read the next commentary and ask yourself how much more of this we can take.

CPP BAILOUT PLAN
MARCH 1997

The federal budget followed so quickly on the heels of the announced changes to the Canada Pension Plan that the CPP almost got lost in the shuffle.

That mustn't happen. The CPP salvage plan is far more important to each of us individually than anything Paul Martin unveiled in his budget. The deal was worked out between Ottawa and just enough of the provinces to allow it to squeak through. It's going to cost younger Canadians a lot of money—and older people, like myself, are going to be the major beneficiaries.

Just to remind you of the horrible facts, the bailout plan proposes to raise the maximum CPP contribution from an employee to $1,635 a year by 2003. This year's maximum, before the changes were made, was just under $945. So the program calls for your contributions to increase by almost 75 percent in seven years.

Of course, that's only half the story. Your CPP contribution is matched by your employer, if you have one. If you don't—and more Canadians than ever are self-employed these days—you must pay the whole shot yourself. That works out to almost $3,300 a year. That's a lot of money by any standard.

There's a real generation problem here. The younger you are, the more this deal is going to cost you. Older people, such as myself, get off almost scot-free. I'll no longer have to pay CPP premiums by the time the new maximum is in place. But I'll receive full benefits from the plan, even though my contributions over the years have been way below those my children are facing.

I find this unconscionable. My kids are struggling with the costs of setting up households, meeting mortgage payments, raising their families, and all the other expenses that young people face. Now they're being asked to pay a huge chunk of their income to support me in retirement—money I certainly don't need. At some point, the young people of this country are going to say, "Enough!" Then what will happen?

The other problem is that no matter how you look at it, the CPP isn't a good deal for younger Canadians. I ran some numbers through my computer that show that someone in his or her twenties would be far better off putting the equivalent of an employer/employee CPP contribution into an RRSP. Let's take someone who is 25 when the new maximum contribution limit is reached. My calculations show that after 40 years that person qualifies for a CPP benefit that's only about two-thirds of the amount that an RRSP/RRIF combination would produce.

Last year, the C.D. Howe Institute put forward a plan that would have dealt with this issue by replacing the CPP with a program of private plans for Canadians. It was a nonstarter in the negotiations that followed, but it may be an idea we have to revisit in the future.

And believe me, we *will* have to revisit the CPP. No matter how you look at, this plan has a lot of problems. At some point, a government is going to have to tackle them head-on and come to grips with such issues as why wealthy seniors can draw full benefits while young people have to deal with a huge financial burden.

Unfortunately, the current crop of political leaders has opted to deal with the matter by throwing money at it—our money, or, to be more precise, our children's money. It's bad policymaking and it will hurt many people.

UPDATE

I guarantee that if I keep doing these broadcasts, a sequel to this book a decade from now will contain a new item that chronicles yet another CPP crisis and yet another decision by politicians to try to solve it by raising the contributions (read taxes) still more. Until we acknowledge that this whole concept is fundamentally flawed and represents a huge, growing, and unacceptable burden on younger Canadians, the Canada Pension Plan is going to be one of the nation's greatest headaches.

CHAPTER

9

Mutual Fund
Mania

The past decade has seen a revolution in the way Canadians invest their money. For years, going back to at least the Great Depression, we've been a nation of ultraconservative interest investors. Savings accounts, guaranteed investment certificates, and Canada Savings Bonds were the backbone of our investment portfolios. Successive governments, frustrated at the lack of domestic capital flowing into our equity markets, tried one tax plan after another to encourage us to change our ways. We stubbornly refused. Give us our GICs and leave us alone—that was the attitude of most Canadians.

But in the 1980s, things began to change. Interest rates, which hit an all-time peak in the early years of the decade, began to fall, and fall, and fall some more. There were occasional blips along the way, but it gradually became clear that we had moved into a new interest-rate cycle. The era of steadily rising rates that characterized the sixties and seventies was gone. The trend line was clearly pointing down.

It took some time for Canadians to react. Most people thought it was a temporary phenomenon, that a return to double-digit rates was just around the corner. In 1989 and early 1990, it looked like they could be right. But then another recession set in and rates began tumbling again. Faced with the prospect of steadily diminishing returns whenever a GIC came up for renewal, investors began to search for alternatives. Mutual funds, which had been a mystery to most people previously, rapidly emerged as the investment option of choice.

When I published my first annual guide to mutual funds at the beginning of the nineties, experts were predicting the industry could grow to over $100 billion by the year 2000. By the spring of 1997, mutual funds held well over $200 billion of our money and were still expanding at a frantic pace. Never in our history has there been such a massive shift of personal savings from one asset class to another in such a short space of time. What we've seen is unprecedented.

The following items chronicle some of the developments that took place over that period, starting in the mid-1980s.

LEVERAGING MUTUAL FUNDS
AUGUST 1986

I saw two items in the newspaper recently that caught my attention. The first was a report that mutual fund sales in Canada are growing at a rate that can only be described as incredible. During the three-month period that ended June 30, the mutual fund industry reported net sales of $1.6 billion. Now to put that into perspective, a year ago at the same time sales were just under $345 million. In other words, mutual fund sales more than quadrupled during that period.

The other item that caught my eye was a warning. It came from the Ontario Securities Commission and dealt with the fact that an increasing number of Canadians are financing their mutual funds purchases with borrowed money. In investment jargon, that's called leveraging. It's estimated that about 30 percent of all mutual funds sales this year have been with borrowed cash. That comes to $800-million worth of fund units.

Now, in principle, there's nothing wrong with borrowing to invest. In fact, it can be a smart business decision in the right circumstances. The interest cost of the borrowed money is tax-deductible, and the additional funds enable you to invest more and increase your profits accordingly. The catch is, you can also increase your losses this way. If you don't know what you're doing, it's a fast route to bankruptcy.

That's what the Securities Commission is worried about. There's a fear that a lot of investors who don't really understand the implications of leveraging may be borrowing heavily in the hope of making a quick killing. If things go badly, though, those people could end up with losses they may not be able to afford.

Let me give you an example of how this could work. Suppose you had $5,000 and you wanted to invest it in a mutual fund. But then you talked to a fund salesperson or read an article somewhere about leveraging. As a result, you decided to borrow an additional $5,000 at 12 percent interest, doubling your mutual fund investment.

Suppose at the end of the first year, your fund increased in value by 15 percent—and that's a fairly modest increase by recent standards. What's happened? Instead of the profit of $750 you would have received if you hadn't borrowed, you now have a profit of $1,500. You have to repay the loan with interest, though. If you're in a 40 percent tax bracket, the net cost of that interest is $360, so your real profit from this transaction is $1,140. That represents a return of about 23 percent on your original $5,000 investment, instead of the 15 percent you would have received if you hadn't borrowed. It's results like that make leveraging attractive. And while mutual funds are doing well, everyone wants to get in on the action.

But what happens when things don't go well? The stock market takes a dive or interest rates soar. Let's say your mutual fund had lost 15 percent instead of gaining it. Then what? Then you'd be in trouble, that's what. Your original $5,000 would be worth only $3,140 after you repaid the bank loan with interest. That means you would have lost about 37 percent of your original investment. That's what leveraging does. It magnifies your gains considerably—but it magnifies your losses even more.

Even without the warning from the Securities Commission, I don't think this is a good time to be borrowing to invest. It's true that interest rates are down and seem to be trending lower. But we're in an uncertain economic period, and that's always a risky time to be going out on a financial limb. If you are thinking about leveraging an investment, I'd wait a bit—and then I'd proceed with great caution.

UPDATE

As it turned out, this was good advice. A year later, in August 1987, the stock market peaked and then went into a sharp decline that culminated in the October crash. Leveraged investors got hammered. That's why I continue to this day to advise most investors against leveraging. Most people become interested in the idea only after markets have had a big run. If you really must leverage, the best time to do it is in the midst of a deep recession, when quality stocks are selling for 50 cents on the dollar. That's when you can make the really big bucks!

INTRODUCTION

In 1986, an innovative Vancouver-based credit union brought a whole new mutual fund concept to Canada—ethical investing. Here's a commentary I did shortly after the launch.

ETHICAL MUTUAL FUNDS
JANUARY 1987

It's called ethical investing and it's an option for people who don't want to own shares in companies that do business with South Africa or that exploit immigrant labour or sell arms to Third World countries. The idea has been around in the United States for more than 15 years, but it's only recently surfaced in Canada. It seems to be catching on, so let's look at the pros and cons of mixing morality with investing.

First of all, you need to understand one basic fact: You're probably going to pay a financial price for sleeping better at night. Most of the socially conscious mutual funds in the United States have not had a particularly good track record. Generally, they've underperformed competitive funds invested with no attention to ethical concerns. Just look at the oldest of them, Pax World Fund, which has been around since 1971. Its returns have been below the average for similar non-ethical funds by any standard of measurement you want to apply—ten-year performance, five-year performance, last year's performance, you name it. The reason is quite simple: With many companies ruled out for moral reasons, the range of investment opportunities is much narrower.

There's no reason to believe that Canadian ethical funds are going to be any different. So if you want to be socially conscious in your investments, you'd better resign yourself to below-average returns. If you're ready to pay that price, you then have to decide what ethical investing really means to you. Exactly what is it you don't want your money to support? Different funds have different definitions of what is important. You'll have to find the one that comes closest to your own standards.

In the U.S., for example, the Pax World Fund has been interested mainly in avoiding companies in the weapons or nuclear-power business and firms involved in tobacco, alcohol, or gambling. On the other hand, the Dreyfus Third Century Fund puts the emphasis on investing in companies that are strong in product and occupational safety, equal-employment opportunities, **and** environmental concerns. As you can see, ethical investing can take different forms.

Here in Canada, the first company into this field has been the Vancouver City Savings Credit Union. If you're from the East, you may never have heard of them, but VanCity has been one of the real pioneers in new financial products in recent years. Their fund, called the Ethical Growth Fund, went national in October, so you should be able to buy it wherever you live. It has five criteria for buying shares in companies: They have to be Canadian, practise good industrial relations, deal only with countries that promote racial equality, be involved in non-military activities, and not be in the nuclear business.

Another fund, called the Summa Fund, is expected to be launched this month by the big Investors Group of Winnipeg. Their criteria will be somewhat different. They're not interested in labour relations, for instance, but they won't invest in companies involved in liquor, tobacco, gambling, or pornography. As I said, you have to decide what's important to you.

I expect we'll see more such funds created over the next couple of years—especially if these two attract a significant amount of interest.

If you think investing should be influenced by moral considerations, then by all means look into them. It will probably cost you money—but then, what price peace of mind?

UPDATE

The socially responsible funds actually performed better than I predicted over the years. Ethical Growth had an average annual compound rate of return of 11.4 percent to May 31, 1997—well above the average for Canadian equity funds. The Summa Fund hasn't done as well, although it's been much stronger in recent years. Several other socially responsible funds have also appeared on the scene, the most outstanding being the Clean Environment family. Their Canadian equity fund has been particularly outstanding, with an average annual compound rate of return of 18.7 percent for the five-year period to May 31, 1997. So I'll eat some humble pie on this one. You can indeed invest with a clear conscience, and make good money while doing so.

INTRODUCTION

One of the key factors in the roaring success the mutual fund industry experienced in the past decade was the introduction of the back-end load—or the deferred sales charge, as it's also known. Previously, all load funds in Canada had been sold with the sales commission payable up front. And the cost wasn't cheap—9 percent was a typical front-end load. Faced with that kind of charge, many Canadians took their money elsewhere. Then, in 1987, Mackenzie Financial came up with a better mousetrap, and the modern era of fund marketing was launched.

NEW HORIZONS
FEBRUARY 1987

It's called a back-end load fund. It's fairly common in the U.S., but so far we haven't seen many of them in Canada. That may be about to change. The newest of these funds, the Industrial Horizon Fund, has been heavily promoted over the past few weeks. If it turns out to have attracted a lot of business when the offer closes, on March 18, you can expect a bunch of imitators to follow.

How does it work? It's quite simple. Instead of paying a sales commission when you buy the fund, you pay when you cash in your units. In other words, you get in for free. You just have to pay to get out. The fund managers don't call this a back-end load. They refer to it as a redemption fee. But it works out to be the same thing.

In the case of Industrial Horizon, the advertising is really quite misleading. There is no mention at all of back-end loads, redemption fees, or anything else. The ads simply stress the fact there is no acquisition fee. It's only when you get the prospectus that you discover you'll be asked to pay when you go out the door.

Now there are different types of back-end loads. The worst are the ones that have a fixed rate. It costs you, say, 5 percent to get out, no matter when that happens. Funds like that can end up costing a fortune. Fortunately, we have very few of them in Canada.

Industrial Horizon works differently. It has a reducing redemption fee. In other words, the longer you keep your money in, the less you'll pay to get out. If you withdraw your funds in the first year, it will cost you 4.5 percent. After that, the fee drops 0.5 percent a year. At the end of nine years, then, you can get your money out free.

There's just one problem with that. Given the volatility we've seen in the financial markets in recent years, you have to be prepared to move your money around when conditions change. The Horizon fund back-end load is a disincentive to switching. But, surprisingly, it's not as big a negative as it might seem at first glance.

I did a few calculations, to see how all this would work out. I compared the Horizon Fund with another of this company's successful funds, Industrial Growth. Both have the same investment objectives, and Industrial Growth has been around for several years, so we know its track record. I assumed a $1,000 investment in each fund this year, and a growth rate of 15 percent over the next several years; that's less than Industrial Growth's ten-year average, so it's not out of line. I also assumed you'd have to pay a 4 percent up-front commission to buy into Industrial Growth today. The posted rate is 9 percent, but a good broker should get it for you for 4 percent or less, even if you have only a small amount to invest. I then figured out how much money you'd have, after all commissions, at the end of each year between now and 1995.

It turns out that, even with this back-end load, you'd be better off with Horizon than with Industrial Growth, as long as you did not cash in during the first year. But even if you did, the difference would be so small it wouldn't matter. The longer you held the Horizon Fund, the better off you'd be. At the end of eight years, for instance, you'd be about $92 ahead of Industrial Growth Fund if you cashed in at that point. What it boils down to is that back-end loads aren't necessarily bad. It all depends how they're structured, and the Horizon plan is quite reasonable.

So if you're looking at mutual funds that charge a commission, don't turn up your nose at back-end loads without checking them out.

UPDATE

All this seems like ancient history now. Horizon was hugely successful. Now almost every load fund in Canada offers a deferred sales-charge option, and an estimated 90 percent of purchases are done on that basis. Hardly anyone pays an up-front commission anymore, even though in most cases now you are rarely charged more than 2 or 3 percent.

INTRODUCTION

The growing excitement over mutual funds cooled somewhat after the 1987 stock market crash. Many investors who had switched their money from GICs were left frightened and confused, and started to redeem their units. That prompted the following commentary.

MUTUAL FUND STRATEGIES
AUGUST 1988

Talk to anyone who's at all interested in investing and they'll say: "Oh sure, I know how a mutual fund works. Doesn't everyone?"

Well, no, they don't. In fact, I suspect that a lot of people who think they know what mutual funds are all about are really quite uncertain about how to invest in them. The latest figures from the Investment Funds Institute of Canada seem to confirm that. They show that about $2 billion in fund holdings were redeemed during the three months from April to June. That's a lot of money. And I doubt whether the investors who cashed in have found a better place to put it.

There are a number of theories about why this is happening, but generally last October's stock market crash gets the blame. The idea is that equity fund investors who held on at that time have now recovered part of their losses. At this point they want to get out before another market fall. That seems like a plausible enough explanation. But if it's true, it suggests there's a lot of uncertainty about how to invest successfully in mutual funds.

Now, I've talked about mutual funds before, but, given what seems to be happening right now, perhaps a quick review of the basics might be helpful. First, remember that a mutual fund doesn't necessarily have anything to do with the stock market. Sure, there are lots of stock funds out there—or equity funds, as they're called. But there are also dozens of mutual funds that have never owned a stock and never will. These invest in such things as bonds, mortgages, Treasury bills, real estate, gold, and even commodities. In a stock market drop, these aren't directly affected at all—in fact, some may actually benefit. So if you own units in a mutual fund and you aren't sure exactly what it invests in, make some inquiries before you take any action. You may be worrying for no reason.

Second, find out whether any funds you're in are part of a family. Does the same company manage several different types of funds? If so, you can switch from one type to another at very little cost. So if you're in an equity fund and you're worried about the stock market, you don't have to cash it in. Simply give the company instructions to switch your money somewhere else, perhaps into a more conservative mortgage fund or a money market fund. This gives you the flexibility to take advantage of changing economic situations—but don't do it too often, because there is a charge involved each time.

Finally, remember that the best strategy for mutual fund investing is to buy and hold. When you go into a fund, you should look at it as a long-term investment, not something you trade in and out of. If you select a well-managed fund and add to your holdings during times when unit values are low, it should perform well for you over the long haul.

Good Canadian stock funds have returned investors an average of between 15 percent and 20 percent a year over the last decade—and there were some major dips in the market during that time. Good bond and mortgage funds averaged between 11 percent and 14 percent. So if you've selected a quality fund, be patient. It'll pay off.

UPDATE

That advice is as good today as it was a decade ago. The principles of sound mutual fund investing don't change.

INTRODUCTION

As interest rates dropped in the early 1990s, the flow of cash into mutual funds accelerated. In 1993, stock and bond markets took off, fund investors scored eye-popping returns, and the mania was under way. Here's a warning I issued to CBC listeners at the end of that frantic year.

TIMING MUTUAL FUNDS
DECEMBER 1993

In the fall of 1990, a major study on the future of the Canadian mutual funds industry was released. It projected that by the year

2000 we'd have over $100 billion invested in mutual funds in this country. Guess what? We passed that mark in October, more than seven years ahead of schedule.

Even the more conservative fixed-income funds did well. The average return for Canadian bond funds during that period was almost 12 percent. The average international bond fund did better than 14 percent. Little wonder investors have been flocking to them.

If you've been considering joining the crowd, one word of warning. You may be told that mutual funds are a long-term invest-ment. Choose a fund, put your money in, and forget about it for five years. Well, don't believe it. Timing is just as important in selecting mutual funds as it is with any other type of security. And once you've made an investment, you should never turn your back on it. Conditions change, and your investment strategy may have to as well.

Let me give you two examples of why timing is so important in buying mutual funds. Let's look first at natural resource funds. These invest in companies involved in our resource industries—mining, forestry, petroleum, and the like. They're hot right now. The worst-performing resource fund in Canada gained over 52 percent in the year to October 31. Some more than doubled in value during that time. I think there are more profits to come, because resource stocks usually do best in the latter stages of an economic recovery. So this is a good time to be in this sector.

But that's not always the case. As one woman said to me recently, "It's about time this fund paid off, because I've had it for six years and it's done nothing until now." That's because resource stocks are notoriously prone to boom-and-bust cycles. They'll lose money in a recession and score big gains in a recovery. If you want to buy funds that invest in the resource industry, the message is obvious. Buy in when times are tough and get out before the next recession begins. When you start to see signs of high inflation, an overheated economy, and sky-high interest rates, it's time to sell.

Bond funds are another example. Many people have made hand-some profits from them in recent years. That's because falling interest rates push up bond prices, creating capital gains in the process. But when interest rates turn around and start moving back up, the opposite happens. Bond prices fall, and the returns on these funds deteriorate. Before that happens, it's time to take your profits and move on.

So don't assume that buying a mutual fund means you can just sit back and watch the profits roll in. It's like anything else—you have to look after your money if you want to get the best return.

UPDATE

Timing is still important in mutual fund management. When markets get toppy, move some of your assets into safe havens and wait.

INTRODUCTION

As money continued to flow into mutual funds, another concern began to appear. People started to ask aloud whether this wasn't the 1990s equivalent of the South Sea Bubble—a giant speculative pyramid that would eventually come crashing down. Here's a commentary I did on those fears.

MUTUAL FUND RISK
MARCH 1994

People keep asking if there's a danger that all the money flowing into mutual funds is creating a speculative bubble that will inevitably burst. After all, it's happened before, back in the early 1970s. So why not again in the nineties?

Well, these are different times. For one thing, there are a lot more mutual funds around, many of which have no investments in the stock market. So there are plenty of alternatives for nervous investors if they want to protect their assets from volatile markets.

Back in the seventies, this wasn't the case. Money market mutual funds, for example, were virtually nonexistent in Canada. These are funds that invest in low-risk, short-term securities such as Government of Canada Treasury bills. Their unit value is fixed—usually at $10—so the chances of an investor's losing money are very low. When times get tough, as they were in 1990 and 1991, money flows to these funds as a safe haven.

That's exactly what will happen again if stock markets get too high and interest rates begin rising. Rather than pull their money out of mutual funds as such, most people will simply shift their assets into low-risk funds that are out of harm's way. That doesn't mean we won't have bad years for stock funds in the future—we will. But when that happens, wise investors will move their money elsewhere.

Obviously, that means understanding the relative risk of different types of mutual funds. So let's take a look at that.

At the bottom of the scale—least risk—are the money market funds I just mentioned. Next up from there are mortgage mutual funds. They're available through most major financial institutions as well as from several independent mutual fund companies. They're a solid, safe, secure investment. I have never come across a case where a mortgage mutual fund lost money for investors in a given calendar year.

Moving up the risk scale, we come to bond mutual funds. Here the risk relates directly to the prevailing interest-rate climate. When rates are falling, as they have been for the past three years, bond funds are very low-risk. That's because when interest rates fall, bond prices rise. So it's pretty hard to lose money in bonds when rates are heading down.

But when interest rates are moving up, it's a different story. Then bond funds become more risky, because as rates climb, bond prices fall—and that can have a negative impact on the value of your bond fund unless the managers are very astute. So the rule here is to be out of bond funds when rates are on the rise. Move your money into some other type of fund and wait for the next opportunity.

Let's move up another notch on the risk scale, to balanced funds. These funds invest in a mix of securities, usually stocks and bonds. The proportion of each is determined by the fund manager or, in a few cases, by a computer program. In some cases, the fund is limited in the amount of stocks it can hold. I know of one fund that limits shares to 25 percent of the portfolio. Other funds may have no limit; they could be 70 or 80 percent in stocks in certain circumstances. So it's hard to generalize about the risk in balanced funds. It depends on the particular fund's investment mandate. But, generally, balanced funds are at about the middle of the scale from a risk point of view.

Next up the list are stock funds, and with these too there are ways to keep your risk to a minimum while you enjoy the profit potential of the stock market.

UPDATE

The comment on bond funds turned out to be appropriate. They went into a deep slump at just about the time this commentary was delivered, when the U.S. Federal Reserve Board raised interest rates. They eventually recovered, but it took almost a year before they regained their former values. Mortgage funds were also hit—not as badly, but my comment about no mortgage fund ever losing money in a calendar year was proven wrong by year-end. A few did drop in value in 1994, although not by much.

INTRODUCTION

A large portion of the new money flowing into mutual funds came from RRSP investors who were switching from interest-bearing securities in the hope of getting higher returns. Unfortunately, some didn't understand the full implications of what they were doing.

MUTUAL FUNDS AND YOUR RRSP
FEBRUARY 1996

It's not an easy time for RRSP investors. Most of their money usually goes directly into guaranteed investment certificates—GICs. But they don't look very attractive right now, with five-year interest rates in the 6 percent range. So what else is there?

Mutual funds, that's what—and a lot of money is pouring into them. I recently saw a forecast that, by the time RRSP season ends, the Canadian stock market will have received a $6 billion boost thanks to money flowing into equity funds.

We saw a similar situation a few years ago, when interest rates tumbled as a result of the recession of the early nineties. That's when the term "GIC refugees" was created for those who were switching their savings from interest-bearing securities to mutual funds. That phenomenon had both good and bad results.

On the positive side, it showed many people that it wasn't all that difficult to build a well-diversified investment portfolio in an RRSP. On the negative side, too many Canadians got carried away with mutual fund mania and invested far too much of their money in high-risk areas like emerging markets and Latin America. When they got burned, many took their losses and fled back to the safety of GICs, vowing never to leave again. Too bad.

It would be nice to say that we've all learned a lesson, and undoubtedly many people have. But I can guarantee that something similar will happen to at least some of this year's GIC refugees. Make sure you're not among them. Here are some tips that may help.

First, plan your mutual fund RRSP portfolio carefully. It should be conservative in its approach and well balanced in its content. Include a mix of good equity and fixed-income funds. I recently looked at the RRSP of an elderly couple in Ontario that was almost entirely in stock funds. That's not what I'd call balance. Although the funds were all good ones, so much dependence on the stock market is far too risky at their age.

Second, don't include speculative funds in your RRSP. If you want to go for the big score, do it outside your plan where you can claim a deduction for any losses. Latin American funds, emerging-markets funds, Japan funds, small-cap funds, and precious-metals funds really have no place in an RRSP. If you must invest in this type of fund in a retirement plan, keep your holdings small—no more than 10 percent of the portfolio.

Third, choose funds that are low-risk. For example, one of my recommended bond funds for RRSPs is the Dynamic Income Fund. That's because the manager puts safety ahead of returns on his priority scale. He wants to protect his investors from losses, and he manages the fund accordingly. As a result, this is one of the few Canadian bond funds that has never lost money over a calendar year. It even managed a solid gain in 1994, when just about every other bond fund ended up in the red. So ask hard questions about the manager's style and priorities. They'll go a long way toward helping you decide if a particular fund is right for your RRSP.

Finally, make full use of your 20 percent foreign-content allowance. International and U.S. funds have consistently outperformed Canadian funds during this decade. Why not put yourself in a position to take advantage of that trend? You'll provide your RRSP with more diversification in the process.

The best choice here would be a broadly based international fund, one that can invest throughout the world. There are lots of them around; Templeton Growth Fund and Fidelity International Portfolio Fund are just two examples.

UPDATE

These observations about using mutual funds in an RRSP remain valid today—and so are the specific funds I mentioned at the time.

INTRODUCTION

As the mutual fund industry grew in size and influence, it was perhaps inevitable that it would create its own star system—managers who were able to attract megabucks through a combination of public persona and above-average returns. One of these was Veronika Hirsch, who created headlines when she decided to change employers in mid-1986, leaving investors who had placed money on the basis of her reputation wondering what to do.

VERONIKA HIRSCH LEAVES AGF
AUGUST 1996

I've never seen anything like it: A banner headline on the front page of *The Financial Post* announcing the signing of mutual fund manager Veronika Hirsch by Fidelity Investments. You might expect that kind of media treatment if a top baseball player like Ken Griffey Jr. switched teams. But a mutual fund manager? It shows just how high the fund industry has climbed in public consciousness in recent years.

Ms. Hirsch, for those of you who were away at the cottage when all this happened, was hired by the AGF fund group last fall. At the time, she was a competent but relatively obscure money manager working for the Prudential funds, which have since been sold to London Life. AGF apparently decided they needed a star, and Ms. Hirsch was going to be it. They spent big bucks to produce a series of TV commercials on the theme of Veronika's investing secrets, which ran all through RRSP season. By the time the campaign was done, everyone with a TV set knew who she was.

There was just one problem. It appears AGF didn't have the foresight to pin down their new manager to a long-term contract before spending megabucks to put her face into every home in the country. That meant she was wide open to a better deal—and Fidelity came along with one. The stories I hear say that Ms. Hirsch was very concerned about the propriety of leaving AGF after just ten months, especially in view of the investment they'd made in her. But in the end she decided to go—whether because of the money, because she was attracted by the career potential, or because of some other reason, only she knows. The bottom line is that her departure left a gaping hole at AGF. They moved quickly to name new managers to take over her funds, but none carry the same weight in the public mind.

So if you're an investor in one of her funds, what do you do now? It's an important question, because a lot of new money flowed into

AGF on the strength of the Hirsch promotion campaign. At the end of September last year, the flagship Canadian Equity Fund had about $367 million in assets. Then came Ms. Hirsch. In the ten months she was at AGF, the fund's assets grew to more than $670 million. That's an increase of more than 80 percent in less than a year! It shows you how effective the AGF campaign was.

But if you're one of the company's new customers, what should you do? Follow Ms. Hirsch to Fidelity? Or leave your money where it is and hope for the best? My advice is to stay where you are, at least for now.

I say that for two reasons. First, most of the new money that has come to AGF has been through the back-end-load purchase option. If you cash out within a year under that plan, you'll face a hefty penalty of 5.5 percent. That's pretty stiff. You want to avoid that unless things get desperate.

My second reason for holding on is past experience. Ms. Hirsch isn't the first high-profile fund manager to move. Several others have moved in recent years; they just didn't get as much media attention. In most cases, the fund they left performed better than the one they went to, at least for a time. There are several reasons why that can happen: The portfolio of the old fund is already in place, the manager has a breaking-in period with the new company, or the mandate of the new fund is somewhat different.

So I suggest a wait-and-see approach. Look at the situation again in six months, see how the AGF fund is performing, and compare it to what's happening over at Fidelity. At that point, you'll be able to make a much more informed decision.

UPDATE

As it turned out, this was just the start of the Hirsch saga. Within three months she had been removed from the new Fidelity fund that had been created for her, following allegations she had acted improperly in a personal stock transaction while at AGF. As of spring 1997, no formal charge had been laid against her by any securities commission. But the incident dramatically demonstrated the high degree of public scrutiny mutual fund managers are now subjected to.

INTRODUCTION

The rapid growth of the mutual fund industry did more than focus public attention on the money managers. It also drew the attention of securities regulators, who felt that some tightening of the rules was required to protect investors from potential conflicts of interest. A number of proposals were unveiled in late 1996, prompting the following commentary.

PROTECTING FUND INVESTORS
SEPTEMBER 1996

The main thrust of the plan put forward by the Ontario Securities Commission is to reduce the potential for conflict of interest when mutual funds are being recommended to investors.

Our fund universe has become huge. There are more than 1,200 of them now available in Canada, with new ones appearing almost every week. It's almost impossible for any individual to sort through all the options and decide which funds best meet his or her needs. That's where financial advisors come in. They review a client's situation, see what the objectives are, and then recommend funds that best suit that person's requirements.

Or at least that's how it's *supposed* to happen. There have been concerns for some time that certain sales practices may influence the recommendations an advisor makes. The proposals put forward by the OSC will go a long way toward eliminating some of those potential conflicts, although they won't disappear entirely. Although they will apply only in Ontario initially, I expect provincial securities regulators across Canada to move quickly to adopt the new rules once they're approved.

Let's take a quick look at some of the most important changes. First, no more special payments or extra financial incentives to dealers. This means that mutual fund companies will not be permitted to make any payments to sales people over and above the commissions outlined in the prospectus. There have been cases where special bonuses have been paid if a certain sales target is reached. That could result in an advisor recommending one company's funds over those of another that didn't pay an incentive.

Second, no more exotic trips. Some fund companies have awarded top sales people with all-expenses-paid trips to "education conferences" in desirable parts of the world. Cruises down the Nile, midwinter escapes to the Caribbean, and meetings in Hawaii are just a few of the rewards that mutual fund sales representatives have enjoyed. Let me be clear about this. These are not rewards to people who are employed directly by the fund company. They go to financial advisors who work for third parties, offering supposedly disinterested advice to clients. Many sales people have told me they would never allow their recommendations to be tainted by the possibility of going on one of these junkets. But the potential has always been there.

Next, tighter rules on marketing assistance. Mutual fund companies will still be allowed to give financial support to dealers and sales people for the preparation of marketing materials and the staging of educational conferences and seminars for the public, but their contribution cannot exceed half the total cost.

Fourth, limits on non-cash incentives. Fund companies won't be able to get around the curtailment of bonus payments by giving non-cash rewards to sales people, such as sporting-event tickets. A cap of $150 a year will be placed on that type of inducement.

Finally, no more redemption-fee incentives. Some fund companies have offered to pay any deferred sales charges that result from an investor's switching to them from another group. The effect was to encourage people to move from company X to company Y, earning a commission for the salesperson in the process. There was quite a bit of this going on a couple of years ago, but the practice will no longer be allowed.

There are quite a few other rule changes, but this gives you the idea. When they eventually go through, you won't see much difference on the surface when you buy a fund. But you'll know that the chances are better that the advice you receive about load funds will be unbiased.

Just remember, though, that mutual fund sales people who depend on commissions for their living aren't likely to tell you about any good no-load funds, and the new rules won't change that. It's up to you to search out those for yourself.

UPDATE

Although the ideas are generally good, it's taking a long time for them to be implemented. The original target was the 1997 RRSP season, but that came and went without formal approval. As of summer 1997, we were still waiting.

CHAPTER
10

There's One Born
Every Minute

The world is full of people who want to separate you from your money. Most of them seek to do it through legitimate means. But a few use more unscrupulous methods. Over the years, I've had many occasions to warn CBC listeners about various scams, both in the financial arena and elsewhere. Here are some examples.

INTRODUCTION

Rising tax rates have prompted more Canadians to seek out tax shelters in recent years. In many cases, they'd have been better off just paying Revenue Canada.

GIMME SHELTER
NOVEMBER 1984

There are two sure ways to tell it's November. One is Santa Claus parades. The stores and shopping centres can barely wait until Halloween is out of the way before inundating us with red-faced clones of the jolly old gentleman.

The other is tax shelters. This is the time of year when the business pages of your newspaper start filling up with ads telling you about the thousands of dollars you can save at tax time by making a smart investment now.

When you stop and think about it, these harbingers of winter have something in common. They're both designed to separate you from your money—and to make you happy in the process. How you deal with the Santa Claus ploy is up to you. Personally, I'm still a sucker for it. Every time I walk through our local shopping mall and see him with a kid on his knee and a couple of elves handing out candy canes, I go all soft at the centre. It was a long time ago, but I still remember when I was one of those kids. It was magic.

Handling the tax shelter pitch, however, is something different. You better not go all soft at the centre at the prospect of saving big money next April, because what's more likely to happen is that you'll lose your shirt. Buying a tax shelter takes a hard head and a lot of research. I have an acquaintance who is one of Canada's leading tax experts. He states, categorically, that he does not know anyone—not one person—who ever made money on a tax shelter deal.

Now, I'm not talking about things like RRSPs and home-ownership savings plans. They're excellent investments. I'm referring to the slickly packaged deals that are being aggressively sold right now—films, MURBs, flow-through shares, things like that. Buying those types of shelters is risky business. Sure, you may save money on taxes. But some or all of the rest of your investment may go down the tube.

Let me tell you what happened to me. Last fall I went shopping for tax shelters for the first time. One of the ones I bought has been a disaster. I purchased shares of a research-and-development stock issue put out by Mitel Corporation, a high-tech company based near Ottawa. The shares were priced at $42.50 each, but by the time the tax savings were taken into account, the real cost was only $20.94. It seemed like a good deal.

Well, a few months ago, after watching the value of the shares plummet like a stone, I finally sold them at just over $15. In other words, I lost over $5 a share on the whole transaction. Some tax shelter! I'd have been far better off just paying the money to the government.

Now, hindsight is wonderful. In retrospect, I should have seen the company was heading for trouble and its stock was likely to take a beating. But, frankly, the tax shelter aspect got in the way. I didn't judge the quality of the investment as carefully as I otherwise might have, because I saw the tax savings as lessening my risk considerably.

That's what you've got to watch out for if you go tax shelter shopping. Every expert will repeat this over and over ad nauseam—and people will continue to ignore it. I'll say it again, and this is from someone who's been burned: Judge the tax shelter on the basis of its investment value alone. If you would not invest money in the project if there were no tax shelter advantages, then don't go into it. I can almost guarantee you'll lose.

INTRODUCTION

Speaking of Florida, Canadians have always possessed an irresistible urge to acquire swamp land in the Sunshine State. Here's what happened in one case.

BUYING FLORIDA HOME SITES
AUGUST 1990

I don't know if you've noticed the articles in the newspapers recently about a company called General Development Corporation. If you haven't, and if you've been thinking of buying vacation property somewhere, you'd better read up on it. General Development is a big—and I mean *big*—Florida land developer. They've been selling property in Canada for the better part of a decade. According to their estimates, as many as 6,000 Canadians bought land or homes from them.

Well, General Development is in real trouble. They're under a federal indictment in the U.S. on charges of selling property at greatly inflated prices. A couple of their former senior executives have pleaded guilty to fraud. And, to top it all off, the company is operating under Chapter 11, a U.S. bankruptcy law that provides protection against creditors. In short, it's a mess.

Now, the thing that really makes this scary is that General Development gave every impression of being a perfectly straightforward operation. They were registered with the Ontario government, their sales literature was slick and attractive, and their development sites really did exist. I've driven through some of them myself. All the veneer of legitimacy was there.

The problem—at least according to the charges that have been laid—was that they sold property at inflated prices based on false appraisals. Now, the truth or otherwise of these accusations will eventually come out in court. But whatever a judge and jury decides, there are a lot of lessons to be learned here.

For starters, it appears that at least some people bought property from this company sight unseen. They apparently relied on pictures and sales presentations for all their information. I find it very difficult to understand why anyone would invest in a house or a piece of land they've never laid eyes on. For all you know, the Interstate runs right behind it or the place is infested with mosquitoes. But, for some reason or other, people still do it. So the first lesson is this: Don't buy any property—vacation or otherwise—without personally checking it out first. If you can't go, don't buy. It's that simple.

The second mistake many buyers made was to pay too much. Sure, they may have been misled by the property appraisals. But there's always another line of defence, which is to check the value of comparable properties in the resale market. One buyer told *The Toronto Star* she'd paid $71,000 for a Florida condo, only to find an identical one later on the same site selling for $44,000. The time to check out the resale market is before you make a purchase, not later.

Finally, think long and hard before you buy an unserviced property. You may get a great price on raw land, but what good is it if you can't get water or electricity and there's no road? If you do decide to take a chance, try to get iron-clad guarantees on when services will be supplied and a commitment from the developer to refund your money if services aren't in place as promised.

The General Development debacle has reminded us all once again that when it comes to real estate deals, it's very much a buyer-beware situation. So don't get carried away by pretty pictures or a persuasive sales pitch. You may regret it.

UPDATE

Florida was the locale for this particular item, but the advice applies anywhere.

INTRODUCTION

High-pressure sales people are found in almost every business. Sometimes you have to be ruder than they are.

HIGH-PRESSURE SALES
AUGUST 1990

A friend of one of my children paid a visit to the Canadian National Exhibition in Toronto this year. He's a young fellow, with very little money—in fact, his job pays little more than the minimum wage. While he was at the CNE, he wandered into the booth of an encyclopedia company. He didn't want to buy anything—he was just interested in the display. What happened next caused him a lot of sleepless nights.

This kid was subjected to some of the most intense high-pressure sales tactics I've heard about in some time. The sales people used every trick in the book—free gifts, easy payments, double-teaming, you name it. He told me later he was so desperate to escape from the clutches of these guys that he would have signed anything just to get away. And sign something he did—a contract to purchase over $2,000 worth of encyclopedias and related products, payable at the rate of $73 a month for the next two years, with interest of 18 percent a year on the unpaid balance. Can you believe it? A young man who earns $5 an hour—and he told them that—hounded into buying thousands of dollars worth of merchandise he doesn't want or need.

Now it's easy enough to say that all he had to do was walk away. But if you've ever been in the grip of a high-pressure sales artist, you know how difficult that can be. Many of us are too polite for our own good in these situations. We don't want to offend anyone, so we allow ourselves to be badgered into buying something we don't want. It's happened to me—and I'll bet it's happened to you too.

A few weeks ago, I criticized the high-pressure sales tactics that some peddlers of vacation property are using. This latest incident is a reminder that no one industry has a corner on unscrupulous sales techniques. Some automobile dealerships are guilty of these practices—not just in selling cars but in pushing such add-ons as rustproofing and extended warranties. I've personally experienced high-pressure tactics and bait-and-switch techniques in furniture and electronics stores. The plain fact is, it can happen any time—but it's more likely to happen, it seems, when the economy is in a slowdown and people become increasingly desperate to make a buck.

What can you do to protect yourself? Well, most provinces have some form of consumer-protection legislation, but it may or may not apply, depending on the circumstances of the sale. If you sign a sales agreement for something you don't want, contact the consumer protection office in your province as quickly as possible to see what your rights are. Don't wait. Often there's a time limit on cancelling an agreement.

If you don't have a legal out, go back to the company that sold you the unwanted goods. Sometimes a reputable firm will cancel the contract if you ask. That's what happened in the case of our friend. He went back to the booth a few days later with a letter stating that he wished to cancel the agreement. The company, to their credit, agreed and he was off the hook—with a lesson, I hope, well learned.

But, in the end, you're your own best line of defence. Exercise your right to say no. Above all, refuse to sign any document on the spot. Insist on taking it home and reading it over for a day or two. That will give you time to think it through. No reputable salesperson will refuse to allow you to do that. If they balk, it's a sure sign they're trying to set you up for a quick kill.

Don't be the next victim.

UPDATE

We learned later that it wasn't the magnanimity of the encyclopedia company that released our friend from his contract. A provincial statute required the company to cancel the deal if it was notified in writing within a certain time. But don't rely on legalities to bail you out. Each province has its own rules.

INTRODUCTION

Is there anyone out there who hasn't been harassed by a time-share salesperson at one point or another? Does anyone actually buy these things? If so, is anyone happy with the investment? I doubt it. If time-shares are such a good deal, why are they using such devious methods to hook people into listening to their sales pitch?

CONGRATULATIONS!
YOU'VE WON!
AUGUST 1990

I received a phone call the other day from a woman who said she had great news for me.

Remember that contest you entered? she asked.

Well, no, actually I didn't.

Doesn't matter. She wasn't going to be put off by that. You didn't win the grand prize, she told me. But you have won a wonderful consolation prize: two nights at the luxurious—she named a motel I'd never heard of—all expenses paid for you and your wife. What nights would you like me to book? No weekends, please.

Well, not having entered any contest, I was just a little bit suspicious. So I asked a few questions—like: What's the catch?

No catch, she assured me. All we ask is that while you're our guest you join us for a couple of hours for a tour of our beautiful new—and she named a big new resort development that I vaguely recognized. We do ask that both you and your wife take this special tour with us, she said. Now, when would you like to come?

That's when I told her we were busy for the next 30 years and hung up.

I've been getting a lot of those come-ons lately, although most aren't as aggressive as that one was. Usually they consist of letters in envelopes marked "Urgent" and "Immediate reply requested." Inside, there's a letter telling me I'm a guaranteed prizewinner—anything from a car to a 35-millimetre camera. All I have to do is pick it up.

Where?

Why, at some resort development, where I'll receive a special two-hour guided tour. Make sure my spouse comes too, the letter says. It's a condition of winning.

On the back of the letter, in very small print, are the odds on winning the various prizes they've listed. The car is one in 175,000. The VCR is also one in 175,000. So is the 20-inch colour TV. Your chances of winning the camera are 174,997 out of 175,000. What does that tell you? If you want to drive for a couple of hours and subject yourself to a hard-sell sales pitch for a couple more, the promoters will give you an inexpensive camera for your trouble. Thanks, but I have better things to do with my time.

I once went on one of these sales tours in Florida, just out of curiosity. It was for a time-share operation, and I have to tell you the pressure to buy was incredible. Those sales people do everything but grab your hand and force you to sign on the bottom line. The reason they want both spouses there is so that one won't talk the other out of the deal later. You've both been subjected to the pitch and, presumably, you've both been sold.

I haven't been to any of the presentations in Canada, but I'm sure they're much the same. A hard sell is a hard sell, wherever you are in the world. So if you get a phone call or a special mailing telling you you've won a big prize, don't get too excited. All you may have won is a headache.

UPDATE

I'm still getting those great prize notices. I still throw them away. You should too.

INTRODUCTION

Ever had someone knock on your door and tell you he could cut your heating bill? Ever wondered what it was all about? Here's the answer.

GAS-BILL CUTTERS
JUNE 1991

You've probably never thought about where your local gas company gets its supply. As long as the fuel is delivered regularly and safely at a reasonable price, most of us couldn't care less.

That was certainly my attitude until a young man rang our doorbell a couple of weeks ago and said we could cut our gas bill by 10 percent or more just by signing a piece of paper. There was no risk involved and I'd continue to deal directly with my local gas utility. I would simply be appointing an agent to acquire a supply of natural gas in my name, at a supposedly lower price than my gas company could. The savings would be split 60–40 between me and the agent.

Well, this was all news to me. But the savings sounded good. Who wouldn't like to knock 10 percent off the heating bill these days? However, being somewhat suspicious, I decided to investigate further. I took the literature to read over. Then I started making some phone calls.

Here's what I found out. You can indeed appoint an agent to buy natural gas on your behalf. It's been possible since the industry was partially deregulated in the mid-1980s. Until now, however, most of the attention has been focused on commercial users, where the biggest potential savings are. The aggressive soliciting of residential users seems to be fairly recent.

If you sign on, you become part of a pool of gas users. Your agent then goes to the producers in Western Canada and negotiates a price for the gas needed for your pool. Right now prices in the short-term market are lower than the gas utilities are paying under long-term contracts. That's where the savings come from.

The agent then directs your local utility to use the gas he's contracted as your source of supply. That makes the utility the middleman, supplying you the gas your agent has purchased. They'll still charge you the same price for distribution. Where you save money is on the supposedly lower price paid to the producer.

The material I received estimated gross savings at present of between 8 and 15 percent, depending on the user. Industries would obviously save more than homes. But that's only on the basic cost of the gas—about half your total bill. The bottom line is a gross discount of, say, 5 percent. If the agent keeps 40 percent of that, you're left with a net saving of about 3 percent. For a gas bill of $800 a year, that works out to a $24 rebate. To get that money, you generally are asked to sign a long-term contract. The one I saw was for five years, with automatic two-year renewals if you don't give a six-month cancellation notice.

Who knows what the price of gas will be in five years? But if it rises, your saving may turn into a loss and you won't be able to do anything about it. You should also realize you're signing what amounts to a power of attorney, appointing the agent to act on your behalf. If he goes belly-up, you may be on the hook for any contracts undertaken in your name.

So if one of these marketing agents rings your doorbell this summer, don't be too quick to sign on. Ask some pointed questions about exactly how much you can expect to save, what guarantees are offered—if any—and how long a contract you have to sign. Also ask about your legal position. If you're unsure about it, you can always check with a lawyer—if you think your potential savings are worth the fee.

And no, I didn't sign up.

UPDATE

These companies are still out soliciting. In fact, one came to my door very recently. No, I still haven't signed and I don't intend to. The price of natural gas has become very volatile. I'd rather rely on the buying power of my utility, thanks very much.

INTRODUCTION

Pyramid schemes are among the oldest scams around. You'd think we would have caught on to them by now, but they keep getting dressed up in new clothes and trotted out for another go-round. And people still fall for them.

PYRAMIDS
JULY 1991

It seems to happen every time the economy runs into trouble. Suddenly, there's a proliferation of get-rich-quick schemes, designed to lure people in with the promise of easy money. This year, there seem to be more of them around than usual, and I get the impression they're casting a wider net. I know several people who have become involved in these deals, and one of my kids has even been approached.

Now, perhaps you're already into one of these schemes. Maybe you've even made some money; I've heard people claim they've grossed over $100,000 a year in some cases. If so, that's great. I have nothing to say to you. But if you haven't yet been recruited—and that's exactly how it happens—maybe I can save you some grief and some money.

I'm talking here about pyramid-sales plans. These are companies that move products by creating an ever-expanding network of sales people, each of whom is encouraged to go out and find other recruits to sell on their behalf. Amway made this type of direct selling famous, but now everyone seems to be getting in on the act. The technique is being used to sell water filters, skin-care treatments, and a lot more.

The pitch to join the team can be very seductive. I recently watched a slick video promotion that featured motivational music, a convincing presentation of the product, and a bunch of testimonials from sincere-looking people telling us how getting involved with this operation had changed their lives. Typically, these companies also organize public meetings that are almost evangelical in their fervour. These folks believe in what they're doing—*really* believe.

Well, fine. But before you become a believer too, ask some hard-nosed questions. See how well it all stands up to scrutiny. For starters, take a close look at the structure of the sales operation. Typically, you'll find that the greatest rewards are earned not by selling the product yourself but by recruiting a large number of people to sell *for* you. The more folks you bring in, the greater your payoff.

Why? Because in most cases, each new recruit has to buy in by purchasing a supply of the product, which he or she is then supposed to sell to the public. In one agreement I looked at, the buy-in price was $1,000. That bought you enough product to get started; if you sold it all, you got a 40 percent return on your money.

If you didn't sell it, you were stuck with it. The $1,000 was non-refundable, and the product was nonreturnable.

Now you see why this is called pyramid sales. The first people in are in the best position to profit. The more people who become involved, the fewer potential recruits there are—and the fewer possible customers. If everyone on your street is trying to sell the same product, who's going to buy? Don't laugh, it can happen. Usually, there's no exclusive sales territory involved. After all, that would limit the number of potential sellers and the money they could pay.

It's rather like the chain letters that flourished back in the Great Depression. When your name came to the top of the list, you'd receive a fortune in the mail. Unfortunately, it never did. Chain letters that ask for money are now illegal in most places.

Some of these pyramid-sales companies have been actively recruiting college students this summer. And, because of the lack of jobs, many students are biting. In most cases, I'm afraid they're going to end up at the bottom of the pyramid. If you or your children are approached, make sure you understand exactly what you're getting into—and the risks involved—before handing over any cash.

UPDATE

We often think of these schemes as hitting mainly unsophisticated investors, as happened in Albania in late 1996. But they can be very persuasive, believe me. Be ultra-cautious if you're approached.

INTRODUCTION

The stock market has become a respected, if somewhat risky, place to invest money. But it wasn't always the case, and there are still some promoters around who give shares a bad name.

PENNY-STOCK PHONE SALES
AUGUST 1992

Has it ever happened to you?

The phone rings. You answer. On the other end of the line someone you've never heard of launches into a sales pitch for a can't-miss stock in a new gold, or diamond, or copper mine. It's the opportunity of a lifetime. A chance to make a killing. It's also an appeal to the greed in most of us. Buy now while the stock is cheap and get rich. The problem is that many people who invest don't get rich—they get hurt.

The Ontario Securities Commission has been trying to crack down on this practice for some time. Last year they published a booklet warning about the dangers of buying penny stocks in this way. Now they're trying to go further by imposing a mandatory cooling-off period for any stocks sold over the phone. They've put forward a plan that would require all dealers that sell in this way to obtain a customer order in writing before the transaction is binding. Only a few companies would be affected—none of the major brokerage firms sells stocks through unsolicited phone calls to non-clients. The ones that do—they're called broker-dealers—aren't happy about the idea. They say the commission is giving their whole industry a black eye when the real problem is with a few individuals who occasionally break the rules.

Maybe that's true. But even if it is, I find it hard to understand why these broker-dealers would object to such a rule if they believe what they're doing is really on the level. After all, a good investment is a good investment. Just because it has to be confirmed in writing doesn't change that.

Perhaps what these dealers are actually concerned about is the possibility that many potential clients will decide, on reflection, that buying penny stocks over the phone isn't such a good idea after all. Maybe they're worried that the other basic emotion of investors—fear—will triumph over greed once the reality of what they've done has a chance to sink in. Whatever their reasons, their initial reaction to the plan was to sharply criticize the Ontario Securities Commission for making what they claimed were "unsubstantiated allegations" about their industry.

I don't know how all this will be resolved, but I hope the proposal goes through. Perhaps illegal or unethical sales practices have been reduced to only a few cases. It's very difficult to know, because no one monitors all the phone calls that go out. But if a cooling-off period can help prevent even a few unsuspecting people from an unwise investment, why shouldn't it be implemented?

Sure, it may cost a few sales. But if the telephone brokers are genuinely trying to upgrade their image, that's a small price to pay. If they're not—well, then it's really time for a crackdown.

UPDATE

Some of these companies have gone under, but a few are still around. I suggest you never buy stocks (or any other securities) over the phone from someone you don't know or do business with on a regular basis.

INTRODUCTION

Sometimes you'll get solicitations from people who actually do want to give you money. But beware—it comes at a price.

MAIL-ORDER CASH
OCTOBER 1993

I received a letter last week. "Dear G. Pape," it began. That was the tip-off that my name had been plucked off a mailing list somewhere. "If you had $3,000 in your hands right now," the letter went on, "would you pay off your bills? Fix up your home? Take a great vacation?"

As I pondered those intriguing options, the letter went on to tell me that I could obtain an unsecured personal loan from Transamerica Financial Services in as little as 48 hours. All I had to do was to sign the enclosed application and mail or fax it back to them. As soon as the loan was approved, my cheque would be sent out.

I can't recall ever receiving a solicitation like this before. It sounds like the sort of thing a fly-by-night operation might do. Transamerica is anything but that; it's a huge company, with over $30 billion in assets. So it seems strange they should be out flogging mail-order loans. But here they are, offering to put $3,000 in my pocket.

They want to be well paid for their trouble, of course. The interest rate on the loan is a whopping 22 percent a year, with repayments spread over three years. At that rate, you'll pay more than $1,100 in interest charges by the time the loan is discharged. Who'd want to do that? Obviously, no one who could borrow money anywhere else.

Let me go back to their letter again, and the various ways they suggest I might use their $3,000. First, to pay off bills. Well, I can think of many less expensive ways to do that. Even credit card rates are a lot cheaper than 22 percent, in most cases, and they're just about the priciest form of consumer credit around. So paying off bills is not a good use for this money.

Next, Transamerica suggests I might want to fix up my home. Well, if I were going to do that, I'd go to my friendly neighbourhood bank and get a home-renovation loan secured by the equity in my property. That would probably cost me a point or two over prime, tops. A lot cheaper than 22 percent!

Finally, Transamerica offers the thought that I might want to use their $3,000 to take a great vacation. I can't think of any worse reason to borrow money. You're not acquiring any kind of an asset; all you're doing is going deep into hock for a couple of weeks in the sun. You'll come back with a tan that lasts a few days—and then spend the next three years repaying the lender at what amounts to an almost unconscionable interest rate.

The bottom line is that only people who are absolutely desperate are likely to have any interest in this kind of offer. That means folks who are really down on their luck, who'll grasp at any straw to get their hands on a little extra cash.

Frankly, I'm surprised to find a company like Transamerica aggressively going after that market. When I talked to someone at the company, I was told it's because they've been very successful doing this in the States so they decided to take a run at the Canadian market too.

And why not? If they can squeeze 22 percent a year out of you, it's good business—for them. It's not good business for you. If you get one of these letters, I suggest you file it where it belongs. If you're truly hard up and feel you have to go this route to get some money, then I recommend you pay off the loan as quickly as possible.

About the only good thing in this deal is that Transamerica allows you to repay the full balance at any time, without penalty. But the bottom line is, you should exhaust all other possibilities before going for something like this. It's very expensive money.

UPDATE

I've never seen another solicitation of this type. Maybe Canadians turned out to be smarter than Transamerica thought we were.

CHAPTER
11

If I'm Supposed to Be Saving, Why Does It Cost So Much?

I'm old enough to remember the good old days, when a visit to your local bank didn't involve a service fee every time you spoke to a teller. Yes, young folks, there were such times. They used to give you free cheques, they didn't charge for asking for your balance, they returned your cancelled cheques at no cost, and lots more. On top of that, they gave you a reasonable rate of interest for the money you left on deposit. As I say, the good old days.

All that has now changed, of course. The banks are second only to governments when it comes to levying user fees. How did the banks put us into this situation? Here are some transcripts from over the years that may shed some light on that question.

BANK SERVICE CHARGES
JUNE 1985

One habit I've acquired in the past few years is asking my bank for a copy of their service charges every few months and reading it over carefully. Try it. There's always something that's more expensive—and sometimes the cost increase in percentage terms is absurd.

The banks suffered a lot of bad publicity a couple of years ago when they went through a period of jacking up service charges on just about everything in sight. Some people were rude enough to suggest they were trying to compensate for the terrible losses they were taking on their foreign loans by hitting retail customers harder. That was indignantly denied, of course. But the service charges still went up.

And they're still going up! Not on everything at once—the banks are being more selective these days, which is perhaps why they're not getting as much attention. But the increases are still there, believe me.

Let me run through a couple I've come across recently at my own bank. If you check, you'll probably find something similar at your bank or trust company. The charge for cheques drawn on a chequing account recently jumped from 27 to 29 cents. Only 2 cents, perhaps. But it's a 7.4 percent increase. That's well above the inflation rate. And it's made even more significant by the fact it's the second increase of this type in slightly over a year. Early in 1984, the charge was only 25 cents. It's gone up 16 percent since then.

The price for stopping payment on a cheque is $5. That's up by 50 cents since the last time I looked, or about 11 percent. Having a cheque certified at my bank now costs $2. A year ago, it was $1.50. That's an increase of 33 percent. Inflation these days is running about 4 percent. Maybe now you see why I'm upset.

Another thing the banks are doing is continuing the process of adding service charges where none existed before. For instance, it used to be that we could write or phone our bank and ask them to switch money from our savings account to our chequing account, or vice versa. No one ever thought about making us pay to do that. After all, it's our money. Well, you guessed it. Now you have to pay. If the amount is less than $1,000, the charge is $2. If it's over $1,000, it's $3.50. One more free service down the tubes.

Another thing that really bothers me is the crackdown that is taking place on so-called "inactive accounts." Last year our daughter had her tiny account confiscated. It's a strong word, but that's what happened. She hadn't done anything with it for six months so the bank seized it. I know it's amazing, but they're actually allowed to do that.

Well, now they've increased the minimum balance in your account that allows them to do this—and they've increased it by 500 percent. It used to be that only accounts under a dollar were affected by the six-month rule. Now if your account is $5 or less and you don't do anything with it, our bank will grab it. If your account is inactive for two years and has $10 or less, they'll take it. For five-year inactive accounts, the cutoff is $20.

If you or your kids have some small accounts, better check what the policy is where you bank—or whether in fact those accounts still exist. If they have been seized, make a lot of noise. Sometimes the bank will relent when they discover someone noticed.

UPDATE

Some of the charges quoted here seem very cheap today—which only shows that the process has continued almost unabated since this commentary was delivered. And, yes, banks still confiscate inactive accounts.

INTRODUCTION

Two years went by, and I was back on the same theme again. Although no one would admit it, there seemed to be a direct relationship between the beating the banks were taking on Third World loans and rising service charges to their retail clients.

SERVICE CHARGES STILL CLIMBING
JULY 1987

I've complained about this before, but here I am again. Our major banks are still jacking up their service charges at absolutely unconscionable rates. I heard someone remark the other day that he was getting tired of paying for bad loans to Brazil every time he used his bank.

Now, that may sound a bit simplistic, but the reality is our banks are getting battered on their loans to Third World countries—so much so that they're setting aside an increasing amount of their earnings to cover their losses. That cuts into bank profits, which doesn't make shareholders very happy.

So how do they get that money back? Well, some of it comes from you. What happens in Brazil or Mexico really does have an impact on your wallet or purse. How do you pay for Third World loan losses? Partly by the bank's increasing the spread between the interest rate it pays on your savings account and the rate it charges you on a loan. And partly by increased charges on all those little services you used to get free.

Let me give you a few examples. Recently I received two notices from the Bank of Commerce, where we have our accounts. One informed us that the charge for our safety-deposit box was going up by $5. That's a 17 percent increase over what we had been paying. Quite substantial.

The other notice was that the cost for having our cheques returned each month was being increased to $1.50. Now, that may not seem like a lot, but it's a 50 percent jump over what we were paying before. That's the sort of thing that really bothers me.

Just to be sure the Commerce wasn't alone in this practice, I checked what was happening at the Toronto-Dominion Bank by comparing their current service charges to last September's. Here's what I found. The charge for NSF cheques returned is up to $12.50—a 25 percent increase. The minimum monthly cost of overdrafts has been hiked to $5. That's a 43 percent increase over last September. It now costs you 95 cents to pay your utility bills at a T-D bank branch—that's a 12 percent jump from last fall. If you transfer money between accounts by telephone or mail, it will cost you $4 to do so. That's a 33 percent hike from last year. And it wasn't very long ago that you could do that sort of thing without charge.

Want some more examples? If you have a T-D Manager Account and your minimum balance falls below $500, you'll be hit with a charge of 36 cents per cheque. That's 13 percent higher than last fall. There's been a similar increase in cheque charges on several of their other accounts as well.

As I said, I'm using the T-D Bank only as an example here. They're all doing the same thing. Just for the fun of it, I went back to 1983 and compared the charges made by the Bank of Commerce then with those of today. Four years ago, it cost $1.50 to have a cheque certified. Now it's $3.50. A 133 percent jump. In 1983 you could phone to have money transferred between accounts for no charge. Today it's $4. In the good old days you were charged $4.50 if you needed to stop payment on a cheque. Now it's $6.50—a 44 percent hike.

I could go on, but you get the message. The banks are really sticking it to you on service charges. If you're using these services a lot, take a close look at what they're costing and see if you really need them. Maybe you're still paying utility bills at the bank out of habit when you could save yourself a few dollars by using some 36-cent stamps instead. That's really the only answer. If the bank services are costing you too much, stop using them.

UPDATE

Many people still don't pay attention to the cost of their banking transactions. If you do a lot of business at your branch, it's usually best to purchase some type of package arrangement that puts a lid on the monthly charges.

INTRODUCTION

A few more years went by. The banks tried to take the heat off by freezing service charge increases for a time, but by the early 1990s the costs were escalating again.

Oops, Sorry, We Didn't Tell You
February 1991

A few years ago there was a lot of publicity about the escalating service charges being imposed by banks, trust companies, and other financial institutions. It finally reached the point where the Commons finance committee looked into it. Their report, which came down in June 1988, concluded that, yes indeed, there were some examples of service charge abuses. The report's main recommendation was that financial institutions be more up-front in notifying clients of increased charges.

Well, the bankers all said *mea culpa*, we promise to do better, and the furor died down. And they have done better in getting notices out to us. We're still being gouged, though—sometimes outrageously so. Let me tell you about a couple of things that happened to us recently. I'm sure your family has similar stories.

First, there was the case of the emergency savings account. This was an account in my wife's name that she kept as a reserve, in case we ever needed it. She didn't pay much attention to it, and took her bankbook in only once a year to get an interest total for tax purposes. Well, the last time she went in, she got a shock.

Somewhere along the way, the bank had introduced a monthly maintenance charge of $1.10 for all accounts with balances under $1,000. She had several hundred dollars in the account, but not enough to escape the charges. As a result, the interest she received was just about totally eaten up by the maintenance charge—which she hadn't even known about. And while she has to pay tax on the interest, she gets no tax deduction for the service fees. Bottom line: She ended up out of pocket.

The lesson here is to make sure you know exactly what service charges you're incurring and compare the cost to the after-tax return from the interest in your account. If you're losing money, check out the alternatives. You might be better choosing an account that pays no interest but that has lower service charges.

My second story concerns our joint bank account. I was going through our most recent statement when I came across a service charge of almost $30. Well, this really threw me. This account normally has a lot of money in it and we never pay service charges. So we made some inquiries. It turned out that for one day in December, the balance in the account slipped below $1,000. Most of the time it was over $10,000. But because of that one day, we were hit with every imaginable service charge for the full month—maintenance charge, withdrawal fees, chequing fees—you name it, the bank took it. We complained, but to no avail. Rules are rules.

The lesson here is to keep a tight watch on your cash flow, especially if you have an account you use frequently and where service charges can really add up if you fall below the magic line. Find out what the policy is at your financial institution and monitor your balance closely to make sure you stay on the right side of that line. Otherwise, it can get pretty expensive. I know.

UPDATE

That's still good advice, although monitoring your day-to-day balance has become much more difficult as a result of automatic deductions to pay everything from property taxes to your cable-TV bill.

INTRODUCTION

Service charges were just one side of the equation. The banks also hit retail customers by greatly reducing the interest paid on their accounts, as this item recounts.

VANISHING INTEREST
JUNE 1991

Next time you're in your bank, ask what interest they're paying on your savings account. If it's more than 5 percent, consider yourself lucky.

Interest rates on deposit accounts have been in free fall lately. A year ago, the big banks were paying 9 percent or more on ordinary savings accounts. Some trust companies were over 10 percent. Today, you'd be fortunate to get half that. In fact, rates have come down so much that you may now be paying more in service charges than you're earning in interest. Check it out.

In times like these, I suggest you keep no more money in a savings account than is absolutely necessary. There are other places to put your cash where you can earn a much better return. And you can still get at your money quickly if need be.

A money market fund is one choice. These are mutual funds that invest in high-quality short-term securities, such as Government of Canada Treasury bills. They're very safe and you can withdraw your cash at any time, usually with 24 hours' notice.

Like savings accounts, the rate of return on these funds has come down. But you can still earn 9 percent or more in many cases, which is a lot better than deposit accounts are paying. Another advantage of a money market fund is convenience. You may not even have to take your cash to another financial institution, just to the next counter. Most of the major banks and trust companies now offer their own money market fund, so it's just a matter of switching your cash from one place to another. Usually, you can open an account for $500 or even less.

A couple of words of warning, though. Money market fund yields will continue to fall as interest rates come down. The rate you get today is not necessarily what you'll receive tomorrow, so there are no guarantees. If you want to lock in a rate, then invest in a GIC. Just remember, you can't cash it in early in most cases.

Also, don't pay any commission for a money market fund. Those offered by the financial institutions are generally no-load. But if you buy from a mutual fund company, a sales fee may be requested. Don't pay it. The return on a money market fund is not enough to make it worthwhile, and there are plenty of good no-load funds out there.

If a money market fund doesn't appeal to you, consider a savings certificate—or cashable certificate, as they're sometimes called. They're offered by a few of the smaller trust companies and some credit unions. They're especially useful to young people who are saving to go back to school in the fall.

Savings certificates work very much like Canada Savings Bonds. The interest rate is guaranteed for a year, but after 60 or 90 days you can cash them at any time with no penalty. You'll receive full interest to the time you cash them, and you can get your money within a day in most cases. Here again, you'll get a much better return than from a savings account. My youngest daughter invested in one recently and received 8.5 percent. They're a little harder to find than money market funds, though. You may have to do some checking around.

Another option is to put your savings into term deposits and roll them over as they come due. You'll improve your return, but you'll lose some flexibility because there will usually be a penalty if you need cash early.

One other point. Ordinarily, I'm not a big fan of Canada Savings Bonds, but if you have any, hold on to them. That 10.5 percent return until next November looks pretty good right now.

UPDATE

The interest rates quoted here look absolutely princely by today's standards. Imagine a return of 5 percent on your savings account! I recently checked a monthly statement on our account. During the period, the balance ranged from a minimum of just under $10,000 to a maximum of over $60,000. The total interest we received: a munificent $5.81! Calculated on the lowest balance that month, that worked out to a return of 0.06%. Annualized, my money was earning 0.72% a year, on the lowest monthly balance. No wonder no one in their right minds keeps any more cash than is necessary in a bank account these days. Money market funds are a better alternative, though their yields too have dropped considerably. Savings certificates are now known as cashable GICs and have become more popular as a savings account alternative.

CHAPTER
12

Introducing . . .

Many innovations in the world of investing and personal finance have appeared over the years. So quickly have events moved that we've lost sight of the fact that many of the financial products and services that we take for granted today didn't exist even 15 years ago, or were available only to very wealthy individuals. Here's a collection of commentaries from over the years in which I brought some of the more exciting changes to the attention of CBC listeners.

T-BILLS FOR EVERYONE
MAY 1984

Today I want to talk about interest rates. Not the fact they keep going up, we all know about that. No, I want to tell you about something new that's happened in the money market that could mean extra cash in your pocket.

If you've ever tried to figure out where to get the best interest rates, you know how complicated it can be. As a result, most of us end up leaving whatever money we have in a bank account or investing in something simple like Canada Savings Bonds. Well, I've got a better idea—Treasury bills. Now, don't panic, this is not as exotic as it may sound. In fact, it's an easy way of getting a much better return on short-term money.

Treasury bills are notes issued by governments as a means of financing short-term operations. In some ways they can be compared to Canada Savings Bonds; the principal is guaranteed and they mature at a certain time, when you redeem them for principal and interest.

You buy them at a discounted price and cash them at maturity for face value. For example, you might pay $970 for a $1,000 Treasury bill that's due in 91 days. When it matures, you collect the $1,000; the difference represents your interest on the transaction.

Now, as I said, these are short-term notes. They're for people who don't want to tie up funds for very long. Maybe you're saving money for a down payment on a house and you want to invest your cash in the meantime. This is an excellent way to do it.

How? Well, you can buy Treasury bills from a bank, but the minimum you have to invest is out of sight for most people—usually $50,000 or $100,000. And you won't get as good a return as you will elsewhere. It's the stockbrokers who have really made Treasury bills an option for the ordinary person. In the past few months, they've dramatically reduced their minimum investment requirements, and they're paying excellent interest rates.

Here's an example. The brokerage firm of Midland Doherty (now Midland Walwyn) will sell you Treasury bills in amounts as low as $1,000. Your interest rate is half a point below the quoted rate for the bill. So if the bill normally yields 11 percent annually, you'd get 10.5 percent. That's far better than what the banks are offering and I don't think you'll find any other short-term interest rates that good.

There's another advantage. You can get your money out early if you need to. You may pay a small penalty, but the flexibility is there.

Treasury bills used to be a rich man's game. They're not anymore. If you're really interested in getting a little extra money for that nest egg, ask a broker about them. It will be worth your while.

UPDATE

T-bills today don't pay anything like the returns they did when that commentary was aired. But they're still a good alternative for short-term cash. Brokers are still the best place to buy them.

INTRODUCTION

Today billions of dollars are invested in stripped bonds, mainly in self-directed RRSPs and pension plans. Here's a commentary I delivered when these useful savings vehicles were brand new.

STRIPPED BONDS—
AN INTRIGUING NEW CONCEPT
AUGUST 1984

A new investment concept has appeared on the scene that I find very intriguing. It's called stripped bonds and if you'll bear with me for a moment, I'll explain how it works.

Let's take a Government of Canada bond—not a Canada Savings Bond but a regular one—with a face value of $1,000, maturing in 15 years, and paying 12 percent interest. If you bought one, you'd receive two things: the bond itself, guaranteeing repayment of your $1,000 in 1999, and 30 coupons, which you cash in semiannually to collect your interest.

In stripped bonds, these have been separated. You can buy the bond itself, without coupons, at a discounted price, and hold it until it matures. You'll be guaranteed a certain rate of interest for, in this case, 15 years. You'll get the full face value of the bond at the end—but you won't collect until 1999. Or you can buy coupons on the same basis. The advantage here is that, because they come due every six months, you can vary the maturity dates to suit your own needs.

This idea has been around for a while, but it's only in the past few months that financial institutions have started marketing it aggressively. They're trying to demystify the concept with hyped-up names, like Cougars and Tigers, that make them sound more like cars than bonds. And some of the ads may give you the impression of a sleazy, fast-buck gimmick: "How to turn $1,000 into $25,000 with no effort." I wouldn't blame you for flipping the page but I suggest you look again.

These stripped bonds carry the magic of compound interest to its ultimate degree. Unlike term deposits, or even Canada Savings Bonds, you can lock in a guaranteed interest rate for 15, 20, even 25 years into the future. That offers some intriguing possibilities. For example, when interest rates soared sky-high a couple of years ago, it would have been very nice to guarantee yourself 17 or 18 percent on your money for as far ahead as you could see. Of course, rates have moved down since. But even now you can lock in returns of 13 to 14 percent, which is not bad.

It's rates like that, multiplied over many years, that make the claims of the ads absolutely true. You can turn $2,000 into over $25,000—if you're prepared to wait 20 years. Wait seven years more and it grows to over $47,000. It's compound interest at work.

Have I got your attention? OK, now let me tell you what to watch out for. First, these are long-term investments. The younger you are, the better they'll work for you.

Second, remember that a good interest rate now may not look so hot five or ten years out. There was a time when 7 or 8 percent on a bond seemed great. You'll have to decide whether you think the rate will be good over the long haul.

Third, there's no secondary market for these bonds yet. I'd be astonished if one doesn't develop. But right now, you could have trouble selling a stripped bond if you needed money in a hurry.

Finally, there are tax considerations. If you buy coupons, you'll have to pay tax on the accrued interest every three years—even though you haven't received one cent of income. Revenue Canada hasn't yet determined how it will treat the bond itself, but you could end up with the same problem. The way around this is to use strips only within an RRSP; you'd need a self-directed plan to do it. In that case, no tax would be payable. You just let the money accumulate until you're ready to cash in.

So there it is. Personally, I like the concept, especially for retirement planning. Take a look at it.

UPDATE

Strips went on to become extremely popular and still are today, even though interest rates are much lower than at the time of this broadcast. The tax issue is an important one, however. If you hold these bonds or coupons outside a registered plan, you'll end up paying tax every year on interest you may not see for a decade or more. Keep them in your RRSP.

INTRODUCTION

Debit cards have become almost as common as credit cards for shopping. It wasn't always the case, and I wasn't very enthusiastic when they made their first appearance, as this commentary shows.

Debit Cards
September 1985

I'm not the world's biggest credit card fan, mainly because of the way too many people abuse them. But I'll say one thing for cards. If they're used properly, they're one of the best financial deals around.

Look at it this way. You want to buy something expensive—say, a new stove and fridge. You go to a furniture or department store, pick something out, and charge it to your Visa or your MasterCard. A couple of days later the appliances are delivered and you have the use of them. But your money is still sitting in your bank account, earning interest.

A couple of weeks later, the credit card statement arrives. But you still have another 21 days before you have to pay it off. In fact, if you timed your purchase right, you could get up to six weeks of interest-free credit. And all the while, the money you earmarked for the new appliances is still earning interest for you.

It's not a bad deal, providing you don't go and spoil it all by failing to pay off the full credit card balance when it comes due. In fact, it's such a good deal that some credit card issuers are busily at work trying to take it away from us. They're on the verge of perfecting what for them would be a wonderful new financial invention—something called a debit card. When they finally get it right, it will probably be trumpeted as a wonderful new breakthrough for consumers. Don't be fooled. It's just a way to get your money faster, and to eliminate that six-week period of having your cake and eating it too.

There are two debit card experiments going on in Canada right now. One is being run by Imperial Oil at selected service stations in six cities. The other is taking place in Swift Current, Sask. It's being conducted by the Credit Union Central of Saskatchewan, using something called a MasterCard II.

The Swift Current test is the most intriguing. It involves a number of local merchants, including food stores. So if you have one of the debit cards, you could use it when you buy your groceries. If the store has an electronic hookup with your credit union, the money would be deducted from your account immediately and credited to the store. If there *isn't* a direct electronic hookup—and in most cases there isn't at this stage—you go through the credit card-type process and walk away with a slip of paper. The difference is the transfer of your money to the store will take place within a day or two. No more bills and cheques. No more six weeks interest-free.

You probably won't be surprised to learn that the people running these tests report a less-than-enthusiastic response from the public. In fact, Imperial Oil has had to add some inducements to get people to use their debit card—small discounts on gas and oil, for instance.

The promoters of these debit cards say they're a more effective way to manage your money and that they'll help keep people from going into debt. Maybe so, although I suspect that people who are debt-prone will find some other way to do it.

The one thing these cards will certainly do, though, is separate all of us from our money more quickly. Let's just hope the experiments flop.

UPDATE

Of course, the experiments didn't flop, although it was some years before the banks got it right. Now we can use our bank cards to pay our bills instead of cash or credit cards. I guess it's a blessing—isn't it?

INTRODUCTION

The banks were being very helpful around this time. They not only developed new ways to help us spend our money, they also devised systems that allowed people to borrow more money from them too—adding, of course, to their interest income.

PERSONAL LINES OF CREDIT
NOVEMBER 1985

For the past few weeks I've been talking about some of the new financial products that have come onto the market this fall. The last one I want to discuss is a personal line of credit, which is one of the hottest items being pushed right now.

Now, personal lines of credit—PLCs, for short—have been around for quite a while. What's different are the new wrinkles that are being added and the aggressive way in which PLCs are being promoted to a broad market. It used to be that a line of credit was something reserved for the wealthy. Well, all that's changed.

Now, don't get me wrong. The banks and trust companies aren't exactly handing these things out like popcorn. They're harder to get than a credit card, for instance, and you have to complete a pretty detailed application form. But if you're creditworthy and have a steady job, the chances are you'll qualify.

At this point you're probably asking yourself: Why would I want one anyway? The answer's simple: It's just about the cheapest way to borrow money today. If you're borrowing for any reason—furniture, a new car, a vacation, to invest—then you should take a close look at a personal line of credit.

How does it work? Well, a PLC is simply an authorization in advance to borrow money up to certain limits. Once you're approved and the limit is established, you receive a special cheque book. If you want to borrow against the PLC, you just write a cheque on that account and it's done. No further authorization is needed.

Once you've drawn on the line of credit, you'll receive a monthly statement. It shows your outstanding balance, the amount of credit you have left, and the current interest rate being charged. The statement will also indicate the minimum payment due that month—typically, it's 3 percent of the outstanding balance.

That's the basic approach. As I said, there are all kinds of new wrinkles being added. For instance, Canada Trust has just introduced what it calls its PowerLine, which has all kinds of gimmicks.

Take, for example, the interest rate. It can be as low as 10 percent, which is as good as corporate borrowers are getting these days. The Canada Trust plan offers two options. If you want the best interest rate, you have to put up liquid security—Canada Savings Bonds, stocks, GICs, anything like that. If you go the secured route, you pay interest at the prime rate, whatever that is at any given time. And you have to pay only the current interest on your loan each month—you can leave the principal untouched if you want.

If you don't have any securities, you can apply for an unsecured PLC. You won't get as good a break on interest rates, especially if you don't borrow very much. In fact, if your balance is under $2,500, you're charged interest at the same rate as a Canada Trust MasterCard holder. But if your balance is over $2,500, the interest rate drops to 11.5 percent right now. It's not as good as prime—but I think you'll find it's less than you would pay for an ordinary consumer loan.

If you're in the market for money, I think it's worth checking out.

UPDATE

Many people have since taken out home-equity PLCs, which allow you to draw cash against the value of your home at a very low interest rate. That can be a useful source of cheap money. However, some people have used these lines of credit to speculate in the stock market, not always with good results. Treat them carefully.

INTRODUCTION

As interest rates declined through the 1980s, more people began searching for alternatives to guaranteed investment certificates. Since GIC business is a huge revenue source for financial institutions, their marketing departments had to come up with new concepts to keep some of that money from drifting away. Here's one example:

A NEW TWIST ON GICs
AUGUST 1987

They've been described as "Safe Excitement" and they're targeted at the person who wants to put money into something just a little more daring than a GIC without incurring much risk.

Royal Trust has done a lot of research and has come to the conclusion that, while we're still pretty conservative when it comes to money, many of us are prepared to take a bit of a chance for a big payoff. What we don't want is to risk losing our original stake.

The trust company thinks its new products are perfectly tailored to that psychology. As a result, it's been spending a lot of money promoting them. You may have seen the full-page ads in your newspaper. If they catch on, it could be the start of a whole new form of investing in Canada.

How do they work? Well, bear with me because while the concepts are simple, some of the details aren't. The first of these products is called a diversified guaranteed investment certificate—a DGIC, for short. As far as I'm concerned, it could also be called a

SSIC, for super safe investment certificate. It's hard to go far wrong with this one.

The only difference between this and an ordinary GIC is that 25 percent of your money goes into the Royal Trust Mortgage Fund. If that fund performs as it has over the past five years, that portion of your investment will give you a better return than if it had been in a GIC. The risk, of course, is that the mortgage fund won't do as well and your return on that part of the investment won't be as good. That can happen, so be aware of it. Royal Trust guarantees you won't lose any of your principal, though, whatever happens. So your risk is that you might get a lower interest rate than if you'd stuck to a plain old GIC. That's not a big risk—but then it's not a great potential payoff either.

The real hot product is called a guaranteed market index investment, or GMII—geemi—for short. This one gives you an opportunity to take a flyer on the New York and Toronto stock exchanges or on the price of gold, all without risking any of your principal.

Here's how it works. You invest a minimum of $1,000 in a six-month term deposit. When you do, you decide how the interest you receive is going to be calculated. It's something like one of those game shows where you have to guess which door the big prize is behind. You can choose the Toronto 35 index, which measures the performance of 35 key stocks traded on the Toronto Stock Exchange. Or you can pick the New York Composite Index, which measures stocks traded on the New York Stock Exchange. Or you can choose the price of gold.

Your interest rate is based on how well your index performs over the next six months, in percentage terms. Let's say you chose the Toronto 35 index and it went up 20 percent during that time. Royal Trust would multiply that by .4, which is the factor they use for the stock exchange indexes. That works out to 8 percent, which is the interest rate you'd receive. That translates into 16 percent over a full year, which is pretty good these days.

If the stock market dropped, though, you'd get nothing. That's the risk you take. Your principal is fully protected, however. In fact, this investment is covered by deposit insurance, so you don't have any worries there.

Should you do it? Well, you would have made a lot of money over the past couple of years, given the strong stock markets we've enjoyed and the surge in the price of gold. But you have to ask yourself how likely that is to continue. As things stand right now, I'd be inclined to take the regular GIC rate and let it go at that. But if you want some safe excitement, be my guest.

UPDATE

Note the date of this commentary—August 1987. That was the month the five-year bull market of the mid-1980s came to an end. Two months later the markets experienced their biggest one-day drop in history. If you'd invested in one of these stock-linked GICs at the time I made this broadcast, your return would have been zero. That's the problem with these exotic GICs, which were heavily marketed again in 1996–97. People tend to buy into them when stock markets are at or near their peaks. The real time to buy is when markets are in a deep depression—but of course no one is selling them then.

INTRODUCTION

Credit cards are one of the main profit centres for financial institutions, so it should come as no surprise that they are constantly being dressed up in new clothes to promote sales. Here's an example.

AFFINITY CARDS
DECEMBER 1987

How would you like to support your favourite charity every time you make a purchase? Or collect credits toward your next vacation trip? Or help your old alma mater build that new library building? Well, now you can. All you have to do is get yourself an affinity card.

If that term is unfamiliar, it won't be for long. I predict affinity cards are going to be one of the hottest new financial products of 1988.

An affinity card is simply a major credit card that's tied in with a particular company, organization, or institution. They've been around in the States for about four years. But it's only in the past few months that they've started to catch on here. Now everyone seems to be rushing to get on the bandwagon.

If you've heard of any of them, it's probably Royal Trust's Canadian Plus MasterCard. It was unveiled in October and has been an instant success. Royal Trust says they're getting far more applications than they expected. This affinity card is tied in with Canadian

Airlines International and is aimed at frequent flyers. The deal is you get one mileage point for every dollar you spend. Add those to the points you accumulate on trips, and you're off to Tahiti a lot sooner than you expected.

While that's the best-known affinity card, there are several others. Universities, for example, are starting to sign up. The Bank of Montreal recently announced an arrangement with Queen's University for a special affinity MasterCard to be issued to Queen's alumni, faculty, and staff. Apart from the usual MasterCard features, the Queen's card offers a $100,000 travel accident policy, an emergency cash feature, emergency card replacement, and a free card for your spouse. On top of that, the bank contributes a small percentage of all purchases made with the card to the university.

The University of Western Ontario has made a similar arrangement with Canada Trust for its graduates. They're offering a gold MasterCard that includes a lower interest rate charge among its range of benefits.

Conservation groups are also signing up. The Bank of Montreal, which is going after this business very aggressively, is issuing a card for members of Ducks Unlimited, a wetlands conservation organization. This one offers such goodies as emergency airline ticket service and waiver insurance on car-rental collision damage. And, again, the Bank will make contributions to Ducks Unlimited based on the extent to which members use their cards.

What's ahead? A lot more of the same. In the States, affinity cards are being used by groups as diverse as doctors and bowlers. Even the unions are getting involved. The AFL-CIO has endorsed a MasterCard that allows its members to skip up to two monthly payments if they go on strike.

So don't be surprised if you get a pitch in the next few months to trade in your present card for someone's new affinity model. Just make sure it's a better deal before you accept.

UPDATE

This program turned out to be a huge success. There are now affinity cards of all descriptions available. You can even get a card that accumulates credits toward the purchase of your next car.

INTRODUCTION

One of the big trends in recent years has been the securitization of assets—the creation of securities based on anything from car loans to coal terminals. Here's one of the first examples that became popular.

Mortgage-Backed Securities
January 1988

They're called mortgage-backed securities, and if you haven't heard of them, you're not alone. They've been around for just over a year now, but they haven't been very heavily publicized, mainly because until recently the demand for them has far exceeded the supply.

But if you're looking for a first-class, conservative investment, you should make it your business to find out more about them. They're especially good if you're about to retire and you want to put your money into something safe that will provide you with a steady monthly income.

Let me explain how they work. When you buy a mortgage-backed security, you're really buying a stake in a pool of mortgage funds that has been put together by a bank, trust company, or some other financial institution. Now these are top-class mortgages—either residential first mortgages or something similar. And they're all insured under the National Housing Act. Even more important from your point of view, the payment of your principal and interest is guaranteed by Canada Mortgage and Housing Corporation. Since CMHC is a Crown company, your funds are guaranteed by the Government of Canada. You won't find anything much safer than that.

Right now, mortgage-backed securities are returning about 10 to 10.25 percent on an annualized basis. So, as you can see, the yield on your investment is respectable—higher, for instance, than the record-breaking Canada Savings Bond issue of last fall.

You receive your money in monthly payments. Now, because these are mortgages, you don't get straight interest, as you do with a guaranteed investment certificate. The cheque you receive is a blend of interest and principal—and the amount of principal you get back each month can vary. That's because if any of the mortgage holders in the pool make unscheduled prepayments, that money flows directly back to the investors.

So you will notice some variation in your monthly payments. And since some of that money is principal, remember that when your mortgage-backed security matures, you won't be paid its full face value. Any principal you've already received is deducted. That's a bit of an inconvenience. But if you're looking for a safe and steady monthly income flow, it's a small one.

It's a myth that it's hard to find these MBS certificates for sale. Most major stockbrokers offer them and you can also buy them through branches of the Bank of Commerce. They're sold in multiples of $5,000, usually for five-year terms. They're eligible for RRSPs and Registered Retirement Income Funds—in fact, they're particularly well suited for income funds.

If you find you need the money later, you can always sell them. There's an active secondary market through brokers. Just be aware that if interest rates rise between the time you buy and the time you sell, you'll suffer a small capital loss.

For most people, though, these are a buy-and-hold investment. I recommend you look at them.

UPDATE

The yields on mortgage-backed securities fell significantly during the 1990s, creating good capital gains for investors. They're still a good place for conservative Canadians to put their money, but they've not gained the popularity of, for example, stripped bonds.

INTRODUCTION

Home equity lines of credit weren't the only new financial product designed to allow homeowners to tap in on cash that had been tied up in real estate. Here's another idea that caught public attention.

REVERSE MORTGAGES
FEBRUARY 1989

I've been getting a lot of questions on phone-in shows about reverse mortgages. People have heard about them, but they aren't exactly sure what they are or how to get one.

Well, I have some good news and some bad news. First, the good news. Reverse mortgages are an imaginative technique for generating tax-free income from the equity in your home while you continue to live in it. The bad news is they're available in their pure form only in the Vancouver/Victoria area, although there are plans to introduce them into Toronto later this year.

The program that's available in B.C. is called the Canadian Home Income Plan—CHIP, for short. It was developed by a Vancouver accountant named William Turner. If you're over 65 and you own your house free and clear, you're eligible.

Here's how it works. You apply for a mortgage on your property through Seaboard Life Insurance Company—they're the only firm offering CHIP right now. Once an appraisal is done, you're told how large a mortgage you qualify for. You can then choose to receive up to 10 percent of the amount in cash. The balance goes to purchase a joint and survivor annuity.

A month later, the first annuity cheque arrives—and they keep coming until both you and your spouse pass away. Those annuity cheques are tax-free. I won't explain why—it's too complex. But Revenue Canada has given its blessing, so it's OK. Also, these payments won't affect your entitlement to such income-support programs as the Guaranteed Income Supplement.

For as long as you and your spouse live, you make no payments against the mortgage. The interest that you owe on the loan simply accumulates as a charge against your house. When you both are gone, the home is sold and the proceeds go to paying off the accumulated principal and interest. If there's anything left over, it goes to your heirs. If your debt is more than the house is worth, the insurance company loses, not your estate—you're never on the hook for more than the selling price of the house.

How much income can you get? Well, someone aged 70 with a $200,000 home could expect about $425 a month. That may not seem like a lot, but remember it's tax-free.

Many older people think it's an interesting idea. But there are some things to be aware of. For one, your income is fixed. Inflation will eat away at the purchasing power while your debt continues to grow. Since you've already mortgaged all your equity to get the annuity, you won't be able to tap into it any more—and you won't be able to sell the house without triggering the repayment of the mortgage. Also, if you live a long time, there probably won't be any equity left in the house to pass to your heirs, if that's important to you.

So if you live in an area where CHIP is available and you're intrigued by the plan, give it some careful thought first. As with anything else, there are pros and cons.

UPDATE

CHIP is still around and reverse mortgages are now available in other parts of the country, although you may have to search a bit. The income you receive is less than I indicated in the commentary, because annuity payments are tied to interest rates, which have fallen considerably in recent years.

INTRODUCTION

Do your banking without ever going to the bank? Impossible! Or is it?

BANKING AT HOME
NOVEMBER 1990

First it was the automatic banking machines. They were supposed to make banking faster, easier, and more convenient. No more standing in long lineups waiting for an available teller. Just stop at the nearest ABM, press a few numbers, and you're on your way again.

Great idea—except that the ABMs have become too popular. Now you often have to stand in long lineups to get at one of them, especially during lunch hours and on Saturday afternoons at your local shopping mall. Kind of defeats the purpose, doesn't it? So now what?

Well, some financial institutions are now experimenting with ways to allow you to do your banking in the comfort of your own home. The Commerce is one of the leaders of the bank-at-home idea. They've got two services you can use to carry out a variety of transactions. One is operated through ALEX, Bell Canada's new in-home computer service.

Now let me say first of all that, although we subscribe to ALEX, we rarely use it. Frankly, most of the services it offers don't impress me very much. I'm really not into games, computer chitchat, or trivia quizzes, which, judging from Bell's ALEX listings, seem to be immensely popular with somebody.

But the idea of doing banking through ALEX intrigued me. Unfortunately, the reality is less exciting than the technology. You can use the ALEX system to obtain account balances, check the status of your Visa account, and make various bill payments. But that's it. They haven't yet figured out a way to enable you to deposit money through the system. Nor have they solved the riddle of how to persuade the computer to dispense $20 bills when requested.

Those are the same problems you'll run into with CIBC's other bank-at-home service, called LinkUp. It does almost exactly the same thing as ALEX except that all you need is a touch-tone phone. Just dial their number, punch some codes into your phone, and a robot-like voice tells you the balance in your savings account or the amount of credit still available on your Visa card.

Now, I admit these are convenient services to have at your finger-tips. But they aren't likely to save you many trips to the bank or to an ABM. And, of course, these in-home services aren't free. You'll pay a charge for each transaction you put through ALEX. If you prefer to use the LinkUp phone system, it costs $3 a month, on top of your normal account charges.

Since the only real transactions you can carry out at present are bill payments, you'll have to decide whether the convenience of doing it all by phone or computer is worth it to you. Checking over the bank's list of participating utilities, I found I would be able to use the service at most only three or four times a month, for paying bills. Using the $3-a-month rate, that works out to a service charge of between 75 cents and $1 for each payment. A 39-cent postage stamp still sounds like a better deal to me.

UPDATE

These early attempts at on-line banking may have flopped, but the banks are still working on finding a method that is generally accept-able. In the meantime they're pushing customers to use ABMs as much as possible. Some banks have posted signs warning customers that they'll be charged for every bill they pay at a live teller instead of through an ABM. We've even seen banks harass customers standing in line for the live tellers by having an employee ask, "Why aren't you using the automated teller today? Have you tried our banking-at-home system?" One family member who was so accosted recently agreed to use the automated teller to deposit his cheques. The machine broke and he had to wait 30 minutes while the bank got someone to open it up and rescue his cheques. He ended up having to make the deposit through a live teller anyway!

INTRODUCTION

Debit cards became such a big success that the banking industry decided to go back to the same well for another product. This one isn't in general use yet, but I predict it will be before the decade is over.

SMART CARDS COMING
JULY 1995

Picture this. You're heading downtown on a shopping trip. To get there, you travel along a toll road—and there are a lot more of *those* in our future. At the tollbooth you insert a plastic card and drive on. No groping for change in your pocket or purse. When you get to your destination, you pull into a parking lot. There's no attendant—just a place to insert your card. You park, lock up, and go into the store.

Inside, you pay for your purchases with the same card. At one point, you decide to call home to say you'll be longer than expected. You don't have a quarter for the payphone, but you don't need one—there's a slot for your card. After the call, you realize you're thirsty. There's a drink machine nearby. You stick in your card, press a button, and out pops a Coke.

Outside the store, you spot a newspaper box. Again no change, but it doesn't matter. A swipe with the card and you take home the *Daily News*. On the way home, you decide to fill the tank. Again, the card handles the payment.

By the time you arrive at the end of the day, you've made a wide range of purchases, some for as little as 25 cents, some for $100 or more. And it's all been done on the one card. You haven't needed a penny of cash.

Science fiction? Hardly. Two of Canada's major banks are launching a test project next year that will pave the way for the onset of the cashless society in this country before the end of the century.

These cards are called Smart Cards. They differ from any of the other plastic you carry around because they're really the equivalent of portable bank accounts. With electronic cash from your regular account you apply to your card any amount you want—$10, $100, $1,000. Think of it as the financial equivalent of putting gas in your car.

Then, each time you use the card, the amount spent is automatically deducted from your balance. When you've spent it all, the card is empty. It has to be taken to your bank or automatic teller machine for a refill.

The advantages are obvious. You can limit your spending by the amount of cash you put into the card, so you'll never blow the budget. If the card is lost or stolen, the amount at risk is limited to the balance remaining on it; the card won't give a thief access to your regular bank account. Plus, the card can be used only if it's been unlocked through a special security code. If you lose a locked card, no one else can draw on it.

Another advantage: You won't have to worry about carrying change for vending machines any more. I don't know about you, but I've stopped counting the number of times I've stared longingly at a soft-drink machine on a hot day because I didn't have the right amount of change in my pocket.

Of course, all this convenience will come with a price tag. The banks aren't doing this because they have big hearts. It's expected there will be a monthly service fee for using a Smart Card. I can't tell you yet how much it will be, but guesses range from $1.25 to $3.

When can you have one? Well, if the pilot tests planned by the Royal Bank and CIBC next year work out as expected, we could see Smart Cards starting to appear on a national scale in Canada as early as 1997, just two years from now. Don't expect all vending machines, payphones, and newspaper boxes to accept them right away. That will involve a massive changeover, and it's going to take a few years.

But it's coming. By the time the 21st century arrives, pennies, nickels, dimes, quarters, and even loonies may be collector's items. Frankly, it can't happen soon enough for me. I'm tired of walking around with a pound of metal in my pocket.

UPDATE

They're not here as this book is compiled. But soon, soon.

INTRODUCTION

The banks weren't the only people creating new financial products in recent years. Securities dealers were active as well.

UNIT INVESTMENT TRUSTS
JULY 1996

They've been around in the States for quite a while, but unit investment trusts are only now starting to make an impact on the Canadian financial scene.

In many ways, they're like mutual funds—but with some important differences. For starters, each trust has a specific investment focus. It may hold shares only in a certain type of company, or it may be designed to generate above-average income, or it may aim for above-average growth. The key is a single, clear-cut objective, and that's what sets these trusts apart from most mutual funds.

Second, the trust will hold only a small number of securities—perhaps 10 or 20. Some mutual fund portfolios may have 100 or more.

Third, there will be very little trading. The trust will buy its positions at the outset and hold them. That approach helps keep expenses well below those of a regular mutual fund.

Fourth, a unit trust has a predetermined life span. You know when you invest that it will be wound up by a specific date and the assets distributed back to unit holders.

Fifth, unit trusts are sold only for a limited period, unlike a regular mutual fund, which is always open to new investors.

Finally, shares in these trusts are publicly traded, either on a stock exchange or in the over-the-counter market. But investors also have the option of redeeming units at their current net asset value from the trust's treasury at any time. That means you can always get your money out, and you may be able to sell at a premium if the market likes what the trust is doing.

Three of these unit trusts have recently been marketed to Canadian investors, and I expect we'll see a lot more in the coming months. The first to appear came out last fall. Officially, it's called the Target 10 Trust, but the more common name for it is "Dogs of the Dow." That's because it invests in the ten stocks that are deemed to be the most undervalued of the Dow-Jones 30 industrials, based on the fact they pay the highest dividends. The list includes firms like General Motors, Exxon, du Pont, and Texaco, so you're getting blue-chip stuff.

Original investors paid $15 a unit. The recent price was $15.69, which represents a gain of 4.6 percent in a little over six months. Not sensational, to be sure, but then this is a trust that's designed for conservative people.

Two more unit trusts have become operational within the past month. The First Premium Income Trust has the goal of generating tax-advantaged income. Investors receive annual distributions of at least $2 a unit, which works out to an 8 percent yield on the $25 purchase price. This return is achieved by a combination of dividends from high-yielding common stocks, such as bank shares, and revenue from writing covered call options. The dividend portion of distributions qualifies for the dividend tax credit, while revenue from call options is treated as a capital gain. So the tax payable is much less than on straight interest income. The trust winds up in 2004, at which time the intention is to return the original $25 to unit holders.

The third unit trust currently on offer is called the Pharmaceutical Trust. It invests in 20 of the top pharmaceutical companies around the world. If you believe that the profits of this industry have nowhere to go but up as the population ages, then this is an investment you might look at.

So far, the unit trusts that have been created for Canada are best suited to conservative investors who want some stock market exposure without a lot of risk. That doesn't mean they'll all be that way, however. So if this is a concept that interests you, be sure to get all the details from a financial advisor before going ahead.

UPDATE

Unit trusts are gradually increasing in popularity as more of them become available in this country. Many of them have produced very good results.

CHAPTER
13

Buyer Beware

With financial services, as with everything else, the rule of *caveat emptor* applies. You have to be very careful when deciding whom to do business with and how much to spend. The following commentaries make this point very clearly.

TAX-PREPARATION FIRMS
MARCH 1984

Tax-preparation firms. You see them on almost every corner this time of year; they've become an even more predictable harbinger of spring than robins and crocuses. Lots of people use them. A survey done by Revenue Canada last year found that 25 percent of Canadians paid professionals to fill out their tax return.

How good are they? That's like asking how good restaurants are. It depends on who's doing the cooking. But the fact is, if you're not careful, you could end up having someone do your tax return who knows less about it than you do.

Tax preparation is a seasonal business. Many of the people in those storefront offices are students working part-time, housewives earning a little extra money, unemployed men and women filling in with temporary jobs. Usually they've had some training, but often it's minimal. Unless they're certified accountants, don't expect them to know all the ins and outs of the tax law. They *can* handle the basics, one hopes—but if your return is the slightest bit complicated, you may be in trouble.

The worst case I've heard of incompetency in tax preparation comes from the Better Business Bureau in Toronto. They uncovered a situation in an ethnic community where a man was charging people

$40 to prepare their returns—and giving the work to his nine-year-old Grade 3 son, who was sitting in an office in the back.

So if you really want someone to do your return, ask some questions. What are the person's credentials? What is the company's track record? A phone call to your local Better Business Bureau can give you that information.

When the return has been done, check it over yourself before you sign. Don't automatically assume all the calculations are correct. Double-check them. You could end up saving yourself a lot of money. Last year the Vancouver *Sun* did a survey of tax-preparation companies, taking the same return to five firms. All the results were different. One company concluded that a balance of almost $1,000 was owed to Ottawa. Another firm said the taxpayer was due a refund of $538. That was closest to the mark, by the way.

Finally, if you're tempted to get a quick refund by using tax discounters, my advice is don't, unless the only alternative is starvation. Most discounters will charge you 15 percent of the expected refund for immediate payment—the maximum permitted by law. For that, you're getting your money maybe two months early—Revenue Canada has promised they'll process our returns faster this year.

So what that amounts to is a two-month loan at 15 percent interest. That works out to about 90 percent a year. If you really need a loan, any bank or even a finance company will do a lot better than that.

UPDATE

I'd give much the same advice today, over a decade later. Check the credentials of the tax preparer, and don't use discounters. If you really want your return done properly, I suggest using a professional accountant.

INTRODUCTION

People are always asking me how to choose a good financial advisor. It's not easy, as the next commentary shows.

FINANCIAL ADVISORS
JULY 1984

I recently had a conversation I'd like to share with you. Last fall, a friend came into a small inheritance and he wanted some expert advice on how to invest the money. After making some inquiries, he contacted a well-known financial counselling firm for assistance.

The first meeting went smoothly enough. The counsellor took all the particulars, then scheduled another session to make recommendations. That was when things began to go sour.

The advisor strongly suggested putting a large chunk of the inheritance into a MURB—a tax-sheltered real estate investment. He had a particular one to recommend: a luxury condominium that was nearing completion.

Well, fortunately my friend knows something about money. He said he wanted some time to think about it. He went home and did his own calculations. The results weren't good. The financial projections for the MURB were based on some pretty shaky assumptions and the whole thing seemed too risky.

But the advisor didn't want to take no for an answer. He kept pushing the MURB, stressing how wise an investment it was and implying that anyone who didn't agree didn't know what he was talking about. It was only when my friend took out his worksheets and started going over the numbers that the advisor backed off.

Was the advisor incompetent? Not necessarily. You see, it emerged later that his firm was acting as a sales agent for the real estate developer behind the MURB. It received a commission on every unit sold, and the advisor got a share of that. Now, he may have honestly believed the investment was sound—but the conflict of interest was obvious.

Imagine how my friend felt. He was paying a high hourly fee for what he thought was independent advice. In fact, he was really paying to be the target of a very sophisticated sales pitch.

This isn't an unusual situation. There are a lot of Canadians who are paying good money for financial advice that is biased and not objective. The problem is there are no widely accepted standards governing financial counsellors. When it comes right down to it, anyone can claim to be a financial planner—it's really a buyer-beware situation. A professional organization has been formed, but its membership is still very limited and it's just beginning to struggle with ethical considerations.

So what should you do if you need financial help? The first rule is: Be wary. Don't end up paying money for a sales pitch. Personal recommendations are a useful place to start your search, but treat them with caution. Most people aren't even aware of this dual role that many financial planners have. The fact that a firm is well known and respected is not a guarantee of independent advice.

I suggest putting some hard questions to any potential advisor. Ask whether they act as sales agents for anyone—especially insurance companies. A lot of them push various insurance-related investments. If a firm is reputable, it should answer such questions honestly. You've no guarantee of that, though, so stay suspicious. If they appear to be strongly recommending something you find dubious, ask the question again. If you're still in doubt, do the same thing you would if you didn't like what your doctor was saying. Get a second opinion. After all, it's your money.

UPDATE

Although professional associations are demanding better disclosure on the part of planners, the situation in most parts of Canada has changed little from the way I described it here. You can still find yourself the target of a sales pitch, without actually realizing it. Most financial planners act in the best interests of their client. That's the most effective way to build a business, after all. But a few still put their personal interests ahead of those of the customer. Don't let one of them sell you an investment you don't want or need.

INTRODUCTION

As I mentioned in the last chapter, home equity lines of credit have become very popular. But they come with a price tag attached.

THE COST OF A PLC
NOVEMBER 1986

Maybe you've noticed the ads in your local paper. Canada Trust, which is the largest trust company in the country, has been vigorously promoting a new financial product, something called a home equity line of credit.

These ads make it sound pretty attractive. They offer a line of credit based on the equity in your home at what they say is by far the lowest consumer loan rate available—9.75 percent. They promote the fact that you can maintain the loan on an interest-only basis—no payments against the principal at all. They stress the convenience— you can use the line of credit at any time, either through a credit card or by writing a cheque. And they tell you all the things you can use the money for—home renovations, a car, a vacation, investing, whatever you like.

Sounds pretty good, doesn't it? After all, where else can you borrow money today at 9.75 percent? In fact, that's the prime interest rate—the rate that banks charge their best corporate customers. It almost sounds too good to be true.

Unfortunately, it is. I called Canada Trust to get some details of the plan and everything sounded fine, except—but I'll get to that in a moment.

First, let me tell you the good points. The interest rate is based on the prime rate, and it will only change when the prime changes. That has to make it the best consumer loan rate around, just as they claim.

Because it's a line of credit, you can draw on the money when you need it. That's different from an ordinary loan, where you receive all the funds up front and have to start paying interest on them immediately. In this case, you pay interest only on the amount you actually borrow. So you may have a line of credit for $25,000 but have only a $5,000 loan outstanding against it. That gives the plan a lot of flexibility. You can borrow money when you need it and pay it off whenever is convenient.

OK, so what's the catch? Remember I said this is called a home-equity line of credit. It could just as easily be called a flex-plan mortgage, because that's exactly what it is. It's mortgage with a difference. If you want to apply for one of these, you have to have a home with some equity in it. If you qualify on that count, Canada Trust sends someone out to appraise your property. That costs you $150.

Let's make things easy and assume you don't have any existing mortgage on your home. Once the appraisal is been done, the trust company enters into a mortgage with you. That means legal fees, which you pay and which probably run to $500 or $600. So your total out-of-pocket costs for getting this line of credit run to as high as $750.

If you go through with the deal, you have a line of credit of up to two-thirds the appraised value of your home. So if you have a

$100,000 house, you can borrow up to $66,000 and charge against it. You don't have to use all that credit, of course. And you pay interest only on what you actually borrow. But the money is there to spend if you want it.

As I said, it amounts to a flexible mortgage. If you need to borrow a lot of money for an extended period of time, those heavy up-front costs might be worth it to get the lower interest rate. But if you're not in that situation, you're probably better off to go for an unsecured line of credit. You'll pay a little more—the Canada Trust rate on those plans is 10.75 percent—but you won't have to shell out $750 up front. That's a pretty big deterrent for any loan.

UPDATE

Nothing has changed. There are still heavy up-front costs involved if you want to set up a home equity PLC. Make sure it's something you really need before you sign any papers.

INTRODUCTION

One of the areas that is most confusing to investors is tax shelters. They appear to offer great opportunities for beating Revenue Canada. But they can be full of traps.

EVALUATING SHELTERS
NOVEMBER 1988

If you're being tempted by all the tax shelter ads in the newspapers, give it some long, hard thought before you go ahead. After all, there's no point saving 50 cents in tax if you lose a dollar on the investment.

I recommend that as a first step you get hold of a copy of the prospectus or offering memorandum for any deal you might be considering. Look first at the amount of money you're actually risking. Then check the profit forecasts and the assumptions they're based on.

Next, read the section on risks. If you're still hanging in after all that, here are some other things to consider.

The tax opinion is critical. If for any reason Revenue Canada disallows your claim, you're really in trouble. And the chances of that are greater now that the tax department has been given new teeth to deal with borderline tax deals.

The prospectus will have a section outlining the expected tax consequences. Read it thoroughly. Then reread it. See if it's based on precedents; if the government has accepted similar deals in the past, the odds are better it will again.

Pay special attention to the author of the opinion. If it's a well-known tax expert or a top-drawer legal or accounting firm, great. If it was prepared by some outfit you've never heard of, you might be a little more cautious.

I can't stress enough the importance of this. I personally know people who have invested in shelters only to find that Revenue Canada refuses to allow their deductions. It happens all the time. Don't let it happen to you.

Another area to look at carefully is the financing. I've seen deals that require investors to sign up for a long-term loan at a high rate of interest, with no possibility of paying it off early. That's a good deal for the financial institution. But it's not so hot for you.

Liquidity is the next hurdle. How easily and quickly can you get your money out? Most flow-through share offers enable you to cash in after about a year. The real estate deals may tie up your money for five or even ten years. If you think you may need your funds, make sure you can get at them within a reasonable time.

If you've come this far and you're still interested, do a little more number crunching. For example, see whether the deal might get you caught up in the minimum tax net.

After all this, you may have concluded that you'd better know a lot about investing before you plunge into a tax shelter. Well, you're absolutely right. If you don't, stay away.

UPDATE

Tax shelters have become much less popular, but there are still some around. This advice still applies.

INTRODUCTION

Deposit insurance is another area that confuses a lot of people, and for good reason. There is some very strange fine print in the rules.

ADDING TO YOUR COVERAGE
JUNE 1989

I get asked a lot of questions about deposit insurance. One of the most common is whether there's any way to beat the $60,000 limit. Of course there is—you just have to know how. Some of the tricks are explained in the CDIC's brochure. Some you have to figure out for yourself.

Let's start with the basic rules. An eligible deposit in any member institution is insured to a maximum of $60,000 per person. Sounds very clear and straightforward, doesn't it? Well, it isn't.

For example, what or who is a person? Clearly, you are, and if you're married so is your spouse. So we have two people, each of whom qualify for the $60,000 maximum as long as they hold money in their own names. That means a couple with separate bank accounts in the same institution can have up to $120,000 in coverage.

But suppose you also have a joint account? That's a separate person, under the CDIC definition, so it's fully covered as well. Now you're up to $180,000.

But it doesn't stop there. Let's assume you and your spouse each have an RRSP in this same bank or trust company. Your RRSPs are considered as separate persons for the purposes of CDIC coverage. So as long as they're invested in eligible deposits, such as guaranteed investment certificates, they each qualify for the $60,000 maximum. Now you're up to $300,000 in coverage between you.

And there's more. Let's say you're approaching retirement. You're under 71, so you can still have RRSPs. But you've also decided to set up a Registered Retirement Income Fund. Guess what? Your RRIF is another separate person for purposes of CDIC coverage. If each spouse has one, that brings the total maximum protection for a couple to $420,000 in one single financial institution.

Now, what's a financial institution? Well, it may surprise you to learn that it's not always what it seems. CDIC won't provide separate coverage for deposits in different branches of the same financial institution. So you can't increase your protection that way. But they will cover deposits in affiliated companies or subsidiaries if they're CDIC members in their own right.

For example, you could have $60,000 on deposit with the Royal Bank of Canada and have full protection for that money. Then you could put another $60,000 into Royal Bank Mortgage Corporation and be fully covered there as well. Obviously, the two companies are closely related. But because they're individual legal entities and they're both members of the CDIC, the deposits they hold are treated separately.

A number of major banks and trust companies have subsidiaries that operate in this way. If you're bumping up against the $60,000 ceiling and you'd like to keep doing business with the same organization, ask them about it.

UPDATE

Some of the rules have changed a bit, but this advice is basically still good today. Get an updated copy of the official CDIC brochure for all the details.

INTRODUCTION

How do you find a good broker? With care and caution. And when you find a good one, treat him or her properly.

BROKER/CLIENT RELATIONS
OCTOBER 1991

The problems that arise between brokers and clients are not all one-sided. Very often the investor is at least partially to blame, partially because he or she didn't follow a few basic rules.

Here they are.

Rule Number One. Know your broker personally. I'm always amazed at the number of people who tell me they've spoken to their broker only over the phone.

This is the person you're relying on to help manage your money. For heaven's sake, find out something about him or her. Have lunch together or at least a meeting in the office. See if you and the broker are on the same wavelength when it comes to investment philosophy. If you're not comfortable with the person, contact the manager and ask to have your portfolio switched to someone else. You're the customer, after all.

Rule Number Two. Accept responsibility for your decisions. A broker's advice should be treated as exactly that—a recommendation, nothing more. The decision is up to you. After all, it's your money.

That means asking for the information you need to determine if this is the right move from your point of view. Ask the broker to explain the rationale behind any suggested trade. Have the company send you research material about the security. Above all, think about whether the trade really fits in with your investment objectives.

If, in the end, you're satisfied the recommendation is a good one, then go ahead. Just remember, it's your decision. Pat yourself on the back if it turns out well—and don't try to shift all the blame to the broker if it doesn't.

Rule Number Three. Read any prospectus you receive. Before you buy certain types of investments, the broker must give you a prospectus describing them—mutual funds are an example.

Unfortunately, prospectuses are dreadfully dull. But you ignore them at your peril. You should read at least the section on costs. It tells you exactly what you're getting into from an expense point of view. Also look at the section on risk, which outlines the potential downside of the investment.

It may not be the way you'd like to spend an evening. But these things are written for your protection. If you want to know what you're putting your hard-earned money into, read them.

Rule Number Four. Review your statements. The brokerage firm should send you a statement of your account every month. Look it over and make sure it's OK.

These documents are computer-generated and it's easy for mistakes to creep in. I got one just the other day that told me my RRSP balance was over $25 million! That would have been nice if true. Unfortunately, the computer had accidentally slipped in a couple of extra zeroes.

I've also received statements that have incorrectly credited me with someone else's dividends or have dropped some securities from my holdings. So make sure your statement is right and advise your broker if it isn't.

Rule Number Five. Follow up with your broker when you do authorize a trade. If you don't hear back by the end of the day, put in a call to see if it was executed. I once missed out on a big profit by failing to do that. I assumed a trade had gone through when in fact it had somehow gotten lost in the computer. The stock made a big move over the next couple of days, and I wasn't there.

So take the initiative if your broker doesn't. That way, there won't be any unpleasant surprises later.

UPDATE

I have nothing to add to this, other than it would make broker/client relations much healthier if everyone followed these suggestions.

INTRODUCTION

Insurance is a real mystery to many Canadians—especially car insurance, where the rules and rates seem to change every year. Here are two recent commentaries on the subject.

YOUR CAR INSURANCE (1)
NOVEMBER 1996

I have a riddle for you. What is it that everyone has but hardly any one knows anything about? Give up?

Automobile insurance.

If you own a car, you have insurance—or at least you'd *better* have. But do you understand how it works? Or how it's priced? Or how to negotiate a lower rate? Probably not—and with good reason.

Most people are totally ignorant about how auto insurance works because of politicians. In many provinces, it's become a political football, with every new government feeling obliged to tinker with it in one way or another. The result is a patchwork quilt of rules and regulations across the country. In some places, no-fault insurance is the rule. Other jurisdictions retain the old, better-understood method of assigning blame in an accident. In some provinces, accident victims can sue. In others, that right is severely limited.

It's important you know how the rules apply where you live. Your insurance company should be able to provide a summary of the regulations for your jurisdiction; just give them a call. But knowing how your insurance works is just the beginning. You should also find out how it's priced and what you can do to reduce the costs.

The pricing of car insurance is basically an actuarial calculation. The number crunchers work out how likely you are to have an accident given your age, driving experience, and where you live. From that base, a series of variables are then built in—the type of car, its age, whether you've had driver training, recent claims, traffic violations, and the types of coverage you want. The end result is a price tag that makes many people gasp when they see it. Let's face it, in many parts of this country, car insurance rates have gone through the roof and insurers are warning there are more increases coming.

So what can you do about it? A lot. You may be able to cut your insurance costs by hundreds of dollars if you go about it the right way. For starters, give some careful thought to exactly what coverage you need. Collision and comprehensive are two areas where you can chip away at your premium simply by raising the amount of the deductible.

Ask yourself: Do you really want your insurance to kick in the moment you sustain $100 worth of damage? That's the amount a lot of policies are written for. Not only do you pay a higher premium for that low deductible, but you also could find yourself making more claims, which in turn may drive up your rate.

Raising your deductible to $500 or even $1,000 means you're absorbing some of the risk yourself. But the offset could be a sizable reduction in cost. Ask your insurance agent for a quote based on a higher deductible.

While you're at it, see what extras your policy offers. For example, does it cover a rental car? Many policies do, but people don't realize it and end up buying the high-priced protection sold by the rental companies.

Another question to ask is whether you'll be provided with a replacement car if yours has to go in for repairs. Some companies offer this as a low-cost optional extra, but they may neglect to tell you about it.

That's what happened to my daughter when she had an accident recently and her car was out of service for two weeks. She thought her policy provided a replacement vehicle. It didn't. So ask.

YOUR CAR INSURANCE (2)
NOVEMBER 1996

Many people don't realize that the type of car you drive makes a big difference in your insurance premium. It's true. If you drive a high-powered sports car, your premium is likely to be substantially more than if you drive a four-door sedan, even though the value of the two cars is the same.

Now, I know that very few people actually make a car-purchase decision with their insurance rate in mind. But you should take it into account, with insurance rates as high as they are today. Every make and model of car is classified by insurers in terms of accident frequency and cost of repairs. So if you have two or three cars you're seriously considering, call your insurance agent before you make a final decision. Ask whether any are in a higher premium category and, if so, what the difference in cost would be. The answer may help you make up your mind about which car to buy.

Another way to cut your insurance bill is to buy used instead of new. The reason is simple: The lower the replacement value of the vehicle, the smaller your insurance premium. You don't have to buy an old clinker. Even a car that's just one year old will probably have a replacement value that's about 25 to 30 percent less than that of the brand-new version of the same model. That's a reflection of the big depreciation hit most cars take in the first year.

The next tip relates to the primary driver of the vehicle. The fact is that some people get better rates than others. Your age, sex, marital status, driving record, and training may all be factors in determining what you'll pay.

If the car has more than one driver, talk to your agent about whether there's a significant difference in the premium if one is designated as the main driver instead of the other. If there is, you may want to change your family driving habits so that the person with the better rating uses the car the majority of the time and therefore qualifies as the principal driver.

Another way to reduce premiums is to use public transit to go to work. Insurers charge a higher rate if the car is used for commuting on a regular basis. By taking the bus instead, you should be able to get your classification revised from business to pleasure and save handsomely in the process. Plus, you won't have to pay for parking.

Taking an accredited driver-training program is another way to bring costs down, especially in the case of younger people with limited driving experience.

Another cost-saving technique is to be a safe driver. Nothing pushes up the cost of your insurance more than a series of traffic violations or accident claims.

If anything happens that could affect your rate, be sure to report it to the insurance company immediately. For example, most companies reduce the premium when a driver turns 25. Now, you'd think their computers would automatically alert them to that event—after all, they have your birth date on the application. But in fact you have to take the initiative. If you don't advise the company when the great day comes, nothing happens. Your premium stays exactly the same.

The same advice applies if you get married. This can also reduce the premium, especially for people under 25. But you have to tell the insurer it happened. That's something they have no way of knowing.

Finally, shop around. Get several quotes before you make a decision on your insurer. There's no point paying more than you absolutely have to.

UPDATE

All these tips continue to be valid today.

CHAPTER

14

Roller-Coaster Rides

The world of finance and investing is full of ups and downs, and sometimes they occur at dizzying speeds. Here are a few examples culled from many I've experienced over the years.

GOLD PLUNGES
JANUARY 1985

I have to admit that gold fascinates me. There's a mystique about it; it's been the symbol of wealth ever since recorded history began. It's also been a symbol of greed. Tombs have been looted for it, ships have been plundered for it, people have endured incredible hardships in attempts to find it. It's the stuff of legends, and they're still being created.

Many people became millionaires in the 1970s when they guessed correctly that the U.S. would end the link between the dollar and gold. That artificial relationship had held the price of the metal to $35 an ounce for more than three decades. When President Nixon finally broke the link in 1971, he unleashed an orgy of speculation that reached its peak early in 1980. That, you may remember, was when gold hit an incredible $875 U.S. an ounce and people were lining up to buy at those absurd prices.

How the mighty have fallen. A few weeks ago, after limping along in the $330 range for several months, gold fell almost overnight to around $300. Gold stocks plummeted in value and sellers were quoted in the press as saying that virtually no one wanted to buy the precious metal.

Well, when I hear things like that I start to get interested. Historically it's been true that the best time to invest in something if you really want to get rich is when it's out of favour. As long as whatever it is has intrinsic value—and gold certainly does—it will eventually come back into fashion and people will start to bid up the price

167

again. So my first reaction when the price dropped was to buy. But when I thought about the world we're living in right now, I backed off. Let me tell you why.

Looking at the possible economic scenarios we might face over the rest of this decade, my feeling is that the most likely outlook for the next few years is continued disinflation—that's when the rate of inflation continues to decline.

There's a lot more evidence to suggest that's what's happening. Interest rates are still falling. Commodity prices such as oil continue to be extremely depressed. Even some of the most pessimistic forecasters are now admitting that inflation will be even lower this year than it was in 1984, despite the huge budget deficits. The Conference Board of Canada, for instance, recently predicted a 3.3 percent inflation rate for us this year, down from 4.4 percent in 1984.

So what does that mean for gold? Well, gold has traditionally been seen as an inflation hedge—a place to protect your money against rapidly escalating prices. But there's no significant inflation to protect ourselves from. And it doesn't look like there's going to be, at least for a while.

In the meantime, interest rates, although they're coming down, are at historically high levels in relation to inflation. When you can earn 11.25 percent on Canada Savings Bonds in a year when inflation is forecast to be only 3.3 percent, you're pocketing a real return before taxes of almost 8 percent. That's unheard of. And it's going to last only until people realize that the economic dragon of inflation is, if not dead, at least in deep hibernation.

That's why I didn't buy gold. I think more people are starting to sense that something quite fundamental has happened, and they're acting accordingly. That means they aren't going to bid up the price of gold dramatically. Instead they're going to put their money where it can earn some of that amazingly high interest.

That's what I'm doing too. There will be a time to buy gold again. But I don't think this is it.

UPDATE

Gold hasn't really done much of anything in the years since that commentary was delivered. It has occasionally shown signs of strength, moving above the $400 mark, only to slip back.

INTRODUCTION

Hardly a year goes by when the Canadian dollar doesn't experience some type of crisis. Here's one from the mid-1980s that you may have forgotten about.

FALLING DOLLAR, RISING RATES
MARCH 1985

If you had any doubts that we're living on a financial roller coaster, the past couple of weeks should certainly have dispelled them. With our dollar plunging to all-time lows and interest rates cranking up again as the Bank of Canada tries to cushion the fall, it's been a pretty hairy time.

The question now is, What next? And what can we, as individuals, do to minimize the damage to ourselves while the bankers and money traders sort out the whole mess?

Well, as to what next, the honest answer is that nobody knows. Our most respected economists can't agree, so how are the rest of us supposed to figure it out? But there's an important indicator and you can use it in trying to decide what you should do.

It's this: Changes in currency values and interest rates tend to move in cycles. What that means is that when interest rates begin an upward movement, the odds are that movement will continue for a period of time. No one knows for how long, or when they will peak. But the trend is clear, and that's the important thing.

It's the same thing with currency values. Once a cycle becomes established, you should expect the trend to continue for a while— sometimes for a long while. Take our dollar, for example. It's been in a downward cycle against the American dollar for several years now. There was a time not long ago when it was worth more than the American buck. When it started down, a friend of mine who is very knowledgeable about currency movements said it could fall all the way to 75 U.S. cents. I snorted. I wish I'd listened. Now some people whose opinion I respect say it could fall as low as 65 U.S. cents. I'm not snorting. I don't know where the bottom is, but my guess is we're not there yet.

That's a long-term cycle. Obviously, there are going to be times when the dollar regains a little strength. But you'd have to be blind to miss the trend. It's the same thing with interest rates. They'll move up for a time, then start downward again.

Now, all of this may sound like interesting theory, but it really does have some practical application. Just think how much more money you'd have today if you'd recognized the downward trend of our dollar several years ago and put everything you own into U.S. currency. Let's assume that the trends we're seeing right now will continue for a while—and there's nothing to suggest they won't. What should you do?

As far as the dollar is concerned, if you'll need any U.S. funds over the next few months, protect yourself against further devaluation. That means buying your travellers' cheques now if you're going south on a holiday. There's no guarantee our dollar won't rally a bit in the meantime. But the odds are against it—the clear trend is down.

However, you're not going to earn any interest holding traveller's cheques, so if you're planning for several months ahead, open a U.S.-dollar account. Many banks and trust companies offer this service, so your money can earn interest until it's needed.

As far as interest rates are concerned, the current trend is up. Again, you should expect that to continue until we get some clear indication to the contrary. That means if you've got a mortgage coming up for renewal, consider locking it in for a longer term. If you've got a variable-rate bank loan, try to switch it to a fixed rate. If you're about to invest some money in interest-bearing vehicles, think about staying short-term for the time being. Buy a 30- or 60-day guaranteed investment certificate and wait. The long-term rates may well be higher when it matures.

You won't always win. There will be blips in the cycles and they may come at the wrong time. But if you recognize the trends and act on them, you'll give yourself an edge. Often, that's all it takes.

UPDATE

If this story sounds familiar, it's because the same scenario keeps being repeated at periodic intervals. Anytime it happens, this advice will still apply.

INTRODUCTION

Roller coasters go down, but they also go up. After the Crash of 1987, many people were worried that the predicted depression had indeed arrived. But just a few months later, the roller coaster was climbing up the track again and the worries were of a different sort.

INFLATION FEARS AND INTEREST RATES
JUNE 1988

Talk about unpredictable! Six months ago everyone was worried about the stock market crash and the coming economic slowdown. Interest rates were lowered in an effort to keep the economy moving and prevent the world from slipping into a major recession.

Well, what a difference half a year makes. The North American economy is humming along just fine, thank you. Unemployment in the U.S. and Canada has fallen to levels we haven't seen in years—in fact, in some parts of the country, such as Southern Ontario, you see help-wanted signs in almost every store window.

The big worry is no longer recession. Quite the opposite. Our policymakers are concerned the economy is overheating and we're about to experience another wave of inflation.

There are some straws in the wind to support that view. Labour unions are becoming more militant: Wage demands are higher and strikes are becoming more frequent. And prices are starting to edge up. The CPI seems to be gathering momentum, especially in key areas like food and housing costs. All of this has the Bank of Canada nervous. The one thing Governor John Crow seems to fear most is a return to the double-digit inflation of the 1970s.

So he's pushing up interest rates to try to slow things down and take some of the steam out of the economy. It's a tough balancing act. Push rates too far, too fast, and we could be suddenly tilted into the much-feared recession. So this policy of higher interest rates could change at any time, depending on events.

What does it mean for you? Well, the general feeling among the experts is that rates will continue to rise over the summer and into the fall. No one is talking about a return to the ridiculous levels of 1981, though—any increase should be relatively modest. By next year, the expectation is rates will start to come back down as the economy slows. Obviously, if a recession materializes they'll come down a lot faster.

If that forecast is correct, it suggests certain strategies for good money management. If you're renewing a mortgage now, you probably shouldn't go long. A one-year term would seem to make the most sense; by this time next year interest rates should be on the decline.

Investors should look at this current run-up in rates as an opportunity to make some money. Short-term rates are excellent right now—Government of Canada Treasury bills are yielding in the 9 percent range. Keep an eye on what T-bills are doing over the summer, especially if you have a fair amount of money tied up in Canada Savings Bonds. Your CSBs are paying 9 percent this year. If Treasury-bill rates rise to the 9.5 percent to 10 percent range, you might want to switch.

If you have a self-directed RRSP, you might consider adding some Government of Canada stripped bonds when rates seem to be peaking. You buy these from a broker at a discounted price; there's no interest payable on them, but at the maturity date you collect the full face value of the bond. I bought some in the summer of 1984 when rates took a temporary jump. They were yielding 13.6 percent at the time and they've been an excellent investment. They're strictly for RRSPs, though. The tax complications outside a retirement plan are horrendous.

Finally, if someone's trying to sell you on the virtues of a bond fund right now, hold off a bit. The asset value of those funds tends to drop as interest rates climb. You may be able to buy in more cheaply in a couple of months.

UPDATE

The advice on stripped bonds and bond funds worked out especially well. Rates continued to rise until mid-1990. At that point they started on a downward trend that lasted several years and made big profits for bondholders.

INTRODUCTION

No chapter on roller-coaster rides would be complete without a commentary on the wild ups and downs the real estate markets experienced in the 1980s and 1990s. Here's one I delivered just as the Toronto market was hitting its peak.

REAL ESTATE FRENZY
FEBRUARY 1989

Our home is in the Toronto suburb of North York. It's a pleasant area, but I've never thought of it as Millionaire's Row. There's an apartment building behind us and a townhouse development around the corner. Just down the street are some semidetached homes that were originally intended to provide affordable housing. A middle-class neighbourhood—at least it used to be.

Last summer, the house across the street sold for $465,000. At the time, I thought that was a ridiculous price. Well, a few weeks ago the house was sold again—for $685,000. Now it's true the new owner had done some renovating. But it was still the same house, on the same street, in the same neighbourhood. And those semidetached homes I told you about—the so-called "affordable housing"? They're now going for a quarter of a million and more. This is affordable?

Then we heard the news that the average price of a new home in North York in December was over $800,000! That's for newly built homes, not resales. But it says a lot about what's happening in my part of Canada.

And it's not just in the Toronto area. House prices have been shooting up in Vancouver. In Calgary, they're finally back to the levels of the early eighties. It seems like many parts of the country are caught up in a buying panic again, something like what we saw in late 1981.

Well, if you have a short memory, let me remind you what happened then. We hit a recession—a bad one—and those artificially inflated house prices collapsed. I'm not saying it's going to happen that way again. But let me tell you the story of tulipmania.

Back in the 17th century, the usually stolid Dutch went crazy over tulip bulbs, which had just been imported into Western Europe from Constantinople. It's hard to believe now, but they bid up the price of these bulbs to insane levels. They traded houses, land, cattle, horses, carriages—anything to get a precious bulb. The idea, of course, was to resell it to someone who would pay even more. A good way to get rich quick—as long as there was someone else to pay.

Well, you can imagine what happened. The whole house of cards came tumbling down. The last ones holding the bulbs had nothing to show for their money but a pretty flower.

Now maybe this housing madness we're seeing isn't a modern manifestation of tulipmania. Maybe homes really are worth the astounding prices being demanded. But history suggests otherwise. All buying frenzies eventually collapse. We'll see what happens this time.

UPDATE

You know what happened. Housing prices in many parts of Canada, especially Ontario, did indeed collapse in the recession of the nineties. Many people who had bought up residential real estate as a speculation (and there were lots of them in the late 1980s) suffered heavy losses. Tulipmania had struck again.

INTRODUCTION

While all this was happening, the Bank of Canada was tightening credit by raising interest rates. The then-governor, John Crow, was adamant that inflation would be wrung out of the economy. But his policies are still blamed today for adding to the severity of the recession of the early nineties.

RATES MUST COME DOWN
JULY 1989

The pressure is really building on John Crow, the Governor of the Bank of Canada. He wants to keep interest rates high—and you can understand why when you look at the latest cost-of-living figures. There's no sign that inflation is letting up. On the contrary, it still seems to be increasing.

As far as Crow is concerned, that means rates have to stay up, the idea being to cool down the economy and put a damper on those inflationary pressures. And, until now anyway, he seems to have the full support of the government. But even with that, it doesn't look to me like he can hold out much longer. There's too much opposition building and events in the U.S. are undermining his position.

We've already seen the Commons finance committee submit a report calling for rates to come down. That report was signed by a number of Conservative committee members, which shows there's unrest within the party over the present policy.

There have also been several speeches by prominent economists calling for rates to come down, most notably one by Douglas Peters, senior vice president and chief economist of the Toronto-Dominion Bank. He said, in effect, that a policy of high interest rates is a losing game. It adds to the federal deficit—the department of Finance estimates that for every percentage-point increase in short-term rates, the deficit increases by $1.6 billion because of the higher borrowing costs. That, in turn, prompts the government to raise taxes, which further fuels inflation. Peters describes this cycle as being every bit as dangerous as a wage/price cycle.

Even if the Bank of Canada continues to ignore all the pressure here at home, I doubt it can ignore what's happening in the States for much longer. Rates are coming down there. Many banks have already cut their prime, and bond yields are down. Even the chairman of the Federal Reserve Board, who has been one of the strongest advocates of high rates, is changing his tune and suggesting that recession, not inflation, is now the main concern. The Fed, as it's known, has already started to ease the rates it controls and there are almost certainly more cuts to come.

I don't think the Bank of Canada can keep hanging tough in the face of falling interest rates in the U.S. Sooner or later, we're going to follow suit. In fact, interest rates in this country have already started to drop in some areas. Mortgage rates are trending lower, some credit cards are reducing the interest they charge on unpaid balances, and bond yields are down here as well.

But as long as the Bank of Canada rate remains high, we aren't going to see any movement in the prime rate—and that's the key borrowing rate for businesses and consumers.

John Crow and Finance Minister Michael Wilson have warned us not to expect any early change in the policy of high interest rates. But my guess is we'll start to see some easing in the Bank of Canada rate over the next few weeks and that the prime rate will be at least a notch lower by autumn.

UPDATE

The governor held out longer than I expected. The prime was pushing 15 percent in early 1990, when the country officially plunged into recession. But even when that happened, the Bank of Canada clung to the policy of high interest rates for several months, as the next commentary shows.

HIGH INTEREST RATES CONTINUE
MAY 1990

People keep asking me when interest rates are going to come down. I wish I knew. Tell me how our constitutional crisis is going to be resolved, *and* when inflation is going to slow down, *and* whether we're going to have a recession and I might be able to give you an intelligent answer. Otherwise, all I can say is—sometime.

It *will* happen, sooner or later. But I can't tell you when. What I *can* offer are some ideas on how to cope with the current situation— and perhaps even profit from it. First, a little background.

We all feel the impact of high interest rates, one way or another. High rates increase the price of the goods we purchase, by making the cost of carrying inventories more expensive. They drive down the value of our homes, by making mortgages less affordable for potential buyers. They put pressure on the federal government to raise our taxes, by increasing the cost of financing the budget deficit.

But the people who feel the effect of high rates most directly fall into two main groups—borrowers and savers. This week I'll talk to the borrowers.

Those of you who listen to me regularly know that, generally speaking, I don't like debt. Owing someone money is a millstone around your neck and makes you very vulnerable when times are tough. The worst kind of borrowing is consumer debt—using other people's money to finance vacations or luxuries you otherwise couldn't afford. But some types of debt *are* acceptable. Not many of us can afford to pay cash for a house, for instance. If there weren't such things as mortgages, we'd all be renting. So there's good debt and bad debt. But either kind is going to cost more when rates go up.

So what should you do if you're a borrower right now? Well, for starters, try not to add any more to what you owe. You're only going to compound your problems. And, if at all possible, pay down your debts. That's good advice at any time, but it's especially valid when rates are high. Start with any non-tax-deductible debt you have, and give priority to the debt with the highest interest rate—that's usually credit cards.

If for some reason you absolutely must borrow right now, then do two things. First, shop around for interest rates. For certain types of purchases—cars, for example—you can often find below-market rates that are subsidized by the manufacturer. Or you may come across retailers who offer inexpensive financing to get your business. Please understand. I'm not recommending you go deeper into debt just because you can get a bargain rate. But if you must borrow, do it as cheaply as possible.

Second, don't lock yourself into a long-term contract at today's high rates if you can avoid it. Rates will come down—remember that. It's just a matter of when. If you lock yourself into paying today's rates for three, four, or five years, you're going to regret it.

Keep that in mind when you're deciding on a mortgage renewal, a car loan, or any other borrowing. And stay flexible. When interest rates *do* decline, make sure your costs do too.

UPDATE

As it turned out, rates started to fall later that year. Those who followed my advice benefited as a result.

INTRODUCTION

When interest rates started the roller-coaster ride down in late 1990, the speed at which they fell astounded just about everyone. As they plunged, mortgage holders whose terms were coming up for renewal wondered what they should be doing. Here's what I told them.

STAY SHORT
FEBRUARY 1991

The last time I talked about mortgage strategies on this program was last fall. At that time, I strongly advised against locking in any new mortgage or renewal for a lengthy term. I suggested staying short, predicting that mortgage rates were sure to come down in 1991.

Well, it's happening. In fact, rates have been dropping so fast it's hard to keep up with them. Last September I took a six-month term at 13.75 percent on a rental property I own. When I renewed at the end of February, the rate had dropped by two full percentage points! That's an incredible decline in such a short time. But I think there's more to come.

Our housing market is still in the doldrums, and it's one of the driving engines of the economy. It needs something to give it a real kick-start, and I think that means five-year mortgage rates in the 10 to 10.5 percent range. It wouldn't surprise me to see them at that level by summer. We're not that far away now.

So if you have a mortgage coming up for renewal or you're in the market for a house, what's the best strategy? I suggest you stay flexible. I think it's still too soon to lock in for the long haul. The best approach right now would be a six-month open mortgage. You'll pay a slightly higher interest rate for it. But in a situation this volatile, that small premium could pay big dividends in the long run.

The reason is that, with an open mortgage, you can convert to a longer term at any time with no penalty. When you think five-year rates are at or near the bottom, you can simply give instructions to your mortgage company to switch over. There may be a small administration fee involved, but that's it.

There's a reason I'm counselling a high degree of flexibility right now. I'm concerned that the window of opportunity for locking in a low long-term rate may be very brief. The Bank of Canada is easing interest rates rapidly in an effort to pull us out of the recession. It's doing this even though there are disquieting signs that inflation in this country is on the upswing again. If the economy does start to recover by summer and inflation is still looming as a major problem, I foresee the possibility of the central bank doing a quick about-face.

That would involve pushing rates back up again, in an effort to keep our growth at the kind of measured pace that would discourage still more inflationary pressures. If that's the way this scenario unfolds—and it certainly looks quite possible to me at this stage— you might have only a few weeks to grab your cut-rate mortgage and run.

When should you lock in? Well, when five-year rates hit 10.5 percent, you should certainly start thinking about it. In recent years, rates below that level haven't stayed around for long.

But keep an eye on the Bank of Canada rate. If mortgage rates are in your target range but the bank rate is still falling 10 or 15 points a week, hold on a little longer. You may end up with the mortgage deal of a lifetime.

UPDATE

Mortgage rates did in fact fall a lot lower than the targets I set out here, but it took a few years to get there, and a temporary spike upward in 1994 rattled a lot of nerves.

INTRODUCTION

By the time we reached late 1992 it was increasingly apparent we were experiencing a decline in interest rates of a magnitude we hadn't seen in Canada since the end of the Second World War. Here's what I told listeners at that time.

LOW INTEREST RATES TO CONTINUE
NOVEMBER 1992

If you're waiting patiently for high interest rates to come back, you may be waiting a long time. We seem to take it for granted that we should automatically get double-digit returns whenever we put money into an interest-bearing investment. If a GIC isn't paying at least 10 percent, we regard it as unusual—a situation that won't last long.

That's why many people aren't sure how to handle their money these days. They have GICs that were paying 10 percent or more coming due and they're shocked when they're offered only 7 percent or so to renew. Well, you'd better get used to the idea. We may not see double-digit rates in this country for the rest of this decade.

Interest rates tend to run in long cycles. Back in the 1950s, double-digit interest rates were unheard of. If you were lucky, you might get 6 percent on your money. Four or 5 percent was more likely.

Then, in the late sixties, things changed. Inflation started to take hold in Canada, thanks in part to some serious financial mismanagement by the government of the day. Rates responded by creeping across the double-digit barrier. It was thought to be an aberration at the time. It wasn't. Rates stayed in or close to double-digit territory during most of the seventies and eighties.

It was only in 1990 that things began to change. The recession forced the Bank of Canada to start bringing rates down in an effort to boost the economy. Just before the referendum campaign began, they'd reached levels we hadn't seen in decades. Many people assumed it was just temporary. When the economy started to pick up, rates would climb again.

I'm not so sure. I think we may be at the beginning of another long cycle of low rates, similar to what we experienced in the fifties and early sixties. In fact, it wouldn't surprise me if single-digit rates were to continue for the rest of this century and into the next.

There are several reasons for this. First, inflation is low—not just here but in many other industrialized countries as well. Low inflation allows central banks to keep interest rates down. In fact, rates in this country are really much too high right now, given the state of the economy and our inflation outlook. It's only a combination of political uncertainty and our unrealistically high expectations that's keeping them up. Otherwise, we'd see the prime rate down in the 5 percent range and five-year mortgages for 7 percent or less—and we may still.

Another reason I believe rates will stay low is the economic outlook. We hope to see clear signs of a recovery in 1993, both here and in the U.S. But it doesn't look like it's going to be a strong recovery—not the kind of snap-back we saw after the 1981–82 recession.

If that's the way it works out, the Bank of Canada will have no reason to push rates back up. On the contrary, it will be doing everything it can to hold rates down to try to keep the economy moving forward.

Then there's the problem of rising government deficits. The higher rates are, the more it costs to service that debt—and governments are strapped for cash these days. The lower rates are kept, the slower the crisis will build. The politicians will have to come to grips with it at some point. But if they can do anything to postpone the day of reckoning, they will.

The bottom line is that I think we're going to continue to see rates trend down for some time to come. There'll be upward spikes along the way, of course, such as we saw in the referendum campaign and as we'll probably see again during next year's federal election, if it looks like we're heading for a deadlocked Parliament. But the overriding trend for the next few years—and perhaps for the rest of the 1990s—will, I believe, be down.

UPDATE

That's how it happened. And we did see a prime below 5 percent and long-term mortgage rates below 7 percent.

INTRODUCTION

Interest rates weren't alone on the roller coaster of the early 1990s. Stocks were there too—but the direction was different.

STOCK MARKET FLUCTUATIONS
SEPTEMBER 1993

If you're going to invest in Canadian stocks these days, you'd better have a strong stomach. I think we're heading for a pretty wild time.

The action we've seen so far this month is just a start. No sooner were we back from the Labour Day weekend than the markets plunged, much to the delight of those who'd been predicting a correction all summer. Then, just as quickly, stocks staged a rally, leaving a lot of people wondering just what's going on.

Well, I'll tell you what's going on. It's uncertainty—something the markets hate. Right now we've got it in spades:

- There's economic uncertainty. Is this semi-recovery really going to take hold or are we about to slide back into recession?
- There's political uncertainty. What's going to happen in the election? Are we going to end up with a divided Parliament, with the Bloc Québécois holding the balance of power, as some of the early polls have suggested? If so, what will that mean for our markets?
- There's price uncertainty. Why did gold run up so fast and then fall so quickly? Where is the price of oil and natural gas going to settle? Are the booming technology stocks over-priced or just starting to move?

When you consider that no one has the answer to any of those questions, it shouldn't be a surprise that our stock markets are behaving like yo-yos gone mad. So where is it all heading—and what should you do about it?

You should be cautious, that's what. It's never a good idea to pay a lot of attention to day-to-day market gyrations. What's normally far more important is the long-term trend.

Under normal circumstances, I wouldn't hesitate to predict the trend is clearly up. We could still be in the early stages of a bull market that will last for quite a while. That's because we're still in the first phase of an economic recovery that looks like it will take several years to unfold.

It's the kind of situation stock markets usually thrive on. As economic conditions improve, consumer confidence builds, corporate profits rise, and stock prices move higher. I think that's the scenario we're looking at in the mid-nineties—as long as we don't blunder into a major political crisis along the way. If that happens, all bets are off.

Take the federal election, for example. The ideal result would be a majority government. A solid minority government won't be as good but probably wouldn't upset the markets too much. But if the polls predict a deeply divided Parliament, watch out. You'll see stock prices begin to fall even before we reach election day. Add to that Premier Bourassa's departure and next year's Quebec election, and there's a real possibility Canadian stocks will go through a rocky period until we get our political future sorted out.

If you're concerned about that, you'd be better off investing your money elsewhere for a while. If you still want to own stocks, look at markets in the U.S., the Far East, and Europe. If we come out of this election with a strong government in Ottawa, then I think the Canadian market will be a good place to have your money for the next several years.

Let's keep our fingers crossed.

UPDATE

The markets went through a rough period in early 1994 but then began a long upward run that carried on right into the first half of 1997. Here's a commentary I did in 1995 as the market was roaring along.

STOCK MARKET RUN
JULY 1995

The TSE moved into record territory earlier this month before slipping back on profit-taking. It's been a heck of a run. So now the party's over and it's time to turn out the lights, right?

No, I don't think so. In fact, I suspect we're just getting started and there's a lot more steam left in this bull market. Early in May, I said on this program that Canadian stocks looked ready for a big move. At that point, the Dow Jones Industrial Average had moved past the TSE 300 Index for the first time and many people were bemoaning the plight of Canadian stocks.

Not me. I felt our stocks were going for bargain prices and predicted the TSE would outperform the Dow over the rest of 1995. It's too soon to know whether that will indeed happen. But we certainly saw a resurgence of interest in Canadian stocks in June and the first half of July. So why do I think there's more to come? Because bull markets don't happen in six-week spurts. They take time to gather steam, and they take time to wind down.

Many people think the last great bull market ended with the stock market crash of October 1987. But in fact it ended more than two months earlier, in August. That's when the markets started to turn down. If you were alert to the signs, there was plenty of time to bail out before Black Monday. I think there will be lots of warning signals again this time—and I don't see them yet.

What should you watch for? One big tip-off is frantic speculation. Markets that are driven by the belief that prices have nowhere to go but up are ripe for a collapse. Think of the Japanese stock market in the late 1980s. Think of the Toronto real estate market about the same time. Think of the gold market in the late 1970s, when the price of an ounce topped $800.

I don't see those signs today. It's true that more people are moving back to stocks and equity mutual funds. But there's an air of prudence and some apprehension about the whole process that's very healthy. Investors are less greedy, more willing to take profits, rather than to hold on for even bigger gains. As long as that sense of scepticism about the stock market continues, the chances of a crash are greatly diminished.

But investor psychology isn't the whole story. The economic outlook is also an important factor. It looks as though the U.S. Federal Reserve Board has pulled off that rarest of feats, a soft landing. The North American economy now appears poised for continued economic growth at a sustainable pace, with low inflation, for some time to come—perhaps into 1997 and maybe beyond.

Those are conditions in which stock markets thrive. They are not conditions that produce crashes. So I'm optimistic. Yes, there will be corrections along the way—they're inevitable in any bull market. But I think this run has a long way to go yet.

UPDATE

The stock market run did indeed have a long way to go. And while Toronto did not outperform New York in 1995, in large part due to referendum jitters, it did outpace Wall Street in 1996.

INTRODUCTION

By the summer of 1996 I was becoming a little less sanguine about the future of the bull market. My commentaries were taking a more cautious tone, as this one illustrates.

STOCK MARKET SLIDE
JULY 1996

What a month it was! Dizzying plunges one day. Big rallies the next. Huge volumes as hundreds of millions of shares were traded every day in New York—and this at a time of year when the markets usually go into hibernation.

In the end, both New York and Toronto were down for the month, but there's a general consensus that it could have been a lot worse.

Regular listeners may recall that I warned you in mid-May about the possibility of a major correction on Wall Street. At the time, I suggested taking some profits if you were exposed to the U.S. market, either directly or through equity mutual funds. I recommended that cautious investors move some of their assets into money market funds and conservatively managed international funds with relatively little U.S. exposure. If you acted on that advice, the July turbulence should have had little effect on your portfolio—and your peace of mind.

So now what? Was that it for the big correction? Or was it just the beginning of a downward trend that will continue for several months?

You may remember that back in 1987 the October stock market plunge actually began a couple of months before—in early August, to be exact. That's when markets hit their peak after an almost uninterrupted five-year upward run. At that point investors became edgy and the markets started to bounce around, rather like they've been doing for the past six weeks or so. It was an early warning signal to head for the high ground. Those that didn't pay attention were clobbered on Black Monday in October, when New York suffered its biggest one-day loss in history.

I'm not predicting that's about to happen again. But there's an old saying that those who don't learn from history are doomed to repeat it.

There are two distinct schools of thought about where we go from here. The first is the "worst is yet to come" theory. This view contends that the July blowoff was just a preview. Much worse will follow after the U.S. presidential election in November. Corporate profits will continue to weaken. Inflation will start to take hold. Interest rates will rise. The bond market will shatter. Stocks will come tumbling down in a rerun of the Crash of 1987, ushering in a new economic downturn.

The second theory says the worst is over. The July plunge was a healthy, midterm correction in a long-running bull market, which may continue to the end of the century. The drop brought prices back to more realistic levels, cooled speculative fervour, and set the stage for a continued upward advance in the major indexes. Proponents of this theory point out there is little evidence the U.S. economy is seriously overheating and that weak commodity prices in most areas will hold inflation down. They also cite numerous forecasts that predict all the world's major economies will be in a growth phase in 1997. Result: prosperity for all.

Being an optimist, I'd like to think this is how events will play out. But still I suggest you be cautious. We do have history working against us. Bull markets don't run forever. And the years following a presidential election have generally not been kind to stocks.

So don't get too aggressive at this stage. Stick with conservative securities and make sure you're well diversified internationally. This isn't a time to try to play hero with your investments. Play it safe until such time as a clearer picture of the future emerges.

UPDATE

The markets rebounded after the midyear correction, going on a tear that took both New York and Toronto to record highs. But then the U.S. Federal Reserve Board raised interest rates in March 1997, the Bre-X fiasco hit the Canadian exchanges, and markets tumbled again.

CHAPTER
15

Saving for the Golden Years

There are three reasons why retirement planning has been a recurring topic in my CBC commentaries over the years. One is the fact that, as the population ages, more Canadians are becoming concerned about providing for their financial independence when they stop work. The second is that the government keeps meddling with the retirement planning rules, causing confusion and uncertainty. The third, and most recent, reason is that Canadians are increasingly concerned that government support programs aren't going to provide much help when they retire, so they had better plan to do it themselves.

Here's a retrospective of a dozen years of retirement planning commentaries. You'll see very quickly how our views of this issue have evolved over that time. I'll start with an item on self-directed RRSPs that contains some advice you can still make use of today.

CHOOSING A SELF-DIRECTED RRSP
JANUARY 1985

Well, it's RRSP season again—that time of year when usually staid financial institutions start to resemble used-car dealers with the shrillness of their pitches for our cash. I suspect the end result of all this sales pressure is widespread confusion. The high-powered advertising campaigns, the claims and counterclaims, really end up, I think, leaving many people uncertain about what's really best for *them*. That's why I thought I'd spend the next couple of weeks trying to make some sense out of the RRSP maze and, I hope, provide some ideas for you to think about.

I'd like to start by talking about self-directed RRSPs, because I've been finding a lot more interest in them recently. More banks, trust companies, and brokers are offering them, and more people seem to realize that they provide greater flexibility than any other type of RRSP.

Now, a self-directed RRSP is exactly what it sounds like—one in which *you* decide what the investments in the plan will be. That immediately scares off a lot of people—they think they have to be financial experts. Well, not true. You can use a self-directed RRSP for common everyday securities. Canada Savings Bonds are an example. The investments can be as simple or as complex as you choose to make them. The key is that you can tailor the plan to suit your own needs.

If you're interested, I suggest you shop around. Right now my wife and I have self-directed plans with three institutions and the differences are significant.

The first advice you'll get when you start out to look for a self-directed plan is to compare prices. That's always important, of course. But to my mind it's not *the* most important thing in choosing a self-directed RRSP. In fact, it ranks well down the list. Here's what I would look for:

First, and most important, is the reporting system. How frequently do you get reports about what's in your plan and what transactions have taken place? And how thorough are those reports? For example, one trust company sends me an itemized statement every month. It gives me a complete inventory, it shows what I've bought and sold in the past month, and it provides my current cash balance—in short, everything I need to know to make decisions.

Another company sends its report only once every six months. That means I'm constantly trying to figure out where I stand at any given time—and that, as you can imagine, is extremely frustrating. Incidentally, I don't intend to keep my plan there much longer.

You see the point. Find out how often you'll receive reports and ask for a sample of what they look like. If they don't come monthly, or they're hard to decipher, go somewhere else.

Another point. Many stockbrokers offer low annual fees to set up a plan with them. That's OK, as long as you understand they will be the *only* ones to deal with your RRSP. That may not always be a good idea. For instance, I like to buy Treasury bills occasionally and I prefer to shop around. Different institutions may offer different rates and maturities at any given time, and you want to get the best deal. If your RRSP has been set up through a broker, you don't have that flexibility. You have to deal with that broker. I prefer being able to look elsewhere.

One final thing to look for—accuracy. I've had 200 shares of a stock vanish from my RRSP because of a clerical error. I got them back, but only because I take the trouble to check my statements carefully. Any company can make a mistake like that. Check your statements. If you find mistakes are occurring too often for your liking, switch your business elsewhere.

UPDATE

Self-directed plans have become extremely popular in the years since that commentary was delivered. The points I made then are still valid, but the reporting systems have improved and I haven't seen as many clerical errors in recent years (although they can still happen).

INTRODUCTION

I have always been an advocate of RRSPs as one of the fundamental components of the portfolio of any Canadian who wants to build a personal fortune. Here's a commentary from the mid-1980s that explains why.

RRSP Trivia
February 1985

The other night after a curling game I was sitting around a table chatting with some friends and the subject of RRSPs came up. I'd been doing some research into RRSPs recently, so I tossed a Trivial Pursuit-type question into the discussion.

I asked my friends to assume they had a relative who was 24 years old. This person was not a member of a company pension plan, and his or her earned income this year allowed for a maximum contribution of about $4,800. Assuming the relative contributed the same amount every year until age 71—that would be a total of

47 years—and supposing he or she could manage that money so as to average a return of 15 percent a year, how much money would the RRSP contain at the end of that time?

Well, I could hear the mental wheels clicking all around the table. Finally, one woman suggested it could be as much as a million dollars. Someone else guessed $1.5 million and then one lady went way out on a limb and offered $5 million. No one took that very seriously.

As it turned out, she was closest—but she was still way off the mark. The amount in the RRSP I described would be—are you ready for this?—over $26 million! I couldn't believe it when I first saw that number; I had to get a financial expert I work with to confirm that, yes, in fact that was right.

Well, as you can imagine, that caused a bit of a sensation around the table. People just don't realize how powerful a savings instrument an RRSP can be until they're confronted with numbers like that.

Now, to be fair, you'd be lucky to average a 15 percent return over 47 years. But even at 12 percent, which is more realistic, at least in today's terms, that person would build over $9 million during that time. And remember, we're not using the maximum possible contribution of $5,500 a year for this example.

The other caveat is what that money will be worth in 47 years. For example, at an average inflation rate of 10 percent a year, that $26 million would buy you an annuity worth about $4,000 a month in 1985 dollars. That doesn't sound quite so grand, does it?

Still, the point I was making remains valid. If you start soon enough, if you make regular contributions to your RRSP, and if you ensure a decent, steady return on your money, you're a guaranteed millionaire when you retire.

So, why aren't we all going to be millionaires? Well, of course some of us just don't have enough years left before retirement—although even if you're in your fifties when you start, you can still build up a comfortable nest egg. And a lot of younger people don't have the extra income to sock away in an RRSP; just raising a family is all they can manage. Finally, too many of us play games with our RRSP, as if it were Monopoly money.

That's why I'd like to leave you with two thoughts today. First, it's worth the sacrifice to find the money to put into an RRSP. In the long run, it's an investment that will pay off handsomely—and that money is always there to draw on if you should run into financial problems. But the longer you put off starting, the smaller that reward will be.

Second, when you're choosing an RRSP, don't be distracted by all sorts of shrill claims. Pick a plan that offers a solid, guaranteed return on your money, and let the magic of compound interest go to work for you. Keep contributing every year, and then sit back and watch it grow. When you've got your first million, you'll thank me.

UPDATE

Many of the numbers here are no longer valid. You can contribute a lot more to an RRSP today (maximum $13,500 a year), but the cutoff for a plan has been reduced to age 69. An average annual return of 12 percent is quite optimistic, although not impossible. Still, the message remains the same today: This is one of the most effective means of building a personal nest egg that I know of.

INTRODUCTION

For many years there were very tight restrictions on how RRSP money could be used when the time came to start drawing on the plan. But in the mid-1980s, older Canadians began to protest they were being treated unfairly—and the politicians finally agreed.

RRIFs UNLEASHED
MARCH 1986

There's a bit of history here. For many years people with RRSPs had only two choices when they reached retirement age. The first was to cash in the plan and take out the money. But that has serious consequences. If you've built up any kind of fund at all, the government will probably take more in tax than you'll collect for your retirement.

The second, and most common choice, was to buy an annuity. That meant handing over *all* your savings to an insurance company in exchange for a steady monthly income that would supposedly support you for the rest of your days. Once you died, or the term of the annuity was completed, that was it. There was nothing left to pass on to your children.

Pretty restrictive, right? Yet for years those were the only choices when you reached age 71 and had to close out your RRSP.

Finally, some senior citizens started grumbling about facing an unenviable choice of whether to give their life savings to the government or to an insurance company. So in 1978 a third choice was introduced—the Registered Retirement Income Fund (RRIF). Not only was it supposed to offer another option, but it was also designed to provide some protection against inflation by gradually increasing the amount paid out each year.

There were only a couple of problems. One was that the plan was so complicated few people could understand it. The second was that it was so burdened down with restrictions as to make it virtually useless to most retirees.

So recently the agitation started again. Only this time there's a difference. There are more senior citizens than ever before. And they're better organized, as last year's successful campaign against the government's proposal to partially de-index Old Age Security payments showed. Now when they speak, politicians listen.

Which brings us back to the budget and RRSPs. Mr. Wilson seems to have launched a preemptive strike here. The campaign to liberalize the rules hasn't really heated up yet, but anyone who's been paying attention could see what was coming. The finance minister is attempting to defuse the issue, on the government's terms, before it becomes embarrassing. He's done so by making the Registered Retirement Income Fund a truly viable alternative, instead of a theoretical concept that very few people used.

That's been achieved in a number of ways. For instance, you can now draw money out of a RRIF in any amount, when you need it. Before, you had to take it out according to a rigid schedule. Hardly a model of flexibility, especially at a time in life when unexpected events, such as a serious illness, might create the need for additional cash.

Another change allows you to hold as many RRIFs as you want. Before, you were limited to just one. The advantage here is that you don't have to tie up all your funds in a single financial institution or in one type of investment. You've got some freedom to move.

Another new rule allows you to start withdrawals from a RRIF immediately. Previously, you had to wait until the following January.

And one other important point. If you've already used your RRSP money to buy annuities and like the sound of this plan, Mr. Wilson has given you an out. He's changing the law to permit you to convert your annuities into a lump-sum payment and reinvest the money in a RRIF.

All of this is a big step in the right direction. It's not as much as some senior citizen groups would have liked. But I think this new approach is going to be very popular. If you've got an RRSP, or an annuity, you should take a close look at it.

UPDATE

It certainly did turn out to be popular. Today RRIFs are the number-one choice by far of people who are converting their RRSPs into retirement income.

INTRODUCTION

As the 1980s went on, it became increasingly apparent that a major overhaul of the pension/RRSP system was needed. Studies for a revised program were started by the Liberal government of Pierre Trudeau and were picked up when Brian Mulroney's Conservatives took power in 1984. By 1986 it looked like the new system was about ready to go.

RRSPs in the Future
November 1986

The really major changes are going to start in 1988. For the next couple of years, the rules governing your pension and Registered Retirement Savings Plan contributions won't change very much, except that RRSP limits will be higher. But after that, it's a whole new ball game.

Let's start by assuming you have no pension plan and that you're relying on RRSP money to provide a large chunk of your retirement income. The first break you get will be higher contribution limits. Starting in 1988 you'll be allowed to contribute 18 percent of your earned income to a maximum of $9,500 to your RRSP. After that, the maximum increases by $2,000 a year each year until 1991. That's when it reaches $15,500.

I've heard some people say those contribution levels amount to a huge tax break for the rich. In fact, the rationale for them is quite simple. Experts calculate that's what it will take to provide a pension of 60 to 70 percent of a person's income—which is the level needed to enable retired people to maintain something close to their previous standard of living.

OK, so what if you don't have that kind of money to put aside? That's where the new carry-forward provision comes into play. That's the rule that begins in 1988 and that gives you seven years to make up any portion of an RRSP contribution you were entitled to but didn't make. But remember, the first year that rule is a factor in your tax planning is 1989—that's four tax years away. A lot of people seem to think it applies right now. It doesn't, so make sure you take your full RRSP deduction this year. Otherwise it's gone for good.

Now let's see what happens if you're a pension plan member. And this is where things get so complicated that even Revenue Canada people aren't completely sure what's happening. What they *can* say is that the system is going to be so complex that most people won't be able to calculate their own maximum RRSP contribution. That's why Revenue Canada is going to do it for us.

Starting in the fall of 1988, we're all going to receive notices advising us what our RRSP contribution limits are for the current tax year. If you're a pension plan member, that figure is going to be calculated by taking the total of all pension contributions made the previous year by you and your employer and then applying what's called a pension adjustment—PA, for short. I won't even try to explain how that's arrived at except to say that the better your pension plan benefits, the less you'll be allowed to contribute to an RRSP once the PA is applied.

If all that has lost you, I'm sorry. I didn't invent this system, I'm just trying to explain it.

There's one other interesting point here. Up until now, your RRSP contribution limit has been determined by your current year's income. But because the new system is so complicated, that too will change in 1988. From then on, your RRSP limit will be based on the previous year's income. So your 1988 contribution level will be based on your income in 1987.

The net effect of all this is generally good. We'll be able to put aside more money for retirement, and people without pension plans won't be operating under the kind of financial disadvantage they've had to contend with until now.

It's just too bad that at a time when tax reform and simplification are being talked about so much, the government couldn't have found a less complicated way to manage all this.

UPDATE

In fact, this plan was delayed, and delayed again. It wasn't until the 1991 tax year that it came into force. Note my comment about a $15,500 maximum RRSP contribution limit for 1991. The current timetable won't have us at that level until at least 2005. That's a 14-year delay, which translates into a huge difference in the retirement fund available to many Canadians. The federal government should be held to account for this (most of the delay was Paul Martin's work), but we've accepted it like meek sheep.

INTRODUCTION

Unfortunately, many people rush to put money into their RRSP before the March 1 deadline and then forget about managing their investments properly. Here are some tips on RRSP management that are as good today as they were ten years ago.

RRSP MANAGEMENT
JANUARY 1987

The decision seems to get harder every year. The government allows you to contribute more money to your RRSP. There are more places to put it. And if you can believe all the ads, every plan out there is the best there is. No wonder people get confused and make the wrong decisions. With so many choices available, you can be sure there are far more bad or mediocre plans than there are good ones.

That's why I think it's important to talk about RRSPs at some length each year at this time. For many of us, it's the biggest single investment we have, apart from the family home. Yet very few people that I know manage their RRSPs effectively. They accept ridiculously low rates of return on their money when they could be building up a tax-sheltered nest egg that enables them to retire in comfort or even luxury.

Over the next few weeks I'm going to try to show you how to avoid that trap. By the time I'm finished I hope I'll be able to cut through some of the advertising rhetoric we're being bombarded with and give you some clear ideas on what to do with your RRSP money this year.

Let me start with some basic rules—call it the Pape Program for Intelligent RRSP Investing, if you like. Some of these may seem like nothing more than plain common sense, but you'd be amazed at the number of people who ignore them each year.

Rule Number One. Never, *never* invest in an RRSP you don't fully understand. If you're not sure of exactly what you're putting your money into, *don't do it!* This is especially true of mutual funds with RRSP eligibility, which can be sold a little too aggressively. There's nothing wrong with mutual funds in an RRSP, but be sure you're buying something you understand, not being sold a product you know nothing about.

Rule Number Two. Diversify your RRSP investments. Don't put them all in one place. Spread your money around—build a portfolio of RRSP investments. Putting all your money into one plan increases your risk and decreases the chances your money will be in the right place for maximum growth.

Rule Number Three. Don't invest in plans with large sales commissions or administration fees. Get your money working for *you,* not for the salesperson or the plan administrator. You'd be amazed at how much some RRSPs cost. Get all the facts before you invest.

Rule Number Four. Don't be afraid to move your money around. Just because an RRSP investment looked good four or five years ago doesn't mean it's still good today. The investment climate is constantly changing. One of the worst mistakes you can make is to put your money into a plan and then forget it. Pay attention to your RRSP. And don't be satisfied with less than top performance.

That's it. Stick to those four basic rules—never stray from them—and you're well on the way to developing a highly profitable RRSP program.

INTRODUCTION

One of the perennial questions about RRSP investing is whether to hold stocks in a registered plan. Here's a commentary I did in the RRSP season of the year of the great crash.

STOCKS AND YOUR RRSP
FEBRUARY 1987

First, let me say that this is not an easy year for choosing RRSP investments. You're going to have to spend a little more time thinking about your options if you're going to get the best return on your money. You're also going to have to spread your money around a bit—diversify your risk and your profit potential.

Where do you start? Let's look at the hottest area of all—the stock market. It's been going crazy since the start of the year and I've had lots of people asking me if that's where their RRSP money should be. First off, you should know that some financial experts say you should never put stocks in an RRSP. They give two main reasons. First, stocks are volatile—what goes up one month may plunge the next. RRSPs are your retirement nest egg, they argue, so you shouldn't be taking risks with your money.

The second argument relates to taxes. For all intents and purposes, capital gains aren't taxable for most of us, and that's where the real money is in stocks. And stock dividends get favourable tax treatment. So why put stocks in an RRSP where you'll lose all those tax advantages? In other words, keep your stock investments outside your retirement plan. Stick with interest-bearing investments in the plan itself.

Now, obviously there's some good sense in both those ideas. I don't personally agree with them, though, for a couple of reasons. First, while it's true that stocks are volatile, it is also true that over the long haul you'll make more money with them than you will with any other RRSP investment—presuming you buy good, solid stocks, of course. I look at RRSPs as a way to build wealth, and stocks are one of the best ways to do that. So I think you should have some stocks in your RRSP—or, more precisely, equity-based mutual funds. And the younger you are, the more important it is.

As far as the tax argument goes, if you've got enough money to be able to build an investment portfolio both inside and outside an

RRSP, then keep your stocks outside. Most of us don't have that much to invest.

OK, let's say you want some stocks for your RRSP. How much? Well, the markets are very high right now. We could be in for a major correction. On the other hand, I recently attended an international investment conference where many of the speakers predicted this bull market will roar on for at least the rest of this year.

Obviously, there's a risk here. There may also be a major opportunity. If you're really interested in growth, I suggest you consider putting up to 50 percent of your RRSP contribution this year into a good, solid equity fund. If you're more conservative, I suggest 20 to 25 percent.

What should you buy? Look for mutual funds with a good record over a long period. Lots of funds have done well in the past few years, but we've been in a huge bull market. Check for funds that did well in the early 1980s, when things weren't so hot.

And give some preference to no-load funds—funds where you don't have to pay commissions up front. You should be able to move your money around to take advantage of changes in financial conditions. If you've had to pay a big sales charge, you're really locked in for the long term.

UPDATE

The predicted correction did come the following fall. But over the long term it was just a blip on the stock market chart, dramatic though it was at the time. In the decade that followed, equity funds proved their worth in the context of an RRSP, and will continue to do so.

INTRODUCTION

Many people still believe an RRSP is an RRSP—that they are all the same. They're not. There are several different types of plans and it's important to choose the one best suited to your needs.

Types of **RRSPs**
January 1988

I see it every year. People become totally confused after being bombarded with all the RRSP advertising and promotion. As a result, they end up putting their money where it's most convenient instead of where they'll get the best return. If you're in that situation, let me try to cut through the rhetoric and see if I can help you make some sense out of all this.

Let's start with the basics. Essentially, you have four choices on how to invest your RRSP money. The first is deposit-type accounts. These are like bank accounts; you put your money in and you're paid interest. The amount you get fluctuates in accordance with what's happening to interest rates generally.

A lot of money goes into this type of RRSP—mainly, I think, because it's easy to understand. Well, don't *you* go along with that crowd. The return on deposit-type RRSPs is extremely low. You can do much better with something else.

The second type of RRSP is the guaranteed plan. Here you agree to lock up your money for a certain period of time in return for a fixed interest rate. Typically this plan takes the form of a guaranteed investment certificate.

There's nothing wrong with plans like this, especially at a time when interest rates are high—as they are right now, at least in relative terms. They build your money slowly but surely, and in complete safety—assuming you're covered by deposit insurance. So if you're not adventuresome and don't want to spend a lot of time managing your money, take a good look at these guaranteed plans.

But be sure to check around before you sign up. The interest rates offered can vary quite considerably from one financial institution to another. If you're going to go this route, do yourself a favour and get the best rate available.

The third type of plan is the mutual fund RRSP. Now, a lot of us associate mutual funds with stocks. But as you may have heard me say before, there are all sorts of other funds as well. If Black Monday has put you off stocks for the time being, you might want to take a close look at bond and mortgage funds. Some of these have performed very well over the years.

Many banks and trust companies offer no-load bond and mortgage funds—that means you don't have to pay any commission when you buy them. I think funds like this can be a good place to invest.

They're relatively safe, and they offer a reasonable return. They're worth taking a look at.

Your final choice is a self-directed plan—one where you make all the investment decisions yourself. This is my personal choice, because a self-directed plan gives you maximum flexibility. But you have to know at least a bit about money management. And you should have at least $10,000 in your RRSP before you set one up.

I think most people should have a self-directed plan sooner or later.

UPDATE

There's now a fifth type of RRSP—a government-sponsored Canada Savings Bond plan. It's suited for conservative investors who like the safety of CSBs for RRSP-building and don't mind the relatively low returns.

INTRODUCTION

Starting early on an RRSP is extremely important, but it's hard to convince younger people to make retirement saving a priority. After all, that's years away. Plus, who wants to think about being old when they're in their twenties?

STARTING EARLY
JANUARY 1989

One of the RRSP questions I get asked most often by younger people is: When should I start? Can I wait until I'm 35 or 40 before setting up an RRSP?

Sure you can. But don't expect your plan to be worth as much when you retire.

I was involved in a TV panel discussion of RRSPs recently and one of the people we talked to was a woman in her mid-twenties. She told us she planned to set up an RRSP eventually, but she was going to wait ten years and save the $3,000 a year she could contribute to a retirement plan for a house instead.

Just for the fun of it, I ran her case through my computer. I used her plan—wait until her mid-thirties, then contribute $3,000 a year to an RRSP until she's 65. I assumed the money in the plan would earn 10 percent a year. The computer told me that the total value of her RRSP at the end of that time would be half a million dollars. Not bad.

But suppose she starts now, and contributes $3,000 a year for the next 10 years. Then she stops, but leaves the money in the plan to grow. What's it worth when she hits 65? Would you believe about $850,000? That's right—she's contributed much less money to the plan. But those extra ten years of compound interest growth make a huge difference in her total return.

So if you're wondering when to start, the best answer I can give you is this: Right now. And if you want to save for a house as well, use the money you get from your tax refund.

That brings me to another common question: Should I contribute to an RRSP or pay down my mortgage? It sounds like a very simple choice. But you wouldn't believe the complexities involved in finding the right answer. There are so many variables here—your tax bracket, the rate of interest on your mortgage, how long you've had the mortgage, the amortization period, and a bunch of others.

In short, there's no easy answer to this one. Every situation is different. As a general rule, the higher your tax bracket and the less time your mortgage has to run, the more the scales tip in favour of the RRSP. If you're in a low tax bracket, and your mortgage still has a long time to run, the mortgage pay-down may be better.

Some financial planners have computer programs that can work out the best option in your own case. Or if you don't want to go to that expense, use the old compromise: Make an RRSP contribution and use the refund to pay down the mortgage.

Finally, a quickie: Is the money in an RRSP covered by deposit insurance? This answer's easy—maybe.

If your money is in savings accounts, guaranteed investment certificates, or term deposits, you're protected up to $60,000. If it's in just about anything else—mutual funds, Canada Savings Bonds, T-bills, stocks, bonds—then you have no coverage. So be careful. It's not money you can afford to lose.

UPDATE

All of this is still true today.

INTRODUCTION

The conventional wisdom is that as you get older you should become very conservative with your RRSP investments. But that thinking can be flawed, as the following commentary suggests.

INFLATION AND YOUR RRSP
SEPTEMBER 1989

I was recently asked by a major newspaper what type of investments I'd recommend for a retired woman who currently had all her assets in guaranteed investment certificates and Canada Savings Bonds. This lady has worked in the civil service for many years. She's now 67 and doesn't want to take a great deal of risk. However, she feels she should be getting a better return on her money. What should she do?

The standard advice in this situation is to be very conservative. You don't want to do anything that endangers your capital base. If anything happens to that, you're in deep trouble. So you'll usually be told to stick with so-called risk-free investments, like CSBs and GICs. What can go wrong?

Unfortunately, a lot. I'm a pretty conservative person, but I think putting all your investments into a protective shell after you retire can lead to trouble down the road. Let's consider the situation.

This woman is 67. Assuming she's in good health, she can expect to live into her 80s. So she has to plan her finances on the assumption she's going to need a steady income flow for at least another 10 to 15 years. So life expectancy is the first point to consider.

The second critical factor is inflation. It's currently running at about 5 percent and, if the Goods and Services Tax does go through, the cost of living is going to take a big jump in 1991. The federal government estimates the GST will add about 2.25 percentage points to the inflation rate, which, based on present levels, would put it over 7 percent that year. This situation underlines the key problem with so-called risk-free investments.

I don't know how much money this lady has in GICs and Canada Savings Bonds. But it represents a lifetime of savings, so let's say it's about $300,000. And let's assume she's averaging a return of about 11 percent on that money right now. That would produce income of around $33,000 a year.

Now remember, the value of those investments is fixed. It will never increase, unless she reinvests some of her income. Ten years from now, she'll still have $300,000 and, if interest rates don't change, she'll still be receiving $33,000 a year.

But what will that buy? If inflation continues at an average rate of 5 percent a year over the next decade, she'd have to increase her income to almost $54,000 just to maintain the purchasing power she has today. She certainly isn't going to do that by leaving all her money in supposedly risk-free investments.

The plain fact is that the rules of the game are changing. We're living long, and inflation isn't going away. So we have to adjust. In financial terms, that means recognizing the risks in what are perceived as risk-free investments. If this lady leaves her money where it is now, her risk is that she'll be below the poverty line within a decade.

UPDATE

The inflation rate dropped as we moved into the 1990s, but the point remains valid. Even at a modest 2 percent a year, cost-of-living increases will eat away at your purchasing power in retirement if you don't plan carefully.

INTRODUCTION

The federal government finally got around to implementing the new retirement planning rules for the 1991 tax year. Although most of the changes were useful, some contained the seeds of potential dangers for RRSP investors.

BEWARE THE CARRY-FORWARD
FEBRUARY 1991

I call it legitimizing procrastination.

It's tough enough for many people to scrape together enough money for their RRSP contribution every year. In fact, fewer than one in four of us actually manages to do it, according to Revenue Canada statistics. So what's Ottawa done? They've made it easier not to contribute, by giving us a ready-made excuse. And, human nature being what it is, a lot of people are going to take advantage of it.

I can hear the conversation now: "Let's go to Florida this year, dear. We'll do the RRSP thing next year." The problem is, next year may never come. It's always easier to spend money than to save it.

Now, I'm sure the people who devised the carry-forward rule were well meaning. They looked at the situation and saw that many Canadians weren't taking full advantage of the retirement tax breaks available to them. So they decided to allow a seven-year grace period for making up unused contributions, starting with the 1991 tax year.

Here's how the carry-forward works. Suppose you're allowed to contribute $5,000 to an RRSP in 1991. But you're short of cash and contribute only $2,000. That means you have $3,000 worth of unused contribution room open to you. Now, let's say that for the 1992 tax year, your normal RRSP limit increases to $6,000. But you're also carrying forward $3,000 from this year, so your total allowance for 1992 is $9,000. If you don't take full advantage of it then, it carries forward to 1993, and so on.

On the surface, this looks like a good idea. But there are two major problems with it. One is the invitation it offers to delay contributing. If you keep putting it off, you could find yourself with unused contribution room of $30,000 or $40,000—maybe even more—in just a few years. Ask yourself how likely it is you'll be able to contribute a lump sum of that amount in one year. What's more likely is that you'll just shake your head in frustration and wish you'd contributed as you went along.

The other major problem with the carry-forward is that, for every year you delay, you lose the power of tax-sheltered compounding within your RRSP. That can knock tens of thousands of dollars off the end value of your plan.

For example, suppose you're 30 years old and you can contribute $4,000 to an RRSP in 1991. You plan to retire at 65. If that money grows at an average rate of 10 percent a year, it will be worth over $112,000 when you retire. Now let's say you decide to use the carry-forward and you make the contribution five years from now. By the time you're 65, that money will be worth only $70,000. By delaying five years, you've lost over $42,000 from the end value of your RRSP.

About the only situation in which the carry-forward offers a significant advantage is if you know you're going to be in a higher tax bracket next year and want to delay your contribution until then to get a larger refund. Otherwise, you're better off pretending it doesn't even exist.

UPDATE

I still feel the same about the carry-forward today. Although it is useful in certain situations, it offers a convenient excuse not to save right away. I'm not suggesting it be abolished, but I do suggest that it be used only if absolutely necessary. Note that the seven-year rule was repealed before it ever came into force, so you can now carry forward unused RRSP contribution room indefinitely.

INTRODUCTION

There are ways you can contribute to an RRSP even if you don't have any ready cash available. The next commentary explains how.

CASHLESS CONTRIBUTIONS
FEBRUARY 1995

The big problem with RRSP season is that it comes right after Christmas. Just when the holiday bills are pouring in, you're faced with the problem of finding a few thousand extra dollars to salt away in your retirement plan before the March 1 deadline.

A lot of people simply can't manage both. That's one reason why so many Canadians don't make RRSP contributions, or don't contribute the maximum amount they're allowed. A recent survey done for the accounting firm of Ernst and Young by the Angus Reid Group found that 43 percent of eligible Canadians won't make any RRSP contributions this year. In the overwhelming majority of cases, the reason given was they don't have the money.

Well, if that's your problem I have two possible solutions. The first I call the cashless RRSP contribution. You need two things to make this work: a self-directed RRSP and some securities you're holding outside a registered plan. These can be almost anything. A GIC, even one that's locked in for several years, as long as it's transferable. Canada Savings Bonds. Mutual fund units. Stock certificates. You name it.

You simply arrange to have the securities transferred directly into the RRSP. It's not a complicated procedure, and you don't have to sell them first. You receive credit for an RRSP contribution based on the value of the securities on the day they go into the plan. If you're using a GIC or a Canada Savings Bond, your contribution is the face value of the certificate plus all the interest earned up to the day you put it into the RRSP. If you have stocks or mutual funds, your contribution is equivalent to the market value on the day they go in. So you receive credit for any profit that you've earned since you bought them.

There are a couple of tax issues to be aware of if you do this. If you contribute a security on which you've made a capital gain, Revenue Canada takes the position that you sold it on the day it went into the RRSP. That means you're liable for tax on the profit at the capital gains rate when you file your next tax return.

If the security has lost money, don't put it into your plan. Our wonderful, even-handed tax system doesn't allow you to claim a capital loss in this situation. That's right—you're taxed on the gains, but you can't deduct the losses. So you're better off selling losing securities and just depositing the cash. That way, the capital loss will be allowed.

If you can't use this technique, then consider applying for an RRSP loan. These are available from most financial institutions at very attractive rates—usually prime or a little more. Interest paid on RRSP loans is not tax-deductible. But even without that, it's a good idea to borrow for this investment, as long as you can afford the repayment schedule and you can pay off the loan within a year, or two at the most. Even if you're in the lowest tax bracket, the tax refund you receive virtually guarantees you make a profit on the whole transaction. That could be several thousand dollars, depending on how much RRSP room you have available.

Normally, I don't encourage people to go into debt, unless it's to build personal wealth. An RRSP loan falls into that category. The money you borrow today to put into your plan will earn tax-sheltered returns for you for years to come.

So if you don't have the cash on hand to make an RRSP contribution this year, consider one of these options. When your tax-refund cheque arrives, you'll be glad you did.

UPDATE

This advice is still valid today. However, very few Canadians know about the contribution-in-kind option, and borrowing for an RRSP still carries something of a stigma. Too bad—both are valuable strategies.

INTRODUCTION

As we moved further into the 1990s, two things happened: More people reached retirement age as the population aged, and I started receiving dozens of questions a month about RRIFs and how to handle them. Here's a commentary in which I answered several of the most common queries.

CONVERTING TO A RRIF
MARCH 1995

The note came from Guelph, Ont.:

"Could you please give some very basic advice to single women who are converting from an RRSP to a RRIF," it said. "We can't leave the assets to a spouse. We can't afford much risk. And we have to depend on a bank or trust company for advice."

It's a short note, but it raises a lot of issues. Let's start with some basics. RRIF is short for Registered Retirement Income Fund. It's one of the options available to you when the time comes to start drawing on your RRSP savings for retirement income.

There are only two fundamental differences between an RRSP and a RRIF. You cannot contribute any money to a RRIF. And you must withdraw a minimum amount each year. You have to wind up your RRSP no later than December 31 of the year you turn 71 (now 69). But there's no minimum age for setting up a RRIF. You can convert whenever you feel you need the income.

OK, now let's consider our listener's specific questions. First, the beneficiary issue—and, by the way, this applies to both single women *and* men. The standard advice is to make your spouse the beneficiary of your RRSP or RRIF. That's because, if you die, the assets of a registered plan pass to your spouse tax-free. But in this case there is no spouse. So now what?

Well, there is one other situation in which RRIF assets can be transferred tax-free after death. That occurs if you have a child or grandchild who is financially dependent upon you. The rules vary, depending on whether there's a disability involved. But the bottom line is that the money remaining in the RRIF can go directly toward the purchase of an annuity for the dependent child, with no tax deducted. If that situation doesn't apply, then the assets of your RRIF are treated as income in the year you die and taxed accordingly. I'm afraid there's no way around that.

Our listener's next question dealt with the subject of risk. How much is appropriate in a RRIF and how should the money be invested? Obviously, risk should be kept to a minimum. Your goals here are to preserve your capital and to generate the income you need to live on in retirement. Where you put the money will depend on what kind of RRIF you have. There are several different types available. Your decision will depend on how much money you have and how keen you are to manage it yourself.

Many people choose guaranteed plans that invest in GICs or term deposits. They're simple and they pay a predictable rate of return— but they offer no protection against inflation. A mutual fund plan or a self-directed plan will allow you to add some growth assets to your RRIF portfolio. I think that's important, even after retirement, but you have to be careful about which securities you choose. You don't want to be adding a lot of high-risk stocks, for example.

Which brings me to the last question. Where do you get advice? Certainly talk to your bank or trust company, if they're the people holding your RRSP. But don't stop there. Your financial institution is going to tell you only about *their* retirement products and services. You need to know what else is out there so you can make an informed comparison.

If you can afford it, I suggest contacting a fee-for-service financial planner who specializes in retirement issues. Ask your friends if they can recommend anyone. These people usually don't sell any products, so their advice is unbiased. They charge for their services by the hour, so you may be looking at a bill of several hundred dollars for a complete plan.

I know that's not cheap—but you could be depending on that RRIF income for 20 or 30 years. It's important it be invested properly.

UPDATE

The issue of retirement cash flow is often overlooked by Canadians who convert their RRSPs to an income stream. It is essential to plan properly; otherwise the money may not be available as you need it to pay the bills. Fee-for-service planners are still an alternative for this kind of analysis, but many banks now offer it free to their clients through specially trained retirement counsellors. Ask about what's available at your branch.

INTRODUCTION

One year after the previous commentary was aired, Finance Minister Paul Martin announced a major change in the rules relating to RRSPs. It took affect in 1997, affecting an estimated 400,000 people initially. Here's what I had to say on the subject.

THE RRIF CRUNCH
MAY 1997

If you'll be celebrating your 69th, 70th, or 71st birthday this year, your RRSP days are numbered. You're heading for what is being called the Triple RRIF Crunch.

It all flows out of the 1996 federal budget. In it, Finance Minister Paul Martin announced that the age limit for having an RRSP would be reduced by two years. Previously, you could keep your RRSPs until December 31 of the year in which you turned 71. Now that's been reduced to age 69, and this is the year it becomes effective.

So three times as many people as normal will have to convert their RRSP to a retirement income program before the end of December. If you or anyone in your family falls into that group, I suggest you start planning now. If you wait until the last minute, you'll not only find yourself in the middle of the holiday season, but you may also have trouble getting professional help. It will be like income-tax time, as thousands of procrastinators rush to beat the deadline.

Basically, you have three choices of what to do with the money that's built up in your RRSP over the years. You can withdraw it all. Very simple, very clean—and very expensive. The problem is that the government will treat your RRSP withdrawal as ordinary income and will tax you on the whole amount. That means you'll probably end up paying taxes at the top marginal rate in your province or territory on at least part of the withdrawal. So the government could take back more than half your savings in one swoop. Painful.

Your second choice is to use the proceeds of the RRSP to buy an annuity. This means exchanging your savings for a guaranteed monthly income, usually for life. The idea appeals to many people, but there are some problems with it.

The first relates to estate planning. When you die, or when the last spouse dies if it's a joint annuity, all payments end. The exception is if you purchase a guarantee at the outset that the annuity will make payments for, say, ten years. So if you want to leave something for your heirs, this isn't the way to do it.

Another problem is that annuity payments are tied directly to interest rates. Right now, rates are very low and will probably continue to be for some time. So if you buy an annuity now, you'll be locking in a low return for the rest of your life.

Finally, in most cases annuity payments don't ever increase. So even with inflation at modest levels, you start to lose buying power over time. You can get inflation-indexed annuities, but the tradeoff is that your initial payments are greatly reduced.

The final choice for winding up your RRSP is to switch the assets directly into a Registered Retirement Income Fund—a RRIF, as it's known. This is the choice most people make, because RRIFs offer a number of advantages.

First, they're flexible. You can take out as much money as you want each year, subject to a required minimum withdrawal that is based on your age. Second, if you die before the RRIF is used up, your heirs get the money. If it's left to anyone other than a spouse, there are taxes to pay. But that's still better than ending up with nothing at all. Third, your investments keep working for you inside the RRIF. So your capital continues grow, providing inflation protection.

As far as I'm concerned, the RRIF is the best choice for most people.

Setting Up a RRIF

May 1997

Switching your RRSP assets into a Registered Retirement Income Fund is as easy as signing a piece of paper. Doing it right may take a little longer.

There's only one real difference between an RRSP and RRIF, but it's enough to change your whole investment approach. You put money *into* an RRSP. You take it *out of* a RRIF. That means at least some of the investments in a RRIF should generate income—not normally a consideration in an RRSP.

Revenue Canada requires you to withdraw a minimum amount from your RRIF each year. But you can take more if you want. So the first order of business is to calculate how much money you'll need from the RRIF each year. That means putting together an income plan that looks at all your sources of revenue—Canada Pension Plan, employer pension plan, Old Age Security, investment income, and everything else. You have to see the big picture to know whether you can stick with the minimum RRIF withdrawal or will need to take more.

Once you know that, you can start doing some realistic portfolio planning. For example, you may want to hold some of your RRIF assets in securities that generate regular cash flow, such as bonds or monthly-pay GICs. The income from these assets should be enough to cover your annual payments. The balance of your RRIF can then be invested in securities with more growth potential. This investment will allow your retirement fund to continue to grow over time, thereby providing a cushion against future inflation.

But you have to be careful in selecting your growth securities. You don't want to take a lot of risk with your money at this stage of your life. Your best bet is to choose equity or balanced mutual funds that are conservatively managed. Stay away from the aggressive, high-performance funds, attractive though they may be. They're usually prone to steeper declines in weak markets.

My next tip is to consolidate all your RRSPs into a single RRIF, if at all possible. You can have as many RRIFs as you like. But you could find yourself getting piddling little cheques from a number of sources, and the management of several RRIFs is a lot more complicated.

Once that's done, you have to decide if you want to manage the RRIF assets yourself or have a professional do it for you. It's more costly to do it that way, of course. But many retired people don't like the responsibility of making their own investment decisions, or they're out of the country a lot and prefer to leave the decisions to someone else.

Virtually every financial institution offers this service, or you can arrange to have it done by a financial planner, an investment counsellor, or some brokers. The fee is usually based on a percentage of the value of the assets in the RRIF.

Final point. Even though you set up a RRIF now, you don't have to keep it forever. And in fact, you may not want to. Here's why.

At some point in time, the payments from your RRIF will begin to decline. Exactly when that happens depends on several factors, including the amount of money you take out each year and the growth rate of the assets in the plan. But, typically, this will happen sometime in your 80s.

Before it does, it makes sense to use some or all of the money in the RRIF to buy a life annuity. At that point, the annuity payments will be much higher because of your advanced age. And they will be locked in for life—you won't ever have to worry about the cash running out.

CHAPTER

16

Prosperity and Success

Over the years, many of my commentaries have focused on sound, practical advice for investing and managing your money. Here's a selection of some of those broadcasts. We'll begin with some tips for investors from the Ontario Securities Commission.

HOW TO INVEST (1)
FEBRUARY 1988

I was wandering around a financial trade show the other day and I happened to pick up a brochure published by the Ontario Securities Commission—that's the watchdog organization that regulates securities trading in the province, and it's generally regarded as the most influential agency of its kind in Canada.

Now, most of the booklet is pretty dry stuff about how securities markets work and that sort of thing. But at the very back are two pages devoted to the basic dos and don'ts that every investor should understand. In fact, this is one of the best lists of investment guidelines I have ever come across.

Since I'm sure most people won't ever see this brochure, I thought I'd tell you about some of the most important items on the list. These are mistakes that people make over and over again. Avoid them, and you'll save yourself a lot of money and grief.

Number one on the OSC list: Don't be pressured into making hasty investment decisions.

I'll second that—I know a lot of people who have acted in haste and repented at leisure when it comes to their investments. And it's so easy. Someone gives you a hot tip at a cocktail party, or you get a phone call from a broker telling you some stock is about to take off, and bang—you're in. Three months later, when you've lost half your money, you wonder what possessed you. So don't rush into anything. Make sure it's the right investment for *you*—and that you fully understand what you're doing.

Next tip: Be wary of schemes that guarantee a quick profit.

Where have you heard that one before? And yet so many people fall for the get-rich-quick approach, month after month. Just remember—any get-rich-quick scheme has one of two problems: Either it's a fraud and you'll get taken, or it's a high-risk venture. You may make a lot of money—but you may lose it all too. Keep that in mind the next time you come across this kind of offer. Be sure it's legitimate. And if it is, be sure you understand all the risks associated with it.

Next piece of advice from the OSC: Don't invest more money than you can afford to lose.

This may not seem so difficult now, but when the stock market is booming there's a strong temptation to borrow heavily to invest. I know one investor, usually very astute, who got caught in that situation on October 19 (the stock market crash of 1987). He lost 60 percent of his assets in a single day. So be careful.

Final guideline for today: Consider whether a particular investment is suitable in light of your general financial needs and overall investment objectives. Is this where you should be right now? And, if so, why?

You'd be amazed at the number of people who put money into investments that are totally wrong for them. I spoke to one elderly woman on a radio hot-line show a few days after Black Monday who had *everything* she owned in the stock market—and I mean everything. She was in a state and I didn't blame her. But the fact is, she had no business being in the market at all. She should have had her money in safe, conservative investments. So be sure what you're investing in is right for you.

HOW TO INVEST (2)
MARCH 1988

I started telling you last week about a brochure published by the Ontario Securities Commission. At the back are two pages outlining a number of basic guidelines that all investors should be aware of. Let's look at some more of these tips today.

Here's the first one: Remember that a good track record is no guarantee of future success.

Boy, is that true. Let me give you a fun example, just to show you how a good track record can mean absolutely nothing. Let's say you've done some time travelling and you're back in 1895. You're offered an opportunity to buy stock in a highly successful company. Now this is a firm that has done *really* well. Its profits are steadily increasing. The business is expanding—they just opened up a new site last year. And a number of promising new contracts are being negotiated. The growth potential looks terrific. What business are they in? Why, they make carriages—and, of course, everyone is going to need their own carriage sooner or later.

Past results are no guarantee of future success. Better check out a guy named Ford who's doing some tinkering in a garage in Detroit. Now that doesn't mean you should ignore the track record of a mutual fund or stock you're looking at. Just remember, it's history. Give some careful thought to the prospects for the future before you jump in.

Next piece of advice: Don't buy anything from high-pressure sales people who call you up trying to sell investments you've never heard of. There are still some of these boiler shops around. I know because I occasionally get phone calls from some brassy type who claims he's got a gold mine to rival Hemlo. Hang up on them. I know of several people who have been sucked in on sales pitches like this and lost a lot of money.

If you've already fallen victim to one of these scams, don't get conned into throwing good money after bad. Often the stock will drop sharply in value after you buy. That will prompt another call from the salesperson, advising you to pick up more shares while they're at a bargain price. Don't do it! If you can unload the stock, cut your losses and get out.

You'll sometimes run into this sort of high-pressure selling with mutual funds as well. Just remember, if you don't know the person on the other end of the line, buy nothing and commit to nothing. You'll save yourself a lot of grief.

One last quick one for today: Don't buy on tips and rumours. Get the facts first.

By the time you hear about them, most so-called hot tips have become cold clichés. Everyone knows about them and the stock has already gone up. You'll probably buy in just at the top and then watch it slide. Do your research, get good advice, and invest in things you understand. It'll pay off in the long run.

UPDATE

The brochure, which is titled "An Introduction to Investing in Securities," has since been updated and is available from the Ontario Securities Commission, Corporate Relations Branch, Suite 1800, 20 Queen Street West, Toronto, Ont. M5H 3S8.

INTRODUCTION

One of the keys to choosing successful investments is to be innovative in your thinking. Here are some thoughts on that subject.

CHECK OUT THE SUPERMARKET
JUNE 1993

One of the best of the recent books on stock market investing is *One Up on Wall Street*, by Peter Lynch. He's the man who managed the huge Fidelity Magellan Fund in the U.S. for many years, so he knows a thing or two about picking winners.

In the book, he tells of how his wife came home from the supermarket one day with some new stockings. She showed him the package they came in; it was shaped like an egg. Lynch was impressed and did some research. The new product was, of course, L'eggs, and he became convinced it would do great things for the manufacturer, Hanes. He bought the stock for his fund, and it took off. Many investors got rich as a result—all because Lynch's wife had gone shopping.

This sort of thing happens all the time. The problem is that most of us don't think about the investment possibilities when we come across something new. If you want to find winning investments, you have to train yourself to think a little differently.

Let me give you another example, this one from my own experience. Three years ago, my wife and I bought a new Toyota Camry. It was the first car we'd ever owned that had antilock brakes, and whenever I drove it I was really impressed with them. The antilock brakes were available only as an expensive option at the time, but I felt this was a technology all car buyers would eventually want. So I made it a point of finding out what company makes antilock brakes.

Imagine my surprise when I learned that the biggest manufacturer in the world is part of what used to be Massey Ferguson, the farm equipment people. You may recall that a few years ago Massey Ferguson pulled up its Canadian roots and moved to the U.S., adopting a new name in the process—Varity Corporation. You'd never guess it from the name, but Varity is very big in the antilock-brake business.

The company wasn't doing very well at the time, and the stock was trading down around $14. No one in the brokerage business seemed to like it much. But I was so impressed with the potential for their antilock-brake business that I bought some shares. Lately, the price of Varity stock has been over $40. I made a nice profit, all because I followed up on a new product that impressed me.

You can do it too. Just pay closer attention to your own shopping habits. Has a new store opened up at the local shopping mall that you really like—one you find yourself recommending to friends? Find out if it's part of a publicly traded company. It could be the next Gap or Body Shop, retailers who make big money for investors.

Are you using a new product frequently—one you haven't bought before? In Vancouver, half the population seems to be addicted to a particular brand of coffee, called Starbucks. The company has shops all over the city. Some people even have Starbucks mugs permanently in their car so they can stop for a fill-up on the way to work.

Starbucks stock went public last year at $17 U.S. a share—it's a Seattle-based company. But very few Vancouverites bought it. Even though they're using the product every day, they failed to see the profit potential it offered. How much profit? Well, the stock has been trading recently at between $45 and $50 U.S. a share—almost three times the issue price. Not bad in one year.

So keep your eyes open. There may be investment winners right under your nose. It's just a matter of recognizing them.

UPDATE

Of course, Starbucks went on to even bigger things and is now the dominant coffee retailer in North America.

INTRODUCTION

One of the problems many families face when tough times come around is that they have no reserve funds to fall back on. Here's some advice I gave on that subject when a family friend (now my youngest daughter's husband) found himself facing a possible strike.

BUILDING AN EMERGENCY FUND
MAY 1996

A close family friend works for the CBC. Obviously, he was very concerned about the possibility of a strike, and was worried about the impact on his family finances if it went on for any length of time.

Fortunately, a strike was averted at the last minute, so he was able to breathe a sigh of relief and get on with his job. But his concern reminded me again about how important it is to have an emergency fund in place, just in case. Many Canadians find themselves facing similar crises every month, whether because of a work stoppage, the loss of a job, illness, or the death of an income earner.

Any of these events can be traumatic enough. But if you have no financial reserves to tide you over, it makes things even harder for everyone. That's why it's so important to build an emergency fund when things are going well. And it should be a fairly large one. You may never need it—but you'll be extremely thankful it's there if you *do* run into a crisis.

Generally, I recommend the fund be equivalent to at least three months' worth of family take-home pay. That may seem like a lot when you're putting it aside, but it won't look like anywhere near enough if you actually have to use it.

The problem for most people is finding the money. Everyone agrees that an emergency fund is a fine idea. But after paying the household bills, the mortgage, the car payment, the dentist, and everyone else, there's nothing left over.

So what do you do? First, you have to make it a priority. You have to decide that this is a financial cushion your family simply must have, and that one way or another you're going to make it happen, even if it means some sacrifices. That commitment is half the battle.

The other half is execution. One good way of achieving this is to set up a pre-authorized savings plan at your financial institution. Tell them to put aside 3 to 5 percent of your income each month—whatever you can afford. Even if the amount is very small, get the process going. Then add to your savings every time a family member gets a salary increase.

Don't keep the money in your chequing account. Direct it somewhere else, where you won't be tempted to draw on it every time you run a little short. One good choice would be a money market mutual fund. They're very safe, pay a better return than a savings account, and you can always get at the cash quickly if it's needed.

That last point is very important. Wherever you put it, keep your emergency fund liquid. Don't invest the money in something like a GIC, which is locked in until maturity. And don't put it in securities like stocks or equity mutual funds, which can fluctuate in value. If you need to get at the cash quickly, you may have to sell at a bad time and take a loss.

One strategy that's worth considering is building your emergency reserve inside your RRSP. That may seem a bit strange because RRSPs are supposed to represent long-term savings. But there are a couple of reasons to consider the idea.

For starters, the RRSP contribution produces a tax refund. In effect, that means the government is contributing to your emergency fund, which takes some of the financial pressure off your family. Second, the fund will grow more quickly inside the RRSP, because any income earned is tax sheltered.

If you're going to go this route, remember to choose liquid investments within the RRSP—a money market fund or a mortgage fund would be best. Also, keep in mind that if you do need to withdraw the money, you're going to have to pay tax when it comes out of the plan. So you're going to need a larger cash reserve inside the RRSP to compensate for that.

On the other hand, if the emergency never arises, you're that much further ahead on building your retirement savings. It's a no-lose situation.

UPDATE

Having a fund like this may save a lot of sleepless nights at some point in your life. Do it.

INTRODUCTION

Finally, here are some financial New Year's resolutions I offered to listeners as we entered 1997.

FINANCIAL RESOLUTIONS
DECEMBER 1996

This is the time for making New Year's resolutions—at least in theory. I don't know many people who actually do it any more, at least not in a serious way. But when it comes to money, many of us could benefit from making some resolutions and sticking to them.

One of the greatest barriers to successful money management is procrastination. We know we should make a budget, or contribute to an RRSP, or set up a savings plan—but there just isn't time right now. We'll get around to it later. Of course, later never comes. A year goes by, and we're still making the same promises to ourselves.

OK, this is it. Resolution number one: 1997 is the year when I put my financial house in order.

To make it easier, I suggest you draw up a timetable. You're not going to do everything at once, and if you try you'll just get discouraged. So set some deadlines. Decide you're going to accomplish one financial objective per month as you go through the year. Then do it.

Your particular goals will depend on your personal situation and your priorities. But let me give you some examples. January is a good time to begin a regular savings program, if you don't already have one in place. Perhaps there's some extra money coming in—a Christmas bonus or a first-of-the-year raise. Put some of that money aside to get your plan going, and decide how much you can add to it on a monthly basis. Even if it's not a lot, get started. Once your savings plan is in place, it will become a routine part of your financial life.

In February, your resolution might be to make your maximum possible RRSP contribution. If you don't have the cash available, look into the possibility of an RRSP loan.

Your March goal could be to pull all your income tax documents together and to complete your tax return. If you have a refund coming, which most people do, the sooner you file, the better.

In April, vow to review all your debts. See if there are ways to reduce interest costs, perhaps by consolidating your credit card balances into a line of credit. Put in place a plan for reducing all your consumer debt to zero within a reasonable time.

May would be a good month to review the family budget—or to prepare one if you don't have a budget already. Get a handle on where the money is going and see if it's being used most effectively. Put the budget in writing—on a computer spreadsheet, if you can—and review the results each month.

Your June resolution might be to go over any investments you may have, either inside or outside a registered plan. See what kind of return you're getting. Decide whether your strategy is going in the right direction. If you don't have a strategy, develop one.

At this point, you can take July and August off and swing in a hammock. You've earned it.

When you come back in the fall, other projects for the rest of the year might be to set up an education savings plan for a child or grand-child, make sure you have a will in place, work out a program for paying down the mortgage, and do some tax planning before year-end.

Sure, it's a lot of work. But I guarantee that if you follow through on these ideas, your financial life will be a lot healthier at this time next year.

UPDATE

Applying these ideas may not ensure an end to all your money concerns, but they'll go a long way toward that goal. Give them a try. And good luck.

CHAPTER
17

A Final Thought

To close this book, I'd like to put all those years of financial comment and advice into perspective. I believe the following transcript does it very well. It needs no further embellishment from me.

A CHRISTMAS MESSAGE
DECEMBER 1989

Normally I talk to you about money. It's a subject that's important to all of us, and one in which I happen to have a special interest. But money isn't everything in life and we should never lose sight of that. There are people at this time of year who may be feeling unhappy because they don't have money to buy gifts for their loved ones, or to put a holiday feast on the table.

Well, I can understand that. But there are things that are more important. The things that *really* count in life are not money or cars or fine houses. They're people. It's the loving relationships we have with our sons and our daughters and our spouses and our parents and our friends—the people who are closest to us.

Too often, we take those relationships for granted. We lose sight of how important they are to us. We get caught up in the demands of our work, or our social life, or even in watching our favourite TV programs. We forget about what really matters. We don't give the time and attention we should to those around us. We're too busy.

Well, Christmas is a time *not* to be too busy. I've always loved this season because it brings our family together in a very special way. We have our own traditions—decorating the tree together, singing carols while our youngest daughter plays the piano, reading "A Christmas at Dingley Dell" from *The Pickwick Papers*. (If that's something your family hasn't read together lately, try it—it's great fun.)

And even though our kids are young adults now, they still won't let Christmas Eve go by without a recitation of "'Twas the Night Before Christmas"—I still pretend to read it from a battered old book, but I know it off by heart.

And they still hang up their stockings by the fireplace, believe it or not.

But I've always tried to remind them as well of the reason we *have* Christmas. It's not just an excuse to pile presents under the tree or to see who can spend the most money on gifts. Oh sure, it's wonderful to give presents, and I always enjoy the golf balls I receive.

But Christmas is much more than that. It really is a season to show love, to express our joy in one another and our thankfulness for being together. And it's a time to remember the Christmas message: Peace on earth, good will to all.

So don't feel badly if you haven't been able to afford expensive gifts for those closest to you. The best gift you can give anyone is to give them a hug and tell them you care for them.

Have a wonderful holiday.

I'm Gordon Pape.

Dear Reader,

I believe so strongly that *Mutual Funds Update* can help you make better, more profitable investment decisions that I've put together a special offer to encourage you to give it a try.

For a limited time only, you can receive a one-year (12 issues) subscription to *Mutual Funds Update* for only $69.95 plus GST, a $20 saving!

That's **22%** off the regular subscription rate and **42%** less than the cover price — **a real bargain**! Plus, this offer is risk-free. If after receiving your first issue you don't agree that *Mutual Funds Update* will help improve the profit potential and safety of your funds portfolio, simply write "cancel" on your invoice and return it without any obligation.

With an offer like that, there's no reason to miss out on what author and fund expert Duff Young described as the "top notch" mutual funds newsletter in Canada in a column in The Globe and Mail. Try it for yourself and see.

Yours truly,

Gordon Pape

P.S. Reply now to take advantage of this risk free offer. You don't have to send any money to start receiving your monthly subscription to my *Mutual Funds Update* Newsletter. Just fill in and mail the attached card.

Gordon Pape's Mutual Funds Update
16715-12 Yonge Street
Suite 181
Newmarket, ON
L3X 1X4